SILENCE, SIMPLICITY & SOLITUDE

ALSO BY DAVID A. COOPER

BOOKS

Silence, Simplicity & Solitude:
A Complete Guide to Spiritual Retreat
(SkyLight Paths Publishing)

Entering the Sacred Mountain: Exploring the
Mystical Practices of Judaism, Buddhism, and Sufism
(Crown)

Renewing Your Soul: A Guided Retreat for the Sabbath
and Other Days of Rest
(HarperSanFrancisco)

God Is a Verb: Kabbalah and the Practice of Mystical Judaism
(Riverhead)

AUDIOTAPE SETS

The Mystical Kabbalah: Judaism's Ancient System for
Mystical Exploration through Meditation and Contemplation
(Sounds True)

The Holy Chariot: Practices on the Jewish Mystical Path to
Higher Consciousness
(Sounds True)

Kabbalah Meditation
(Sounds True)

SILENCE, SIMPLICITY & SOLITUDE

A Complete Guide to Spiritual Retreat

DAVID A. COOPER

Walking Together, Finding the Way

SKYLIGHT PATHS Publishing

WOODSTOCK, VERMONT

Originally published by Bell Tower, an imprint of Harmony Books, a division of Random House, Inc.

Library of Congress Cataloging-in-Publication Data
Cooper, David A., 1939–
Silence, simplicity & solitude : a complete guide to spiritual retreat / by David A. Cooper.
p.   cm.
Includes bibliographical references and index.
ISBN 1-893361-04-7
1. Retreats. 2. Spiritual exercises. I. Title. II. Title: Silence, simplicity, and solitude.
BL628.C66   1999
291.4'46—dc21   99–17384
                    CIP

10 9 8 7 6 5 4 3 2 1

Manufactured in the United States of America

Cover design by Drena Fagen

Walking Together, Finding the Way
Published by SkyLight Paths Publishing
A Division of LongHill Partners, Inc.
Sunset Farm Offices, Route 4
P.O. Box 237
Woodstock, VT 05091
Tel: (802) 457-4000   Fax: (802) 457-4004

www.skylightpaths.com

CONTENTS

CONTENTS

PREFACE

Silence, Simplicity & Solitude: A Complete Guide to Spiritual Retreat and *A Heart of Stillness: A Complete Guide to Learning the Art of Meditation* were originally published in 1992. They were intended to be self-help guides for people who wanted to learn about and practice meditation in the comfort of their own homes without instructions from a particular teacher. It is true that teachers are important resources for one's spiritual path. The guidance and care offered by a good teacher is invaluable. Yet it is also true that we can quickly acquire on our own, with minimal guidance, the skills of various styles of meditation, and in addition we can design a self-guided spiritual retreat to explore what mystics have experienced for thousands of years. Thus, people interested in meditation and retreat are often advised to keep on the lookout for a compatible spiritual friend, guide, or teacher, but not to delay the process of learning on their own.

The purpose of these books is to go beyond communicating the potential of the meditative experience, but also to encourage readers to delve into the depths of their souls, to explore the boundaries of their hearts, and to discover the nature of their minds. For thousands of readers who are familiar with *Silence, Simplicity & Solitude* and *A Heart of Stillness*, the approach of emphasizing personal experience has been powerful. Many people have written heartfelt letters describing how their lives were changed by the meditative and retreat experiences outlined in these books.

Human inquiry into the nature of the mind has been a consistent theme since the beginning of history. From the moment of the first "Aha!"—when someone realized there was some kind of thinker behind a personal thought—we have probed and scrutinized our internal process in an effort to understand how it works. The basis of this search, I believe, is our intuition that a momentous secret of creation will be revealed when we finally comprehend the origin of thought.

Although science has significantly multiplied our base of knowledge during the twentieth century, little has been added to the wisdom of thousands of years regarding the function of the mind and the inception of thought. Clearly, science has opened new avenues of inquiry; it has developed tools of measurement and methods of evaluation. Yet, the central effort of self-inquiry is always personal, and is better accomplished by individuals working in silence and solitude than in laboratory or academic situations.

A great deal of today's scientific and philosophical knowledge is difficult to acquire. We must engage many years in specific fields of inquiry to gain a working framework, and even then our endeavor may be limited to a single limb on a tree of knowledge that includes hundreds of other branches of study. Thus, most human intellectual achievement is inaccessible to the average person except on the most cursory level.

The opposite is true of self-inquiry. Each of us has the potential to dwell in realms of understanding of the highest order; each of us may achieve the qualities of personal development that were realized by the greatest masters known to humankind. This does not necessitate learning great volumes of information, nor does it require special intellectual aptitude. Admission to the school of self-inquiry is dependent rather on our motivation, willingness, and effort to explore the inner dimensions of our being.

In the last ten years, meditation and retreats have become far more popular in various parts of the nation and around the world. Yet, for many people, the practice of meditation remains mysterious and somewhat unapproachable. Too often, one who is exploring the possibility of learning meditation encounters claims that particular ideologies, dogmas, or spiritual personalities are the only true path to enlightenment. This can be discouraging to the beginner, particularly when accompanied by the implication that serious meditators need to abandon their spiritual roots to engage in meditative practice.

Nothing could be further from the truth. The meditative experience is universal. Every spiritual tradition has explored it. When we become skilled in the art of learning how to quiet ourselves, we discover new levels of inner truth, and we begin to connect with our world in amazing ways. This does not require any special beliefs; it is the natural result of one's personal, direct experience with higher levels of awareness.

Thus, many readers have appreciated the eclectic nature of the presentation in these books. You do not have to be of a particular faith to benefit from meditation practice. Indeed, the most common experience described by meditators is that it deepens their relationship with their own root traditions, it opens their eyes to new possibilities, and it sharpens their experience of daily life in the richness of each and every moment.

I discovered soon after the initial publication of both books that they had become my teachers. Interestingly, they continue to teach me. Often when I am on retreat, I glance through one of the books and discover something I wrote ten years ago that is pertinent today. In fact, at times I am so inspired, I wonder, "Who wrote that?"

Part of the spiritual path is to be reminded of things we already know. We forget our lessons so easily. Life is too busy. It tends to overwhelm us. If we get caught in the swirl, we lose our balance. So, we must give ourselves an opportunity to quiet down on regular occasions, to reflect, and to remember who we are, what we are doing here, what we have promised ourselves, and where we are going. This is what meditation and self-guided retreats are all about.

The reader is invited to explore the range of opportunities for inner work. You will find that some practices are far more appealing than others. When you do, try to master greater proficiency in a few practices rather than superficial skills in many. As your practice deepens, you may want to devote an entire day or long weekend to a particular experience. This is where your spiritual practice will truly improve. A self-guided retreat can be done readily, without financial expense, by following the instructions offered in these two books.

Many blessings for success on your inner quest. The discovery of one's personal truth remains the most exciting adventure in the history of human consciousness. Moreover, each step in this direction brings the world closer to its ultimate potential. May you add your own insights to this path, a path clearly marked by the efforts of untold numbers of spiritual adventurers over thousands of years. Welcome.

ACKNOWLEDGMENTS

This book is dedicated to the millions of anonymous retreatants who over the ages have been silent warriors in the eternal struggle to attain higher consciousness.

There have been many teachers along my path to whom I owe an enormous debt of gratitude: My primary teacher and rebbe, Rabbi Zalman Schachter-Shalomi, Rabbi Shlomo Carlebach, Ram Dass, Pir Vilayat Inayat Khan, Bilal Hyde, Father Theophane, Joseph Goldstein, Sharon Salzberg, and Jack Kornfield. All have freely shared wisdom teachings in a variety of traditions, and have given me personal attention and support.

Also important on the path are the people who taught me in other ways—I call them teachers of the heart: Rabbi David Zeller, Asha Durkee Greer, Tzvi Avraham, Gil Eisenbach, Miriam Goldberg, Marilyn Hershenson–Feldman, Abby Rosen, Ulrich Seizen Haas, and my lifelong friend, Reuben Weinzveg.

Many of my spiritual guides are no longer in their physical bodies but remain alive with me through the publication of their offerings. These teachers are too numerous to mention, but I do feel it is important to acknowledge the many authors, editors, and publishers who have provided the general public with the essential teachings of a wide variety of sages. This is often done at considerable personal sacrifice and with little monetary gain because of the belief that it is important to assure the dissemination of these wisdom teachings. As a result, the average person today has at her or his fingertips more resources for spiritual development than ancient kings, emperors, or even erudite scholars of the last century.

A special thank you to Toinette Lippe, who originally edited these books, and who had the faith and persistence to bring them to fruition. She was the perfect literary partner in the development of these books. Also, I am grateful to Stuart Matlins, who continues to be a light of his own in his commitment to bring excellence to the world of publishing.

My business associate, Alan Secrest, has consistently provided invaluable support and resources. His high ideals, unfailing integrity, and continuous support allow me to devote my undivided efforts to the spiritual path.

The most important blessing, by far, is my wife, Shoshana. She often joins me in retreat experiences, or protects my solitude during frequent inner journeys. She is not only a great helpmate and companion in the activities of daily life, she is also a wonderful teacher. She is steadfast in her constant encouragement, and sharp in her sympathetic criticism when it is most needed. She is a great partner, friend, defender, and lover as we navigate together the mysterious path of human awareness.

THE
TRADITION OF
SPIRITUAL
RETREAT

PATH OF THE MYSTICS

Forty days have passed in silence. My room is empty of furniture, except for a pile of foam and cushions for sitting and sleeping. In one corner is a washbasin, in another a one-burner stove and a few cooking utensils. There is one bowl, one knife, one fork, and two spoons. A few blankets are neatly folded near the foam. They keep me warm, day and night. This is paradise.

A bowl of fresh fruit and vegetables sits next to a large jug of water. I use the water for washing, cooking, and drinking. If used sparingly, it needs refilling only once a week. I learned about water on my sailboat. That was a different kind of retreat. This one is a voyage within. The landfalls of my imagination have been exotic, bizarre, at times dangerous.

There have been islands bathed in gentle sunlight and long stretches of empty beach by a tranquil sea. The palm fronds wave slowly in the breeze. There are no footprints in the sand or ships on the horizon. There is nothing to remind me of the past or the future. It is perfect just as it is.

Other anchorages have been filled with rocks and jellyfish. Sometimes clouds creep over the horizon. On one, when I visited the jagged coral beach, I saw eyes peering at me from the jungle. A monster crashed out and chased me. I barely got away in time. On another, strange creatures flew about as I crouched, huddled in a small shelter. In a single moment, paradise can be transformed into hell.

These inner voyages are not confined by any boundaries. Limitations of time and space are not relevant. There are some maps, a few charts for general navigation, but vast areas remain gray. In every corner and at all the edges the map is marked: Unknown Territory.

These were notes from one of my forty-day retreats. Throughout history, explorers have ventured into this inner world. It is an experience that almost always transforms the traveler and is often so personal that it cannot be transmitted to others except by vague hints. It is called a mystical experience.

A few of these voyagers did find a way to share something of their illumination. They brought back treasures that have changed the course of history. The expression of their experience resonated deep in the fiber of humanity.

However, the only real way to appreciate this transmission is through direct experience. Without this experience, we read stories about treasures that are difficult to describe, and we tend to envision them within our own limited reality. Imagine for a moment that you are told, "Here is a treasure chest. Open it up. Reach inside your imagination and explore." You will discover pictures forming in your mind. Ideas and preconceived notions of what a treasure looks like. Perhaps you will see the image of jewels, gold, and silver spilling out of a strongbox. Maybe a peg-legged pirate is standing alongside. Most of us have limited ideas about treasure chests.

The mystical treasures from the reaches of human inquiry break all the boundaries of imagination. When we read about them in spiritual literature, we sense that something of enormous significance is hidden there, but we cannot discover what it is without tasting a similar experience ourselves.

This is why I undertake a hermitage each year. Some years I am able to do more than one. At times I am alone, sometimes with a group of fellow retreatants. It takes courage to do these retreats, but I have discovered that silence holds many of the secrets of the mystical experience. Each of my retreats has been an adventure into unexplored realms and I too have had glimpses of the mystical treasures.

In daily life, moments of insight may arise spontaneously and have a major impact on our lives. A spiritual retreat is like a large magnifying glass, excluding many of the details of life that distract us, filtering out extraneous material and revealing the base elements. Thus there is a much greater frequency of these insights and our awareness may expand dramatically.

Attuning our awareness to the way we function and our relationship to the universe is the primary aim of most spiritual practice. Many teachings point out that our main enemy is ignorance. Awareness is our only defense against ignorance. This is why the practice of silence in spiritual retreat is so beneficial—it raises and expands our awareness.

The experience of a retreat compresses and focuses our efforts for spiritual development. In some instances, a seven- or ten-day retreat can be the turning point in our lives; for most people, however, it is an intensification process that helps provide insight for daily living. We continue to change from one retreat to the next, ever moving to new levels of spiritual refinement.

Our experiences of sharpened perspective and new depths of awareness are not something special about us as individuals; everyone has the potential for mystical insight. Many people report that each retreat experience results in greater appreciation of the accounts of the great mystics. A new universe opens up, transcending both paradise and hell; it is a world beyond the furthest stretch of imagination.

Forty days have been spent in silence and solitude. It has been a time filled with spiritual practice and meditation. All day is passed inside this room, except for brief excursions to the outhouse or to pick up food supplies at the drop point. The days begin early, between two and three in the morning. I sit quietly in meditation; I pace quietly in meditation; I sit again. An observer peeking through the window might think, "He is doing nothing at all. He must be terribly bored. What a waste of time!"

Inside this world the experience is often just the opposite. It is true that there are times filled with boredom. Yet, there are also periods filled with light when everything seems exquisite and nothing is trivial. At those times, when I do something as simple as moving my arm I am often amazed. Volumes could be written about this simple movement. If it were studied in infinitesimal detail, the template of the universe would be revealed. I gaze at an ant moving across the floor. It is fascinating. Marvelous ideas arise that I never previously contemplated. At those times, I am in a state of rapture. The universe is so extraordinary, I wonder why most of us spend our lives in a way that ignores the nature of creation. If I were able to look out the window upon the world of busy people, the thought might arise, "They are doing and appreciating so little, they must be terribly bored!"

I discovered the secret of silence and solitude long ago. Most of my retreats have been three to ten days long, but quite a few have been longer. Some retreats have been very difficult, almost torture; some have been euphoric, beyond any of the things that turn most people on, including sex or drugs.

People often ask, "What do you do there?" I try to answer, but I see in their eyes that there is no comprehension. It is impossible to communicate. Imagine you have just experienced the most profound insight or the most incredible sexual experience you can remember and your best friend asks, "How was it?" What do you say? There is also the other side. Sitting still, alone, for long periods is very hard work. We encounter demons, anger, frustration, pain, anxiety, and yes, there can be hours when nothing seems to happen. People understand this side of the retreat better. When I say, "Oh, it was frustrating and boring," I see twinkles in their eyes. When I say, "It was pure ecstasy," I see clouds of doubt arising.

Obviously, spiritual retreat is not for everybody. Yet many of the group retreats that are currently offered in North America and Europe are filled to capacity soon after they are announced. The retreats attract people of all ages and occupations. I often note a large proportion of professionals and executives, including physicians, lawyers, nurses, psychologists, and social workers. When I see a diverse group of people struggling in their spiritual practice, I sometimes wonder what the common denominator is that draws them together. They are from all walks of life and have varied cultural backgrounds. They seem to be of different temperaments—some outgoing, some reflective. What is the binding thread?

It has something to do with an aspect within each of us, something unknown to science, a part of us that longs to be at peace. There may be a psychological dimension, but this longing seems to dwell more in the transcendent realm of spiritual aspiration. In my investigation of retreats throughout history, I discovered that the combination of silence and solitude is the primary path for mystics in almost all traditions. Many great religious leaders experienced the inner silence and spiritual solitude of retreats, and most religious traditions are actually founded by people who received their inspiration, insight, or revelation while on retreat.

In Western theology the archetype of the spiritual retreat is the image of Moses on the mountain, in direct communion with God. "He was there with the Lord forty days and forty nights, he did neither eat bread, nor drink water. And he wrote upon the tablets the words of the covenant, the ten Words. And it came to pass, when Moses came down from Mt. Sinai with the two tablets of Testimony in Moses' hand, when he came down from the mountain, that Moses knew not that the skin of his face shone while he talked with him. And when Aaron and all the children of Israel saw Moses, behold, the skin of his face shone; and they were afraid to come near him."[1]

Tradition records that Moses actually went up the mountain twice, some say three times, forty days each, without food or water, on the most awesome spiritual quest undertaken by humankind—to gain a new level of intimacy with the Creation.

This then is the mystical thread. We have a yearning to know what life is all about, but the answer remains elusive. It is not something we are able to discern through simple logic. We know that there is a truth that extends far beyond our limited mental capacity. We just know it somehow; it is part of our essential nature.

We also know that it is not easy to uncover. If it were, we would all be enlightened. Indeed, just as we have a yearning to understand our lives, we also each have within us aspects of doubt and cynicism. Spiritual aspirants often experience an inner battle. Doubt tells us that the part that yearns is a fool. The cynic tells us that it is all a delusion. When our pessimistic side gains power, we tend to believe that people have been struggling throughout history to gain an ephemeral understanding that, in fact, does not exist. We are just going around in circles and there is no deeper truth.

Yet something inside continues to whisper to us. It says, do not believe the cynical and doubting thoughts. Indeed, they are an integral part of the search for truth. An aspect of our ultimate realization depends upon understanding and overcoming the misgivings that tug us away from our efforts to know the true nature of life. As long as we surrender to them, they retain their power. However, if we persevere in our spiritual practice we will come to taste the mystical nectar. One sip of this and we gain an entirely new perspective on our negative thoughts.

This is why mystics throughout the ages have found the resources to overcome their own powerful internal opponents. Once the deeper truth is experienced, and we have penetrated the barriers of our ignorance, we gain enormous strength to continue on the path of wisdom. It becomes a self-perpetuating process. Mystical revelation nurtures our efforts in the continuing search for truth.

The story of Moses on the mountain, as told in the Bible, is only half-complete. The collection of Jewish folklore, called the Midrash, gives us the other side. There we read that Moses not only saw "all of the seven heavens, and the celestial temple," hearing the angels praising God as they sang, "Holy, holy, holy is the Lord of Hosts," but also, "when he started to descend and beheld the hosts of the angels of terror, angels of trembling, angels of quaking, and angels of horror, then through his fear he forgot all he had learned."[2]

The idea expressed here is that despite the experience of complete illumination—the highest enlightenment known to humankind of conversing with God face-to-face, so to speak—Moses lost this state of "knowing" when he encountered overwhelming spiritual opposition. This forgetting, however, did not change the absolute shift in consciousness that had taken place as a result of his profound experience.

The same paradigm applies to us. Once we have experienced a flash of insight, we are no longer the same. We may forget things over and over again; indeed much of our lives is spent remembering things we already knew, but each new insight gives momentum to the ongoing enlightenment process.

A seven-day retreat will often shift my perspective on life to an entirely different track. This always comes unexpectedly—a new way of seeing things. It is a natural process. When I clear away all the nagging commitments of daily life, set them aside for a few days or a week, the ensuing space allows for a new awareness. On a physical level there is a total revitalization; on the spiritual level, there is a strengthened appreciation of the interconnectedness of all life and a sense of affirmation.

There are many types of retreat. An army may retreat from the battlefield; a businessperson may join with others on a retreat to focus efforts on a project without the distractions of the daily office routine. A vacation is a type of retreat from our normal busy lives. A spiritual retreat, however, has a character entirely its own.

A spiritual retreat is designed to reconnect us with our inner being. A well-designed retreat will begin to clear blocked passageways of repetitive thought forms; it will traverse the internal barriers of our fixed ideas and open the gates of wisdom. It is difficult to define the benefits because they are not intellectual. By the end of an intense retreat of a week or longer, something is different, something has changed. Yet we may not be able to describe the change because it takes place in a realm that is commonly called "mystical."

The words *mystic* or *mystical experience* have worn thin through overuse. They are used frequently in contemporary literature, with various meanings. I follow the classical definition expounded by one of the major explorers of the phenomenon of the spiritual experience, William James.

In his well-known lectures on *The Varieties of Religious Experience,* William James listed the two main characteristics that defined for him the mystical state: ineffability and the noetic quality. Ineffability stems from the fact that the experience defies expression. It cannot be transmitted to anyone who has not had a similar experience, and communication with one who has is made only through vague expression rather than explicit description. The noetic quality is the insight revealed through the experience, an insight that is also hard to describe. However, the truths understood by a person in a mystical state, although inexpressible, may have an extraordinary effect on his or her entire life.[3]

James mentions two additional characteristics: transiency and passivity. Transiency is the normal brevity of the experience, which rarely lasts for more than a few hours and often passes in moments. Nevertheless, an exquisite moment is often experienced as eternal.

The characteristic of passivity is the inability to enter the mystical experience at will, or remain in it through our own efforts. Wanting it is not enough to assure its presence—but we will see that a high level of desire and effort makes us more receptive to the experiences when they come our way.

The word *mystic* is derived from the Greek *mystes,* a term used to denote initiates in the Greek mystery religions. Dr. Rufus Jones, who in the early part of this century published a book entitled *Studies in Mystical Religion,* discussed mysticism in a religious context. He wrote, "Mystical devotion means direct, firsthand fellowship with God, and the deepened life-results which emerge."[4] Jones described mystical religion as putting "the emphasis on immediate awareness of relation with God, on direct and intimate consciousness of the Divine Presence. It is religion in its most acute, intense and living stage."[5]

For the modern reader, this definition falls somewhat short. It does not include the vast number of Eastern mystics, whose practice is exclusive of a personal God. It does not include the many artists, writers, musicians, and poets who express inner dimensions that touch the souls of their audiences. It also tends to separate the mystic from the rest of mankind, as if mystical experiences were accessible only to a select few.

Some people believe that there are only a handful of authentic mystics at any moment in time. This is not correct. Our everyday lives are filled with experiences that would be mystical according to James's definition. The experiences we have when seeing a newborn infant, a tearful child, a playful pet, a drooping plant, a good friend in pain, or a blossoming tree are mostly inexpressible. Our feelings when we meet new people or notice the mood of friends and family mold our lives, but nobody can explain clearly how this works. Indeed, the predominant experience of all communication or relationship is ineffable.

When daily activities or experiences also stimulate the noetic quality, fulfilling the second part of James's definition, they can be considered mystical. Often the effect within us is subtle. It is not the thunder and lightning we associate with profound revelation; rather it is more of a whisper that becomes part of the ongoing flow of insight that continuously influences how we view and relate to the world. Thus, much of what we call common sense or intuition develops from life experience that fits a broad mystical category. We do not realize how much of our worldview is influenced by these experiences because we are usually oblivious to what is happening around us and within us.

When our minds are busy, engaged, and constantly thinking, our perception becomes more intellectual, and much of the day passes without our really noticing what is going on. The busy thinking mind generates the "veils" often mentioned in spiritual literature. These veils are by-products of thought and emotion, and they block our inner perception (which is non-intellectual) of the true nature of everything around us.

Once we slow the constant creation of new veils by minimizing our thoughts, we begin to notice how much they shroud and constrict our inner perception. This helps us to gain even greater inner silence and then, interestingly, we begin to experience stimuli in a new way: colors take on a fresh shimmer, sound becomes almost sensual, nature feels abundant and awesome. This all occurs as a natural result of experiencing things as they are rather than filtered through the veils produced by continuous thought. The opening of our nonintellectual perception is sometimes called *knowing*.

Time and again, teachers East and West have pointed out that the basic nature of man is this place of *knowing*.

It is a state accessible to every human being and is not limited to a select few. Upon reflection, most of us already know the feeling, the yearning, the impulse of this soul force. It calls to us in ways that are not necessarily recognizable, drawing us toward the sea, the forest, the desert, or the mountains. Sometimes it calls to us in artistic and poetic form, either as the receiver who is uplifted by creative work or as the artist who *needs* to create. Occasionally the pull is so overwhelming that we put on robes, make a vow, and devote our entire life to the full-time practice of spiritual discipline.

All of us have a deep reservoir of mystical experience that sustains the part of us some call the soul. The soul yearns to be nourished, and if the reservoir begins to run low, we can feel ourselves becoming dull, empty, brittle, and arid. If it sinks lower, we enter into states of angst, despair, and depression.

Once the reservoir is replenished, there is greater harmony and balance. The soul continues to yearn—this incessant tugging toward perfection may be a definition of the soul force—but more gently now that it is being nourished, more balanced now that it is more connected to the universe.

This nourishing can be done in many ways. It sometimes happens spontaneously, but usually we must make an effort to obtain food for the soul. Just as we stop what we are doing to eat regular food to nourish our bodies, so too must we find a way to stop ourselves, to allow the time and space for spiritual nourishment, to breathe, perhaps to sigh, to open our hearts.

In this busy world, the ability to stop is becoming increasingly rare. Often we awaken to the sound of a radio, which fills us instantly with agitating news. We may read a newspaper while eating breakfast or drinking a quick cup of coffee, which is all we have time for as we rush to take care of the kids or leave for work. We run for the bus, hurry to catch a train, or dash off in the family automobile only to find ourselves snarled in traffic. We bolt through the day and return home in the evening having no idea what happened to all the time.

Our daily office or house work is filled with details, schedules, appointments, maintenance. The day is congested. Evening comes and it is time for food and television. Even now we are usually talking, reading, or watching. This is how we relax. The mind is constantly engaged. When do we truly stop to simply be, observe, perhaps meditate a little? We know we must feed this machine called the body or it will quickly die. But feed the soul? Who has the time?

After a while the jaws of this trap close upon us. This is the time demon. We convince ourselves that we have barely enough time to live our lives. Who can think about something as ephemeral as meditation? Sit and do nothing? We stay so busy that we become numb to the complaints of the weeping, famished soul. We lose our ability to pick up these subtle signals. We turn on our automatic response buttons and function like machines. Yet the soul continues to call incessantly.

How is it that the classical spiritual teachings, the great mystical experiences of others, set up such a resonance within? It must be that something in us feels at home in other realities. The more we encounter these worlds, the more we come to realize the degree to which our daily experience is saturated with potential spiritual nourishment. Nonetheless, our minds keep us in a spinning fog, dulling our senses, obscuring the true experience.

A spiritual retreat is medicine for soul starvation. Through silence, solitary practice, and simple living, we begin to fill the empty reservoir. This lifts the veils, dissolves the masks, and creates space within for the feelings of forgiveness, compassion, and loving kindness that are so often blocked.

The retreat is not an end in itself; it is simply a method to help us slow down and stop. We are like globes attached to a center point by an elastic thread. The faster we spin, the farther we get from the center. When we slow down, we draw in to the center. If we are able to stop, we rest exactly at the midpoint.

The midpoint is the source of light. When we are quickly spinning, our globes receive only a small fraction of this light. The closer we come to the center, the brighter the glow. At the center, we integrate with the source of unimpeded awareness. Even a moment of this is enough to refresh and revitalize us, to release us so that we may flow more easily in the conduct of our full lives.

A retreat requires extraordinary effort and inner strength. On retreat we do not watch television, write long letters, read books or newspapers, sleep the day away, or lie on the beach. We do not dine in fine restaurants, engage in conversations, or go off fishing. Instead, we make a serious commitment to a period of silence and solitude—and this is often very hard work.

A retreat invariably implies some degree of solitude. In the extreme, this translates as living alone in a cave, deep jungle, desert, or on a mountain, often for an extended period. There are also forms of retreat that create solitude surrounded by a community—in a monastery, convent, or other supportive gathering.

There are more moderate forms of retreat where we work together with others while maintaining the psychic space of aloneness. We can be alone, yet part of a group working toward a common goal. This has been the model of the Essenes, the Sufis, and many Buddhists, among others. Finally, sometimes retreat conditions are provided serendipitously when we fall ill, have an accident, or are sent to prison.

The spiritual quest has always been a heroic journey. On it, we must deal with primordial energy, images, revelations, and insight. Often it is an exceptionally lonely path, with very few like-minded travelers for companionship and hardly any reliable guides.

In this book we will find testimonies of various retreat experiences. Some of them will have a familiar ring. Some will seem as though they come from another planet. Many will be intriguing, describing places we will want to visit. These accounts have been organized by religion; however, if there had been no division we would not be able to tell which experience comes from which tradition. As the quality of selflessness is pervasive in all mystical tradition, there is a sense of unity rather than separation. Mystics usually transcend religious barriers, sensing a common bond with the whole family of creation. One of the characteristics of the mystical experience is its universalism.

Mystics also do not like to draw attention to themselves; they tend not to speak about their experiences. This comes from a wisdom teaching that people not only empower but also drain power from one another. Loving thoughts are empowering; critical and negative thoughts are disempowering. As people are generally more critical than loving, mystics tend to be shy. Thus, there are often oaths of secrecy among Kabbalists, Sufis, Buddhists, and many other groups and individuals. The descriptions in this book, therefore, may represent only a tiny segment of the world of mystical experience.

Nowadays, especially in large cities, there are many

resources for someone who wants to begin spiritual exploration—a wide selection of books, teachers, and classes is available. Very little, however, is available on the process of retreat. How do we develop the practice of inner silence? What are the conditions necessary for spiritual solitude? How do we define simplicity?

This book is intended to be a resource for people who are interested in experiencing the spiritual benefits of silence, simplicity, and solitude, but who do not know how to prepare themselves for a group retreat experience or set up an individual hermitage. It takes more than simply closing ourselves off in a room and locking the door. There are retreat fundamentals—essential characteristics that give a retreat its special quality.

The first part of this book provides background information, which gives us an understanding of the enormous impact the practice of retreat has had on human consciousness. Five major religious traditions are explored from the perspective of retreat. We discover that none of them would have developed without this practice. It is a curious fact that more material is currently available to Westerners on Eastern mysticism than on the mystical and contemplative foundations of our own Christian and Jewish traditions. Therefore, the first section provides more information on these Western traditions than the others.

The next part of the book deals with the structure and logistics of a retreat. Every element of the process of spiritual effort involves new levels of awareness. Here we not only discuss the "how-to" level of preparing for a retreat, but an effort is made to probe into the essential substance of each underlying component.

The final part of this book offers a broad survey of practices that may be done on retreat. The purpose is to provide a prospective retreatant with an overview of the wide array of possibilities available. It does not take much to begin the practice of spiritual retreat. We do not need to find a teacher at first; we do not need to go anywhere. There is no expense, nothing to buy, nothing to prepare. All we need to do is take time for ourselves—and the reluctance to do that, as we will see, is the most common excuse that blocks the way. Yet the awakening experience provided by retreat is something available to everyone. The question is whether there is a sufficient spiritual imperative to make the necessary effort.

It is up to us. The teacher is not out there somewhere but within each of us. Enlightenment is not a state we achieve; it is a continuing process. Retreat is a simple practice to begin, but it is not easy to continue. It takes work and determination.

The rewards are subtle, but one day we will understand something that can never be intellectualized; we will have direct experience of a deeper truth. This will open new levels of awareness and provide the energy for our continued spiritual efforts. That is all there is to it. The process continues to unfold, the path fills with ever-increasing light, and our lives are changed forever.

BUDDHISM

In Eastern tradition, the Buddha provides a major archetype of the "Buddha within each of us." The original Buddha upon whom the tradition is based was Buddha Shākyamuni*, who was determined to pursue the spiritual quest, abandoning a life of privilege, wealth, and comfort. For many years he was an ascetic, pushing his body to extremes as he fasted and performed exceptional tests of endurance. All this was to no avail. He finally realized that abuse of the body would lead to death, not enlightenment, and he changed his direction to the well-known "Middle Path," somewhere between extreme deprivation on the one side and self-indulgence on the other.

It is important to realize that the Middle Path is itself not without extraordinary effort. We can appreciate this from the Buddha's words as he sat beneath the Bo tree: "Though only my skin, sinews, and bones remain and my blood and flesh dry up and wither away, yet never from this seat will I stir until I have attained full enlightenment."[6]

---

* In order to help readers pronounce unfamiliar words in other languages, I have added macrons to show which vowels are long. These are the only diacritical marks I have used. Often words are mispronounced because we are unaware of the length of the vowels and which syllables need stressing.

If the Middle Path involved an effort of sitting still in meditation, day after day, determined not to move until enlightenment or death, we can only wonder what the asceticism was that the Buddha rejected. This becomes one of the most significant inquiries for the spiritual aspirant as well as anyone involved in short- or long-term retreats. How far do we push ourselves and how do we know when to quit or at least ease off? How do we keep from being fanatical and yet not fall into the trap of self-indulgence?

The yearning to know the Truth, to be at one with creation, is a vital drive in humankind. It causes us to push against our limits, real or imaginary, time and again in the ultimate quest. As long as we feel separated, this motivation pushes us, causing a sense of falling short and missing the mark; it is a constant source of frustration.

Still, the true seeker will often acknowledge that life without meaning is worse than death. A small voice within incites us to ever more extensive explorations into the unknown territories of the inner world. When we do not have a personal teacher, the path can be winding, rocky, and often treacherous. Even with a guide, the process is always extremely demanding, without any assurance of attaining the goal.

Indeed, many prominent teachings point out that the idea of progress is itself limiting. The desire for enlightenment, by definition, keeps us from becoming free. Consequently, we are greeted with the paradox of acknowledging the immense, virtually overwhelming primitive force that urges union with the universal Oneness, while simultaneously recognizing that "desire" and the sense of "becoming" are major impediments that strengthen the idea of a "self." This idea must be completely relinquished if we are to attain divine union.

So we see that the innate drive for being at one with creation must be tempered somehow so that it does not lead to fanaticism. Buddhism solves this problem in a unique way through its basic ideology. The drive to be united with the divine rises from an ego center. The Buddhist view is that this ego center does not really exist.

The entire thrust of Buddhism has to do with three major principles: everything in the universe is constantly changing; everything is ultimately unsatisfactory; and there is no "self." There is nothing to desire for there is nothing to become; moreover, the nature of desire produces a concept of "I/me" that does not exist. On an intellectual level, these principles are interesting, but when we actually have direct experience of no self, for example, the realization completely alters our consciousness.

Buddhism, in its own way, has done far more investigation and experimentation into the nature of mind than any modern science. The intricacies of the human process, the devious nature of mental constructs to maintain the illusion of reality, the extent to which we are willing to go to assert our existence, are all subjects of penetrating exploration in Buddhist wisdom teachings. For the retreatant, Buddhism provides high precision tools for inquiry into the nature of things. It provides an unsurpassed spiritual technology that has been under continuous development for twenty-five hundred years.

One of the notable paradoxes of the spiritual quest has to do with the nature of enlightenment. We tend to believe that the seeker follows a path that leads to ever-increasing awareness. From a Buddhist perspective, this is only half of the process. An investigation into the very force that pushes the seeker on the path reveals that the center point of the force itself resides in the sphere of enlightenment. That is to say, the urge to greater awareness is an essential aspect of enlightenment; some even go so far as to say that the expression of the urge is enlightenment itself. Shunryu Suzuki Roshi, a prominent Zen master of the twentieth century who was influential in bringing Zen teachings to the West, notes that the essential act of meditation is assuming a posture on a cushion and is not related to any idea of gain or becoming something. He observes: "Just keeping the right posture and being concentrated on sitting is how we express the universal nature. Then we become Buddha and we express Buddha nature."[7] If this is so, we come to realize that there is as much quality of "enlightenment" in the first effort we make on the spiritual path as there may be after years of practice. This is an amazing idea, especially for the beginner meditator.

We can demonstrate that the experience of steady practice influences the quality of our lives, but the nature of the essential urge toward enlightenment is enlightenment itself. The very fact that we are intrigued with the spiritual quest stems from the source of the Light, so to speak. Consequently, enlightenment is not an end; it is truer to say that it is the beginning.

Most people think of enlightenment as a kind of magical attainment, a state of being close to perfection. At this level, one can perform amazing feats, see past and future lives of others, and tune in to the inner workings of the universe. This may be possible for a number of special beings, but for most of us enlightenment is much more in line with what Suzuki Roshi describes. It means having a quality of "beginningness," a fresh, simple, unsophisticated view of things. To have "beginner's mind" in how we approach things is a major teaching. In many ways, the process of enlightenment is clearing away the thoughts, beliefs, and ideas that cloud our ability to see things as they really are in their pristine form.

The founder of the Sōtō school of Zen Buddhism, Dōgen (thirteenth century), after more than ten years of intense practice in Japan, undertook a journey to China in search of enlightenment. He went to many different monasteries until finally arriving at the T'ien-t'ung monastery, where he found his master, Ju-ching. For the reader unpracticed in the Zen mind, it is virtually impossible to appreciate that after all these years of practice, Dōgen's enlightenment came from overhearing Ju-ching scold another monk who had been caught sleeping. He said, "The practice of *zazen* [Zen meditation] is the dropping away of body and mind. What do you expect to accomplish by dozing?"[8]

What is meant here is that any conception we may have of our own body or mind must be eliminated. Dōgen attained his liberation through hearing these words. We find a typically Zen rendering of this illumination in the story of the exchange between Master Dōgen and Ju-ching just after this experience. Dōgen went to Ju-ching's room to confirm that his enlightenment was authentic. He burned incense and prostrated himself before Ju-ching:

"What do you mean by this?" Ju-ching asked.

"I have experienced the dropping away of body and mind," Dōgen replied.

Ju-ching, realizing that Dōgen's enlightenment was genuine, then said, "You have indeed dropped body and mind!"

Dōgen, however, remonstrated, "I have only just realized enlightenment. Don't sanction me so easily."

"I am not sanctioning you so easily."
Dōgen, still unsatisfied, persisted, "What is the basis for your
saying that you haven't sanctioned me easily?"
Ju-ching replied, "Body and mind dropped away!"[9]

After this profound experience, Dōgen continued his
zazen training for another two years before returning to
Japan. This is significant for anyone who believes that
enlightenment is an endpoint. Here we find that the
founder of a major school did not stop his daily practice
for there is no distinction between practice and enlightenment in Sōtō Zen.

Zen is but one of many expressions of Buddhism that
have developed over more than two thousand years. It is
well known, in fact, that each time Buddhism encounters
a new culture, it adapts in a fresh way. In the West, three
forms of Buddhism have made a considerable impression:
Zen, which comes from Mahāyāna Buddhism (the great
vehicle, the path accessible to everyone); Tibetan, which
comes from Vajrayāna Buddhism (the diamond path
which can cut through anything); and Vipassanā, which
comes from Theravāda Buddhism (the lesser vehicle, the
path of the elders). All of these have strong traditions in
meditation and retreat. Although they are all Buddhist,
they differ significantly from each other in practice.

A retreat in the Zen tradition is called a *sesshin*, where
students sit in *zazen*, usually for a week, but sometimes
longer. The word *za* in Japanese means "to sit," and *zen*
comes from the Sanskrit word *dhyāna*, which means "to
concentrate." Thus, "sitting in concentration" would be
a literal translation of *zazen*. However, Zen practitioners
have different concentrations. The form of meditation
used by Rinzai—one of the two main schools of Zen
Buddhism—begins with the breath but ultimately focuses
on a *kōan*, a paradoxical query that does not have an

objective answer. Sōtō—the other main school—might understand *zazen* as "sitting in emptiness," because the meditator concentrates on the breath and nothing else. Zen practice will often include periods of community work, but the main focus of a *sesshin* is sitting quietly. The mind is empty, with the exception of the *kōan* practice; but even with a *kōan,* the solution must come out of a non-intellectual realization. Zen has no mantras, visualizations, or *mudrās.* In Japan a *sesshin* is often done in great austerity, while in the West there may be creature comforts like heat in the winter or mattresses on which to sleep. Yet under any circumstances, a *sesshin* is extremely demanding.

Tibetan Buddhism is more devotional, oriented to esoteric practices. Like many other forms of Buddhism, a central practice is following the breath, but it also uses visualization extensively and often utilizes a *mandala,* a diagram representing the enlightened state of mind, for concentration. The meditation practice includes the repetition of *mantras* (sacred sounds) and the use of *mudrās* (physical gestures).

Students of Tibetan Buddhism are familiar with retreats of varying lengths. One of the most common retreats is called *dathun,* a month of intensive practice. More serious students undertake a three-month retreat and a major goal for the most committed students is the three-year retreat, which actually lasts three years, three months, and three days.

On retreat, practitioners of Tibetan Buddhism follow the meditation practices listed above. They may have accepted the Vajrayāna Preliminary Practices, called *ngondro.* These require a stringent discipline that can take over two years to complete, including practices such as one hundred thousand prostrations, the repetition of a hundred-word mantra a hundred thousand times, the offering of one hundred thousand mandalas made of colored rice, and a guru supplication repeated one million times. A retreatant may also be involved in scholarly research of other schools of Buddhism, the Tibetan language, and classes in hatha yoga.[10]

Theravāda is the "Southern" school of Buddhism, established mainly in Burma, Thailand, and Sri Lanka. One of its meditation methods is *Vipassanā*, meaning "insight," a method completely devoid of secret formulas or esoteric symbols. The meditation instruction is simple and direct. Its purpose is to rid us of the defilements that cloud our perception of the true nature of things.

In *Vipassanā* practice, retreat plays a highly significant role, with continuous meditation from morning to night. Tens of thousands of practitioners in Southeast Asian countries take retreats every year, including the "rains" retreat, which lasts three months. This is in many ways a national pastime and is performed by people of all ages who go on retreat as casually as Southern Californians hold a barbecue.

In the United States and Europe there are many retreat centers for Buddhist practice. The majority are Zen-oriented, but centers for Tibetan practice or *Vipassanā* are available for short- or long-term, individual or group practice. Most retreat centers schedule group retreats at different times during the year.

CHRISTIANITY

In the West, the path of solitude and silence has deep roots in the Christian tradition. Contemplative prayer is a path many follow when seeking to deepen their devotional practice. A large number of churches have retreat facilities for individuals and groups and retreats are often part of the annual schedule.

Simplicity is one of the hallmarks of Christian ideology, exemplified by the teaching in the Sermon on the Mount: "Blessed are you poor, for yours is the kingdom of God."[11] Many commentators clarify that "poor" refers not only to material wealth but to the simple, humble, or childlike. For example, the fourth-century Desert Father, John of Thebes, is reported to have said: "The monk must be before all else humble. This is the first commandment of the Lord, who said: 'Blessed are the poor of spirit. . . .' "[12] Also, in the Gospel of Matthew, we read that Jesus invited a child to stand by him and said to his disciples: "Truly I say to you unless you turn and become like children, you will not enter the kingdom of heaven. Whoever humbles himself like this child, he is the greatest in the kingdom of heaven."[13]

Most Christian saints lived in conditions of utmost simplicity. Monks, nuns, and even lay people undertook long periods of intensive introspection in lonely, isolated shelters. At the heart of the tradition, we find that Jesus himself retired to the desert to contemplate an awesome revelation.

At the moment of his baptism, Jesus had a profound experience: "He went up immediately from the water, and behold, the heavens were opened and he saw the Spirit of God descending like a dove, and alighting on him; and lo, a voice from heaven, saying, 'This is my beloved Son, with whom I am well pleased.' "[14]

Jesus then set off on a forty-day retreat in the wilderness to fast and pray. The Gospel according to Mark reports: "The Spirit immediately drove him out into the wilderness. And he was in the wilderness forty days, tempted by Satan; and he was with the wild beasts; and the angels ministered to him."[15]

The forty days in the desert marked the turning point for Jesus. One of the main characteristics of a mind-altering retreat experience is confrontation with what is often called the "Other Side," the side of darkness and evil. Jesus had three encounters with the devil during these forty days and through this archetypal battle a new inner strength emerged.

Paul, who was almost the same age as Jesus, also experienced a tremendous light and went into seclusion for an extended period. In three chapters of Acts, we read about his well-known encounter on the road to Damascus. In all three, a great light knocks him to the ground, and a voice speaks to him from heaven. This pivotal experience brought about Paul's conversion. The fact that he went into retreat immediately afterward, just as Jesus had done, suggests that the ancients used silence and solitude to assist the process of transformation.

This idea of inner silence and retreat is expressed in the early seventeenth-century writings of Jacob Boehme, who experienced his major illumination at the age of thirty-five. He was "surrounded by the divine light, and replenished with the heavenly knowledge," and reported that "In one quarter of an hour I saw and knew more than if I had been many years together at a university. For I saw and knew the being of all things . . . through the divine wisdom."[16]

Boehme wrote in a style that was common in the seventeenth century—an imaginary dialogue between a scholar and a spiritual master:

Scholar: How may I come to the supersensual life, that I may see God and hear Him speak?

Master: When thou canst throw thyself but for a moment into that where no creature dwelleth, then thou hearest what God speaketh.

Scholar: Is that near at hand or far off?

Master: It is in thee, and if thou canst for a while cease from all thy thinking and willing thou shalt hear unspeakable words of God.

Scholar: How can I hear when I stand still from thinking and willing?

Master: When thou standest still from thinking and willing of self, the eternal hearing, seeing, and speaking will be revealed to thee, and so God heareth and seeth through thee. Thine own hearing, willing, and seeing hindereth thee, that thou dost not see nor hear God.

Scholar: Wherewithal shall I hear and see God, being He is above nature and creature?

Master: When thou art quiet or silent, then thou art that which God was before nature and creature, and whereof He made thy nature and creature. Then thou hearest and seest with that therewith God saw and heard in thee before thy own willing, seeing, and hearing began.[17]

The ideas expressed by Jacob Boehme have fascinating parallels in classical Eastern mysticism. At one point, he says, "*I have nothing,* for I am utterly stripped and naked; *I can do nothing,* for I have no manner of power, but am as water poured out; *I am nothing,* for all that I am is no more than an image of Being, and only God is to me *I AM.*"[18] This is very close to the Buddhist idea of no self, despite the theological differences between Buddhism and Christianity about God. This is a common occurrence. Although many traditions have clear theological or philosophical differences, the mystical experience often transcends these points of dispute.

St. Ignatius of Loyola, the sixteenth-century founder of the Jesuit order, is another who had widespread influence as the result of his illumination. He was a knight known for his chivalry and skill in the martial arts. At thirty, he was wounded in the leg by an enemy shell and during his long recuperation became converted through reading the *Life of Christ* by Ludolph of Saxony and books about the saints. Soon after this, he went to Manresa in Spain, and "he secluded himself in an isolated cave where he abstained from meat and began a life of begging for alms. Every day he would kneel in prayer for six or seven hours. In time, by the grace of God, he had a number of deep mystical experiences, which . . . were brought together into a small book called the *Spiritual Exercises.*"[19]

It is written:

> *Saint Ignatius confessed one day to Father Laynez that a single hour of meditation at Manresa had taught him more truths about heavenly things than all the teachings of all the doctors put together could have taught him. . . . On [one] occasion . . . his spirit was ravished in God, and it was given him to contemplate . . . the deep mystery of the Holy Trinity. This last vision flooded his heart with such sweetness, that the mere memory of it in aftertimes made him shed abundant tears.*[20]

St. Ignatius is known for his belief in strict obedience (the Jesuits are one of the few orders that take vows of obedience to the Pope), his highly disciplined spiritual practice, and the method of visualization he developed. Every Jesuit takes a month-long retreat, often a number of times. The retreat is based on advice given by St. Ignatius in *Spiritual Exercises* and follows his practices of purification, self-examination, meditation, attentiveness to prayer, carefulness in posture, and one-pointed concentration. A Japanese Jesuit priest, Kadichi Kadowaki, has shown the close relationship between the thirty-day retreat and a Zen *sesshin* in his book, *Zen and the Bible.*[21]

John Yepes, better known as St. John of the Cross (sixteenth century), was on the spiritual path as a Carmelite friar, but his breakthrough occurred when he was imprisoned for many months in a Toledo dungeon. Here he began the composition of one of the most famous and influential works in Christian literature, *Spiritual Canticle.*

St. John said that the aim of the poem was to

> describe the soul's . . . progress [to the highest state]. . . . First of all it exercised itself in the trials and bitterness of mortification, and in meditation. . . . Afterward it passed through the pains and straits of love. . . . The soul then relates how it has received great communications and many visits from its Beloved, wherein it has reached ever increasing perfection and knowledge in His love, so much so that, passing beyond all things, and even beyond itself, it has surrendered itself to Him through union in love in the Spiritual Betrothal.[22]

Many mystics describe similar stages of development. Each description seems to follow an individual process, but most have the general principles of purification (mortification), concentration (meditation), effort (pains and straits of love), and mastery (increasing perfection and knowledge in His love). These are key elements for the spiritual path.

One of the most revered Christian contemplatives, St. Teresa of Avila was twenty-seven years older than St. John. She followed a path of constant prayer over a long period, moving ever higher as the gates of divine awareness opened for her. She is best known for providing details on the seven levels of unfolding she experienced, which she referred to as the inner castles. Although there are many mystics who delineate a specific turning point of enlightenment, St. Teresa described an ongoing process filled not only with rapture but with fear and dread.

Throughout her early years, St. Teresa suffered a great deal from serious illness. She had seizures; one lasted four days and her tongue was "bitten to pieces." Another dramatic experience included a paralysis that continued for almost three years, during which for eight months she could hardly move. Yet she describes a deep joy that came out of this: "When I began to get about on my hands and knees, I praised God. All this I bore with great resignation and, except at the beginning, with great joy; for none of it could compare with the pains and torments which I had suffered at first."[23]

In her autobiography, St. Teresa describes fainting spells and heart problems during her first year as a Carmelite nun, at age twenty-one. She spent her first long period in solitude (almost nine months) around this time, using a guidebook for the practice of prayer, *Third Spiritual Alphabet*. Some people have the good fortune of being guided by a teacher, but like St. Teresa, many must find their own way.

I did not know how to practice prayer, or how to recollect myself, and so I was delighted with the book [Third Spiritual Alphabet] *and determined to follow that way of prayer with all my might. As by now the Lord had granted me the gift of tears, and I liked reading, I began to spend periods in solitude, to go frequently to confession and to start upon the way of prayer with this book for my guide. For I found no other guide (no confessor, I mean) who understood me, though I sought one for fully twenty years subsequently to the time I am speaking of.*

She goes on to say,

This did me great harm as I had frequent relapses, and might have been completely lost; a guide would at least have helped me to escape when I found myself running the risk of offending God.[24]

Her account continues:

I was quite resigned to the will of God, even if He had left me in this condition forever. My great yearning, I think, was to get well so that I might be alone when I prayed, as I had been taught to be—there was no possibility of this in the infirmary. I made my confession very frequently, and talked a great deal about God, in such a way that all were edified and astonished at the patience which the Lord gave me; for if it had not come from His Majesty's hand it would have seemed impossible to be able to endure such great sufferings with such great joy.[25]

Solitude and prayer remain the keystones of the spiritual practice of Teresa of Avila. Year after year of practice brought her to the seventh, highest inner castle. It is difficult for us to grasp the subtleties of this level of awareness.

The difference in this dwelling place is . . . [that] there are almost never any experiences of dryness or interior disturbance of the kind that was present at times in all the other dwelling places, but the soul is almost always in quiet. There is no fear that this sublime favor can be counterfeited by the devil, but the soul is wholly sure that the favor comes from God; for . . . the faculties and senses have nothing to do with what goes on in this dwelling place. . . . Every way in which the Lord helps the soul here, and all He teaches it, takes place with such quiet and so noiselessly that, seemingly to me, the work resembles the building of Solomon's temple, where no sound was heard. So in this temple of God, in this His dwelling place, He alone and the soul rejoice together in the deepest silence. . . . I am amazed as well to see that when the soul arrives here all raptures are taken away. . . .[26]

The literature of Christian mysticism is prolific. Many Christians who had mystical experiences were cloistered, living lives of relative solitude in walled communities. These descriptions are ecstatic, filled with light and beatific visions of the divine. An anonymous letter, written in Germany or the Netherlands in the sixteenth century, says, "In me such a light blazed up from the clarity of the Lord that I could see into the middle of God's heart and could well recognize his great love and his heavenly counsel concerning me. Though I did not see him outwardly, I recognized him inwardly, for his light was in me, and I became full of the joy of God, so that I almost died of it. For where the Lord God is, there is his wisdom and joy."[27]

Often there comes with the ecstasy a kind of suffering, pain that can last for a long time. It is said of a fourteenth-century nun, Jutzi Schultheiss, that "she penetrated deeper into the eternal nature of God, of this she could not speak, nor did she know it, for she had lost herself so completely that she did not know if she was human. . . . In the seven years that God worked this miracle with her she did not come into a common room for five [of those] years, and she never remained for long with people when she could avoid it. . . ."[28]

Perhaps the most famous account of the Christian mystical experience was recorded in the fourteenth century in an anonymous book, *The Cloud of Unknowing.*

This is a small classic of advice to someone who has chosen the spiritual path as a lifetime commitment. The author says in the beginning: "There are four states or kinds of Christian life, and they are these: Common, Special, Solitary, and Perfect. [The first] three of them may be begun and ended in this life; the fourth, by the grace of God, may be begun here, but it goes on forever in the bliss of Heaven! . . . The Common state is living with your friends in the world. . . . The Special life [is to be] a servant among servants [one who is committed to the spiritual path]. . . . [The] third stage [is] the Solitary. It is in this state that you will learn to take your first loving steps to the life of Perfection, the last stage of all."[29]

Another anonymous account, of a woman who began her deeper path through illness, is recorded in a landmark study, *Cosmic Consciousness* by Dr. R. M. Bucke, published at the turn of the twentieth century. The woman is known only by her initials: C.M.C. She deeply related to her Catholicism and was basically happy, but "there was always that undercurrent—a vein of sadness deep down, out of sight. Often as I have walked out under the stars, looking up into those silent depths with unspeakable longing for some answer to the wordless questions within me, I have dropped down upon the ground in a perfect agony of aspiration."[30]

C.M.C. has a beautiful, expressive style and her story speaks to many of us. She is not a saint, nor a religious leader. She is the lady next door, someone we might see on the street, not realizing what is happening inside her. She lived a hundred years ago, but her insight speaks to us as though it were only yesterday.

C.M.C. was married at twenty-two, had children, and

lived a fairly ordinary life until middle age. She says,
"Something in life had been missed which it seems *ought*
to be there; depths in my own nature which had never
been sounded; heights I could see, which had not been
reached. The chasm between what I was and what I need
to be was deep and wide. . . ."[31]

At forty-nine years of age:

> *An illness, combining extreme bodily prostration with equally*
> *extreme mental and emotional disturbance, revealed to me the depths*
> *in my own nature. After some months my strength was restored and*
> *my mental condition to some extent improved, but the deep unrest*
> *remained. With the power to suffer came the power of sympathy*
> *with all suffering. . . . I had been living on the surface; now I was*
> *going down into the depths, and as I went deeper and deeper the*
> *barriers which had separated me from my fellow men were broken*
> *down, the sense of kinship with every living creature had*
> *deepened. . . .*[32]

After this C.M.C. records that she had an uneventful
period leading up to

> *the supreme event in my life. . . . The pain and tension deep in*
> *the core and center of my being was so great that I felt as might*
> *some creature which had outgrown its shell and yet could not*
> *escape. What it was I knew not, except that it was a great*
> *yearning—for freedom, for larger life—for deeper life. There*
> *seemed to be no response in nature to that infinite need. The great*
> *tide swept on uncaring, pitiless, and, strength gone, every resource*
> *exhausted, nothing remained but submission. So I said: There*
> *must be a reason for it, a purpose in it, even if I cannot grasp it.*
> *The Power in whose hands I am may do with me as it will! It*
> *was several days after this resolve before the point of complete*
> *surrender was reached. Meantime, with every internal sense, I*
> *searched for that principle, whatever it was, which would hold me*

when I let go. At last, subdued, with a curious growing strength in my weakness, I let go of myself![33]

This "letting go" was the fulcrum of C.M.C.'s life. From this moment, her relationship with everything in her world grew in exquisite harmony.

Never before had I experienced such a feeling of perfect health. . . . I had never before realized how divinely beautiful the world was. . . . Presently what seemed to be a swift, oncoming tidal wave of splendor and glory ineffable came down upon me, and I felt myself being enveloped, swallowed up. . . . Now came a period of rapture so intense that the universe stood still. . . . In that same wonderful moment of what might be called supernal bliss, came illumination. How long that period of intense rapture lasted I do not know—it seemed an eternity—it might have been but a few moments.[34]

The afterglow of this experience lasted for a few days, and then came a period of quiet and assimilation.

What astonished me beyond all else was, as the months went on, a deepening sense of a Holy Presence. There was a hush on everything, as if nature were holding her breath in adoration. . . . Nature touched me too closely; I sometimes felt oppressed by it, such extreme exaltation exhausted me, and I was glad when I could have a common day. I looked forward with somewhat of dread to the summer, and when it came its light and its profusion of color, although delightful, were almost more than I could bear. We think we see, but we are really blind—if we could see![35]

In fact, early that next summer,

I went out in happy, tranquil mood, to look at the flowers, putting my face down into the sweet peas, enjoying their fragrance, observing how vivid and distinct were their form and color. The pleasure I felt deepened into rapture: I was thrilled through and through, and was just beginning to wonder at it, when deep within me a veil, or curtain, suddenly parted, and I became aware that the flowers were alive and conscious! They were in commotion! And I knew they were emitting electric sparks! What a revelation it was! The feeling that came to me with the vision is indescribable—I turned and went into the house, filled with unspeakable awe.[36]

At the close of her account, C.M.C. splendidly describes her internal state.

Another very decided and peculiar effect followed the phenomena above described—that of being centered, or of being a center. It was as if surrounding and touching me closely on all sides were the softest, downiest pillows. Lean in what direction I might there they were. A pillow or pillows which fitted every tired spot, so that though I was distinctly conscious of that lightest touch there was not the least resistance or obstruction to movement, and yet the support was as permanent and solid as the universe. It was "the everlasting arms." . . . The consciousness of completeness and permanence in myself is one with that of the completeness and permanence of nature. . . . My feeling is as if I were as distinct and separate from all other beings and things as is the moon in space and at the same time indissolubly one with all nature. Out of this experience was born an unfaltering trust. Deep in the soul, below pain, below all the distraction of life, is a silence vast and grand—an infinite ocean of calm, which nothing can disturb; Nature's own exceeding peace, which "passes understanding." That which we seek with passionate longing, here and there, upward and outward, we find at last within ourselves. The kingdom within! The indwelling God! are words whose sublime meaning we never shall fathom.[37]

C.M.C.'s experience is particularly interesting for several reasons. First, it is the report of an everyday person that would never have been known but for its recording in an unusual book. The fact that C.M.C. remains anonymous is a testament to the millions who have touched the inner depths in their quest for purpose and meaning, discovering their own profound wisdom, yet have never been revealed to the world.

Another quality of C.M.C. is that she is not a young, romantic poetic ideal; she is a middle-aged woman, with family and friends, who searched in her early years but is now somewhat resigned "into this life, past its meridian and apparently fixed for good or ill."[38] Perhaps if she had not experienced her illness and its resultant intense period of reflection, she might not have broken through. That, of course, would be the story for most of us. The fact remains, however, that she did gain a powerful, growing insight into the nature of her being and her relationship with the world.

How it happened that C.M.C. was "chosen" is one of the mysteries of the spiritual path. Untold numbers of people have embarked on the quest of spiritual evolvement without experiencing anything. The mystics say it is a kind of grace to be called to higher plateaus. Where this grace comes from, and why to one and not another, remains one of the great questions of spiritual life.

Finally, C.M.C. represents the vast population who live normal lives, but who still have spiritual aspirations. It has not been their destiny to take religious vows or travel barefoot to India or the Holy Land, yet their souls continue to yearn for something deeper. Many of these people have a regular spiritual discipline of some kind. They may turn deeper into their discipline because of accident or illness and be graced with a profound insight. They may also voluntarily intensify their regular practice through the process of retreat.

Since the fourth century, Christians have been beckoned by the lure of solitude. Monasteries and nunneries have not only invited in novices, they have often opened their doors for lay people in search of spiritual refuge. An underlying theme in Christianity may be summed up by the saying of a Desert Father over fifteen hundred years ago: "Abbot Pastor said: Any trial whatever that comes to you can be conquered by silence."[39]

Currently, under the leadership of Father Thomas Keating, in Snowmass, Colorado, there is an upsurge of a Christian contemplative practice that started in the days of the Desert Fathers. The contemporary form is called the "centering prayer." A number of books have been written about this practice by Basil Pennington, one being *Centering Prayer: Renewing an Ancient Christian Prayer Form* (Doubleday, 1982).

In the Western world today there is widespread availability of Christian-oriented retreat centers and sanctuaries. There are hundreds of different orders, some strictly contemplative, like the Carmelites and Trappists, others less so, like the Benedictines, Franciscans, and Dominicans. Many have private retreat facilities that are available to individuals and groups, whether Christian or not. At times they offer retreat guidance; for the most part, however, they simply provide a facility and spiritual support for retreats in an atmosphere of tranquillity and devotional prayer. For a guidebook to many of these retreat centers, see *Sanctuaries* (Bell Tower, 1991).

HINDUISM

India has long been a heartland for the spiritual seeker and its inhabitants have evolved in an atmosphere of continuous spiritual introspection. India gave birth to Buddhism over twenty-five hundred years ago, but a thousand years before that India had planted the seeds of Hinduism.

Hinduism is one of the few major religions that does not have a dominant personality with whom the tradition is identified. In fact, it is not actually a religion, per se, but a way of life that permeates the cultures where it exists. There is a large cast of divinities in the Hindu perspective of creation, but each of them personifies an attribute of the ultimate source.

India is known for its yogis, ascetics, and fakirs—individuals who will go to any lengths to crash the barriers separating them from the divine spirit. For thousands of years, holy men have walked away from the comforts of ordinary life into the deserts, mountains, and forests of India to live in extreme conditions of austerity. Almost all of these holy men lived and died in anonymity, but they left behind a rich heritage of spiritual consciousness.

In the last two centuries, the world of India has opened to the West and many enlightened men and women have been acknowledged—a wealth of teachings have been uncovered from previous centuries. Because the spiritual quest is common in India and so many people are well advanced in their individual development, it takes a special achievement for anyone to stand out from the crowd.

One of the most renowned modern Hindu gurus was Shivapuri Baba, born in 1826. At the age of eighteen he began to prepare for his life as a *sannyāsin,* renouncing all material things. He was trained by his grandfather until he was twenty-five, when he undertook an extraordinary retreat. He walked for weeks, deeper and deeper into the Indian jungle. The last two weeks of his journey, he did not encounter a single human being. There he stayed, far from contact with other people, for almost a quarter of a century. There is no record of what happened to him during this time. He spoke very little about it later except to relate that the supreme moment during all these years "came in a flash," in which "God was seen and all problems were solved."[40]

At the age of forty-eight, when Shivapuri Baba emerged from his retreat, he undertook to walk around the world, a pilgrimage he had promised his grandfather he would make once he had attained God-realization. On his travels he met the distinguished Indian sages, Ramakrishna and Aurobindo, both of whom were deeply impressed by Shivapuri Baba. He met with the leaders of various countries, including the Shah of Persia, Kaiser Wilhelm II, Queen Emma of the Netherlands, and Queen Victoria of England, whom he visited eighteen times during the years he resided in England. While living in the United States, he met Theodore Roosevelt and then continued on to Mexico and South America, the Pacific Islands, and Japan. Finally he returned to India, having walked round the world, except for sea passage. The trip took forty years, from 1875 until 1915, and he was almost ninety years old when he returned.

His story does not stop here. The *sannyāsin* wandered for the next ten years in India and finally went to Nepal where he settled near the Shivapuri Peak and became known as Shivapuri Baba. He then continued to live in partial retreat, occasionally receiving visitors, but for the most part rejecting the idea of an ashram where he would be the center of attention. He remained in this partial retreat another thirty-eight years, dying in 1961, reputedly 137 years old.[41]

Shivapuri Baba's teaching is uncomplicated and straightforward:

> Mind is filled with various impressions, passions, and thoughts. All these should be emptied from the mind. God-thought alone should roam in the mind. . . . Moral discipline is [practiced] to create peace in the mind. Without peace, prosperity becomes meaningless. Meditation on God becomes impossible when there is no peace in the mind. When any desire remains, meditation is not possible. One's sole concern in life should be God-realization. Life should become secondary.[42]

He continues:

> My teaching is that one should know what is life, why is life, and how is life. Without knowing these things life can never be lived properly. To know these things we should know God first. So one's aim should be to see God. To know God one should be possessed by that one idea of God exclusive of all other ideas. Therefore, one should always meditate on God. Now, in an impure mind, meditation becomes impossible or distracted. For that, moral discipline is essential. But again, without a purified body, purification of mind also becomes impossible. To have a purified body one should do simple essential things. One should regulate all his duties and these regulated duties should be done with complete success. Hence disciplined actions.[43]

Another venerated Hindu teacher of this century was Sri Ramana Maharshi, born in 1880. At sixteen he had a transforming experience. While sitting alone in a room, he began to ponder his own death. As the thought gripped him more and more powerfully, he became immersed in the experience of visualizing his actual death. Whereas most of us have imagined our death to some extent, the experience of Ramana Maharshi was so intense that he soon left his home, was mysteriously guided to the mountain of Arunāchala in southern India, and for the next fifty-four years never strayed more than two miles from it.

The first few years after he arrived on the mountain, he went into deep retreat and quickly entered a state of *samādhi* (total absorption) to the extent that insects chewed away portions of his legs, his fingernails grew exceptionally long, and he almost wasted away for lack of food. He remained in this phase for a couple of years, and it took several more years to regain his physical health. From this point on, Ramana Maharshi was a teacher of ever-increasing reputation, ultimately becoming quite famous worldwide.[44]

These examples of extreme deprivation, years of isolation, and mental states oblivious to surroundings are not intended to be models or even ideals. Indeed, descriptions of them may be counterproductive if the reader comes to believe that enlightenment requires such extreme conditions. All the outstanding teachers deny this as a necessity; none recommend following the path they themselves experienced. The idea is to learn from the masters, but to find our own way.

A major point made by Ramana Maharshi deals with surrender. When asked how to hasten along the path of awareness, he answered, "Leave it to God. Surrender unreservedly. One of two things must be done. Either surrender because you admit your inability and require a higher power to help you, or investigate the cause of misery by going to the source and merging into the Self. Either way, you will be free from misery. God never forsakes one who has surrendered."[45]

He goes on to give a basic principle and the essence of spiritual retreat: " 'Be still and know that I am God.' Here 'stillness' is a total surrender without a vestige of individuality. Stillness will prevail and there will be no agitation of mind. Agitation of mind is the cause of desire, the sense of doership and personality. If that is stopped, there is quiet."[46]

The idea of surrender is one of the foundation stones of spiritual work. It is our main tool for bringing the ego into line. Without surrender, we will be stuck in a place of separation. With it, we gain the long sought-for unification with the source of life.

Ramana Maharshi notes that we can realize our spiritual progress as it is happening.

The mind, having been so long a cow accustomed to graze stealthily on other's estates, is not easily confined to her stall. However much her keeper tempts her with luscious grass and fine fodder, she refuses the first time. Then she takes a bit, but her innate tendency to stray away asserts itself and she slips away. On being repeatedly tempted by the owner, she accustoms herself to the stall until finally, even if let loose, she does not stray away. . . . The degree of freedom from unwanted thoughts and the degree of concentration on a single thought are the measures to gauge the progress.[47]

Another prominent Hindu guru who lived in the nineteenth century was Ramakrishna (1833–1886). As a child he would go into trances for hours at a time, in communion with Kālī, the Great Mother. He spent twelve years practicing extreme ascetic exercises. It is reported by his disciple, Vivekananda, that Ramakrishna never slept soundly during these years. It is also said that throughout the twelve years his eyes were always open and fixed.[48]

Descriptions of extreme inwardness are common in Hindu mystical literature. From a Western perspective, it is quite possible that a psychiatrist examining Ramakrishna during his ascetic period would have institutionalized him as catatonic. It is difficult for Westerners to grasp the extent to which a yogic practitioner can surrender. Although the practice begins as something voluntary, the yogi submits completely, no longer expressing a will for anything, including his or her own survival. These ascetics are not practice ideals for Westerners, but they broaden our perspective of the possibilities of total faith, devotion, and surrender.

One teacher in India in this century did not go to the extremes mentioned above, yet his impact in sociopolitical terms remains a lasting testament to his intrinsic spiritual power. Mahatma Gandhi is linked to other distinguished teachers in his willingness to put personal needs aside or to sacrifice his life. However he is unique in the history of spiritual endeavor in that he was the first to use a basic practice—fasting—not for his own development, but for raising the consciousness of those around him.

Some of Gandhi's fasts were made in jail. He was one of the most outstanding public relations geniuses of this century, and he achieved what he did without the benefit of modern communications. He would begin a fast, let just a handful of people know, and in a matter of days, by word of mouth, most of India would be aware that Gandhi was fasting.

His political opponents would say that Gandhi used fasting as an exploitative tool, as intimidation, as a power play. From their perspective, this has substantial truth. From a mystic's perspective, Gandhi understood a universal principle, the relationship of inner and outer, micro and macro. He understood how to involve a large number of people in the process of expanding awareness. Like-minded or not, friend or enemy, secular or religious, whoever was touched by Gandhi, either personally or through the issues in which he was engaged, had to reflect upon and often dramatically change his or her own innate attitudes or opinions.

Most retreatants work on their own spiritual development; Gandhi constantly worked on the awareness of those around him. He spoke out often and engaged the world, but his most powerful, thought-provoking, transformative acts were the inward moves he made. He discovered the secret of utilizing and radiating spiritual power. Gandhi understood how to use his expanded awareness to soften the minds of people around him, to move them from their own limited world view, so that personal boundaries would collapse and compromise became possible.

Gandhi is another illumined being who regularly experienced long periods of solitude, which were at times voluntary, but often not. In South Africa he was jailed for two to three months three different times, for political activities, before beginning his life's mission in India. It is reported that "he made such good use of his time in jail with study and prayer that he was able to declare that 'the real road to ultimate happiness lies in going to jail . . . undergoing sufferings and privations there in the interest of one's own country and religion.' "[49]

His efforts in his homeland also brought him extensive

periods of incarceration, totaling 2,089 days, in the aggregate close to six years in jail.[50] Jail is not the place for most of us to attain enlightenment. It is usually a miserable, crowded, angry environment. Nonetheless, occasionally, it is this very misery that feeds and pushes the spiritual side. We saw that this was true of St. John of the Cross. It can occur in modern times as well. The American teacher, Ram Dass, relates: "Once I met a Black Panther. I was impressed with the clarity of his eyes. I said to him, 'How did you become so clear?' His answer was, 'It was solitary, man.' He had been in solitary confinement for a long time and had used that punishment as a chance to deepen his own being."[51]

Gandhi performed another powerful practice in addition to fasting. He kept a full day of silence each week. He would not speak to anyone, for any reason, on Mondays. "Years ago," he explained, "I started my weekly observance of a day of silence as a means for gaining time to look after my correspondence. But now those twenty-four hours have become a vital spiritual need. A periodical decree of silence is not a torture but a blessing."[52] He would keep to this discipline of silence even if it meant not speaking at an important political conference.[53]

The other unusual practice of Gandhi's during most of his later years was daily spinning two hundred yards of cotton thread. Even though he would on occasion discuss matters while spinning, there is no doubt that this was a daily meditation practice. It once again had a practical benefit, for he wore homespun cloth and provided for others. Most of all, spinning was his symbol of emancipating the poor, a way whereby they could gain more economic independence. He was so loyal to this practice of spinning that he would work late at night if it had been missed during the day, and even traveling on trains he could be seen spinning while the train slowly moved through the countryside.[54]

At a number of ashrams in the West it is possible to arrange for individual retreats. Some have programs for guided retreats. India, however, remains the goal for spiritual aspirants who wish to explore Hinduism at a deep level. There one will find a plenitude of retreat facilities, mostly primitive, and a large number of guides at various stages in their own development.

ISLAM

Islam is the traditional religion for almost a billion people in today's world. Only Christianity has a larger number of adherents. Like all large religious traditions, it is divided into many areas of discipline, many diverging paths of belief and practice. Our focus is on one group, the Sufis, who are not necessarily representative of mainstream Islam, but who clearly carry the mantle of mysticism in the Islamic tradition.

The Sufis themselves are divided into many different groups, but they are unified in the goal to annihilate the ego. Sufi poetry often describes the burning desire to be in an intimate relationship with God. A famous image is of a moth flying into a flame, consumed by its yearning. Another well-known image is that the Sufi develops an immediacy with God closer than his own jugular vein, closer to the core of being than his own life.

The Sufis long ago developed an institution of forty-day retreats as a form of initiation. In the eleventh century Hujwiri wrote that the forty-day retreat is derived from the forty-day fast and ascent of the mountain by Moses. Indeed, the ascent of Moses is found not only in the Book of Exodus, but also in the Koran, the holiest book of Islam: "We [Allah] promised Moses that We would speak with him after thirty nights, to which We added ten nights more: so that the meeting with his Lord took place after forty nights. . . . And when his Lord revealed Himself to the Mountain, He crushed it to fine dust. Moses fell down senseless, and when he came to himself said: 'Glory be to You! Accept my repentance. I am the first of believers.' "[55]

It is recorded that Muhammad (seventh century) himself retreated to the desert, spending exceptional lengths of time, often in a cavern on Mount Hara, near Mecca. He experienced many visions, ecstasies, and trances, as is common when one does intense practice in solitude; his breakthrough came when he was forty years old.

Muhammad's illumination occurred on one special night still celebrated by Muslims. As the story reports:

> It was his habit to retire to a cave in the mountains in order to give himself up to solitary prayer and meditation. . . . One night in Ramadān about the year 610, as he was asleep or in a trance, the Angel Gabriel came to him and said: "Recite!" He replied, "What am I to recite?" The order was repeated three times, until the angel himself said, "Recite in the name of your Lord who created, created man from clots of blood. Recite! Your Lord is the Most Bountiful One, who by the pen taught man what he did not know." When he awoke, these words . . . [were] "inscribed upon his heart."[56]

Out of this experience came the Koran, but nonetheless, we are told that Muhammad

> came trembling and agitated to Cadijah [his wife] in the morning, not knowing whether what he had heard and seen was indeed true, and that he was a prophet decreed to effect that reform so long the object of his meditations; or whether it might not be a mere vision, a delusion of the senses, or worse than all, the apparition of an evil spirit.[57]

Even the greatest spiritual teachers had difficulty verifying their own experiences; there is no measuring rod.

Only a fine line may separate authentic revelation from complete self-delusion. Modern science tends to lean toward the assumption of delusion—it is easier to explain. However, one must wonder where humanity would be without these empowering visions, without religious belief, without our mythology and our sense of the divine. To be sure, some of this belief has been to humankind's detriment, but on the whole, it has given us the richness of life, the color, the drama, and indeed its sense of purpose.

It would appear that the majority of humankind has integrated—on the most rudimentary level, perhaps even as part of our RNA/DNA structure—a universal mystical language, which seems to cross all cultural barriers. When a spiritual teacher speaks in this language, a curious awareness arises within us. We are certain there is something beyond our understanding, a truth we may be able to reach only through experience, and this alone empowers our continuing quest.

In any case, it is wise to be extremely cautious before drawing conclusions about unusual experiences that come out of spiritual practice. The more we work on our spiritual development, the more we understand the extent to which we live in an illusory world. Often the most devoted practitioners are the ones who have the least to say. Many teachers, in fact, require secrecy as a part of the discipline. This not only helps to contain the power of the experience, it also protects the student from falling into the trap of self-delusion.

Most Sufi practices are performed in strict secrecy. There are hints in books that one main practice involves the constant repetition of the name of God. There are a number of accounts of retreats in modern times where the retreatant chants a *dhikr* throughout the entire retreat period, often lasting forty days. A *dhikr* is a special kind of mantra, often repeating the Arabic phrase, *"Lā il'lā ha illā Allah-Hu"* (There is no God but God).

The *dhikr* is sometimes accompanied by whirling the head in a characteristic circular motion, drawing down the divine energy. The movement begins facing upward, and then sweeps around clockwise, reaching the point of looking upward once again. This is done while chanting the first four syllables, *"Lā il'lā ha."* Then the head drops straight down on the sound *"illā,"* chin to the chest, filling the heart with the sound. Finally the head lifts with the sound of *"Allah"* and completes the cycle facing upward, drawing from the heart a final sigh of the unsounded *"Hu,"* one of the unutterable holy names of God. This is one round that may be repeated hundreds or even thousands of times.

There are many other ways to perform *dhikr.* Some involve movement, others are done simply on the breath. *Dhikr* should never be attempted without the guidance of a competent teacher. It quickly alters our mind state and can soon become overwhelming.

Whirling dervishes add another dimension to this practice. Whereas the *dhikr* described above is usually performed seated, either alone or in a circle of fellow participants, the whirling dervishes stand and twirl their entire bodies. The whirling rapidly induces a state of altered consciousness to the extent that some teachers will test a student's absorption by plunging a long needle through the disciple's arm. In a deep, altered state, the student feels no pain and hardly bleeds. There are many Sufi groups that disapprove of this level of rapture and strongly adhere to sobriety in their practice.

Among the few recorded Sufi autobiographies is one of

the eleventh-century leader, al-Ghazzālī. A physician who began his exploration of Sufism as an intellectual, he soon realized that he could appreciate the tradition only by direct experience. He left his successful medical practice, his fortune, his family, and "went to Syria, where I remained about two years, with no other occupation than living in retreat and solitude, conquering my desires, combatting my passions, training myself to purify my soul, to make my character perfect, to prepare my heart for meditating on God—all according to the methods of the Sufis, as I had read of them."[58]

Al-Ghazzālī's story has a familiar ring despite having happened almost a thousand years ago.

> *This retreat only increased my desire to live in solitude, and to complete the purification of my heart and fit it for meditation. But the vicissitudes of the times, the affairs of the family, the need of subsistence, changed in some respects my primitive resolve, and interfered with my plans for a purely solitary life. I had never yet found myself completely in ecstasy, save in a few single hours; nevertheless, I kept the hope of attaining this state. Every time that the accidents [events that broke the solitude] led me astray, I sought to return; and in this situation I spent ten years.*[59]

This is the man who was considered "the greatest Muslim after Muhammad"[60] and "the most influential theologian of medieval Islam."[61] He teaches us:

> *The first condition for a Sufi is to purge his heart entirely of all that is not God. The next key of the contemplative life consists in the humble prayers which escape from the fervent soul, and in the meditation on God in which the heart is swallowed up entirely. But in reality this is only the beginning of the Sufi life, the end of Sufism being total absorption in God.*[62]

In the seventeenth century lived a Sufi named Tevek-kul-Beg. He relates:

I followed the prescription of my master to the letter, and from day to day the spiritual world unveiled itself to me more and more; the next day [after the initial experience with his master] I saw the forms of the prophet and his chief companions, and legions of angels and saints passed before my inner sight. Three months passed in this way; then the sphere in which all color dissolves was opened to me, and all images disappeared. During this time the master did not cease to expound to me the doctrine of union with God and mystical sight; but the absolute reality still would not reveal itself to me. The knowledge of absolute reality in relation to the comprehension of my own existence came to me only after a year's time. In that moment the following verses were revealed to my heart, from which they passed, as it were, without my knowledge, to my lips:

I knew not that this corpse was anything other than water
*   and earth;*
I know not the powers of the heart, of the soul, of the body.
What misfortune that without you this time of my life passed
*   away!*
You were I, and I knew it not.[63]

Much of the Sufi literature is expressed in metaphors, analogies, tales, and stories rather than in explicit description. Although the references may be somewhat oblique, we can read between the lines. Bāyezīd Bistāmī (ninth century) relates: "For twelve years at a stretch I was the smith of my own being. I laid it on the hearth of asceticism, heated it red-hot in the fire of ordeals, set it on the anvil of fear, and pounded it with the hammer of admonition. Thus I made it into a mirror that served me to gaze at myself for five years, during which I never ceased to dissolve the rust from this mirror by acts of piety and devotion." Moreover this Sufi said, "For thirty years I went in search of God, and when at the end of that time I opened my eyes, I discovered that it was he who had been looking for me."[64]

There is a Sufi Order of the West, which should not be confused with traditional Sufis. It was founded in 1910 by Hazrat Inayat Khan, who was sent by his teacher to bring the Sufi message to the West. Just as Buddhism has adapted to the nations where it has been transplanted, so too the Western-oriented Sufi movement has adapted to an eclectic approach. Its basic theme is that all spiritual paths lead "toward the One" ultimate source.

Several offshoots from the original Sufi Order of the West exist today. Some emphasize meditation, others explore such practices as singing the sacred names of the divine from all traditions, or dancing the "Dances of Universal Peace." This is a popular variety of Sufism with which many Westerners are familiar. Most of the retreats in the United States or Europe that mention Sufism are affiliated with the lineage of the Sufi Order of the West.

It is more difficult for Westerners to participate in a retreat associated with traditional Sufism because it usually requires some form of commitment to Islam. The regular experience of an Islamic devotee involves complex procedures in preparation for prayer as well as prayer itself five times a day. In addition, it is necessary to observe an extensive body of law that covers all aspects of normal life. When this is added to requirements of meditation and other practices, we find that traditional Sufism is a highly disciplined way of life that permeates every thought and every cell of the individual.

A few traditional Sufis in the West make some of the practices available, particularly *dhikr*. These teachers can be found in some of the larger cities. Retreats in the Sufi tradition are rarer but may be discovered with persistence. Once one learns the basic practices, it may be possible to develop an individual retreat program under the guidance of a teacher. This can be a powerful, transformative practice.

JUDAISM

Jewish mystics, particularly Kabbalists, have remained among the most hidden from the historians of mystical literature. The foremost authority on Jewish mysticism, Gershom Scholem, tells us that Kabbalists have "an overwhelmingly strong disinclination to treat in express terms of these strictly mystical experiences. Not only is the form different in which these experiences are expressed, but the *will* to express them and to impart the knowledge of them is lacking, or is counteracted by other considerations. . . . The Kabbalists are no friends of mystical autobiography. . . . It is as though they were hampered by a sense of shame. Documents of an intimate and personal nature are not entirely lacking, but it is characteristic that they are to be found almost wholly in manuscripts which the Kabbalists themselves would hardly have allowed to be printed."[65]

Nonetheless, a prophetic tradition explicitly discusses the path of spiritual retreat: "Ancient Hasidim [pious ones] . . . retired into the caves of rocks and into the desert, withdrawing from all social intercourse. Some of them were *hermits in their own houses,* living [at home] as in a desert and praising their Creator without interruption, day and night, with the study of Torah and the Psalms of David . . . until their mind cleaved with a mighty force and passion to the supernal lights."[66]

There are fragments that offer hints about the practices and experiences of ancient Jewish mystics. In one instance—the writings of Abraham Abulafia—considerable detail is revealed on a unique kabbalistic method. Abulafia, born in Saragossa, Spain, in the thirteenth century, developed an unusual meditation on Hebrew letters, mentally merging them in various combinations and permutations. This was a kind of visualization, which elicited a profound rapture and a feeling of complete absorption in the divine. Once again, the method is dependent upon solitude and silence.

> *Be prepared for thy God, oh Israelite! Make thyself ready to direct thy heart to God alone. Cleanse the body and choose a lonely house where none shall hear thy voice. Sit there in thy closet and do not reveal thy secret to any man. If thou canst, do it by day in the house, but it is best if thou completest it during the night. In the hour when thou preparest thyself to speak with the Creator and thou wishest Him to reveal His might to thee, then be careful to abstract all thy thought from the vanities of this world. Cover thyself with thy prayer shawl and put tefillin [phylacteries used in Jewish prayer] on thy head and hands that thou mayest be filled with awe of the Shekhinah [the aspect of God to which we can relate] which is near thee. Cleanse thy clothes, and, if possible, let all thy garments be white, for all this is helpful in leading the heart toward the fear of God and the love of God. . . .[67]*

At this point, Abulafia describes his method in detail; it will be discussed in the chapter on visualization. Then he says,

> *And know, the stronger the intellectual influx within thee, the weaker will become thy outer and thy inner parts. Thy whole body will be seized by an extremely strong trembling, so that thou wilt*

think that surely thou are about to die, because thy soul, overjoyed with its knowledge, will leave thy body. And be thou ready at this moment consciously to choose death, and then thou shalt know that thou hast come far enough to receive the influx [a flow of insight].[68]

Abulafia's methods for attaining ecstasy were difficult, yet he influenced many Jewish mystics following him. Here is an account of an anonymous disciple, who wrote at the end of the thirteenth century:

> *One night, after working for many months in the method, I noticed that the candle was about to go out. I rose to put it right, as oftentimes happens to a person awake. Then I saw that the light continued. I was greatly astonished, as though, after close examination, I saw that it issued from myself. I said: "I do not believe it." I walked to and fro all through the house and behold, the light is with me; I lay on a couch and covered myself up, and behold, the light is with me all the while. I said: "This is truly a great sign and a new phenomenon which I have perceived."*[69]

At this point the disciple was given advanced instructions from his teacher, but he decided to go even further:

> *I set out to take up the Great Name of God, consisting of seventy-two names, permuting and combining it. But when I had done this for a little while, behold, the letters took on in my eyes the shape of great mountains. Strong trembling seized me and I could not summon strength, my hair stood on end, and it was as if I were not in this world. At once I fell down, for I no longer felt the least strength in any of my limbs. And behold, something resembling speech emerged from my heart and came to my lips and forced them to move. I thought—perhaps this is, God forbid, a spirit of madness that has entered me. But behold, I saw it uttering wisdom. I said: "This is indeed the spirit of wisdom."*[70]

The next day the disciple was reprimanded by his teacher, but he pleaded to be given the power to cope with the experience. The teacher replied, "My son, it is the Lord who must bestow such power upon you for such power is not within man's control."[71]

The disciple then related, with some humility, the following experience:

> That Sabbath night also the power was active in me in the same way. When, after two sleepless nights, I had passed day and night in meditating on the permutations or on the principles essential to a recognition of this true reality and to the annihilation of all extraneous thought—then I had two signs by which I knew that I was in the right receptive mood. The one sign was the intensification of natural thought on very profound objects of knowledge, a debility of the body and strengthening of the soul until I sat there, my self all soul. The second sign was that imagination grew strong within me and it seemed as though my forehead were going to burst. Then I knew that I was ready to receive the Name.[72]

He continues now into uncharted waters:

> I also that Sabbath night ventured at the great ineffable Name of God [the tetragrammaton—the unpronounceable name Y-H-W-H]. But immediately that I touched it, it weakened me and a voice issued from me saying: "Thou shalt surely die and not live! Who brought thee to touch the Great Name?" And behold, immediately I fell prone and implored the Lord God saying: "Lord of the universe! I entered into this place only for the sake of Heaven, as Thy glory knoweth. What is my sin and what my transgression? I entered only to know Thee, for has not David already commanded Solomon: 'Know the God of thy father and serve Him'; and has not our master Moses, peace be upon him, revealed this to us in the Torah saying: 'Show me now Thy way, that I may know Thee, that I may there find grace in Thy sight?' " And behold, I was still speaking and oil like the oil of the anointment anointed me from head to foot and very great joy seized me which for its spirituality and the sweetness of its rapture I cannot describe.[73]

We must pause for a moment after reading such a description to reflect upon our natural mind filters. Some of us will automatically try to categorize the experience. Some of us may be skeptics and not believe his report. We may try to explain in scientific and psychological terms how such a person could become deluded. Some of us will assess and compare this experience with others we have read about. We look for a niche and try to give the experience a name.

Some people may be disturbed by the messianic flavor of this account, others by the intimacy with God and the typically Jewish chutzpah revealed here in arguing with God. Some may feel distanced from the experience, as if it is something wholly beyond them. It is worthwhile to explore our feelings as we read these kinds of passages. We will begin to learn more about ourselves than the material we are reading. We will begin to gain insight into our own areas of resistance. These are the areas that will often be major stumbling blocks in the early periods of building a meditation and retreat practice.

Finally, we may have already had experiences of our own. Then it is likely that we will recognize in this account the familiar essence of what is called the "mystical fragrance," a common insight in authentic mystical descriptions.

The thirteenth-century disciple speaks directly to the reader, the skeptic, the philosopher, the doubter, the psychologist, the judge, and the mystic:

All this happened to your servant in his beginnings. And I do not, God forbid, relate this account from boastfulness in order to be thought great in the eyes of the mob, for I know full well that greatness with the mob is deficiency and inferiority with those searching for the true rank which differs from it in genus and in species as light from darkness.

Now, if some of our own philosophizers, sons of our people who feel themselves attracted toward the naturalistic way of knowledge and whose intellectual power in regard to the mysteries of the Torah is very weak, read this, they will laugh at me and say, "See how he tries to attract our reason with windy talk and tales, with fanciful imaginations which have muddled his mind and which he takes at their face value because of his weak mental hold on natural science." Should however Kabbalists see this, such as have some grasp of this subject or even better such as have had things divulged to them in experiences of their own, they will rejoice and my words will win their favor. But their difficulty will be that I have disclosed all of this in detail. Nevertheless, God is my witness that my intention is in majorem dei gloriam *[for the greater glory of God] and I would wish that every single one of our holy nation were even more excellent herein and purer than I.*[74]

There have been many Jewish luminaries who have followed practices of seclusion, either as Kabbalists, or through deep yearning in their souls. The most influential Jewish mystics almost all recommended practices of spiritual solitude, inner silence, and simplicity. For example, Chaim Vital (1542–1629), the leading disciple of Isaac Luria (discussed below), is the source of the exposition of Lurianic Kabbalah. Vital describes the path of divine illumination as follows:

It calls for a person to repent with great earnestness of all wrongs he has committed. Then he is to perfect his life by performing positive commandments and by directing his prayer toward their highest purpose, and by zealously pursuing the study of Torah, for its own sake, as an ox bows its head to the yoke, until his strength is sapped; and by confining himself to few pleasures, and little eating and drinking; and by rising at midnight or a little earlier, and by turning away from all unbecoming traits, and withdrawing from people, even from idle conversation.

Then he is to cleanse his body by continuous immersion [in a mikva—*a body of "living" water used for purification]. He is to isolate himself for periods of time and contemplate the fear of God,*

*putting the divine name Y-H-W-H before his eyes always while
making sure to empty his thoughts from the follies of this world; and
he is to be attached to God's love with great yearning.*[75]

Vital was a mystic's mystic. Isaac Luria said that Vital
was one of the few people who could integrate and be
completely at one with Luria's cosmic kabbalistic perspective. In Vital's instruction to the seeker, he used what
we today would call a holistic model of the Creation. The
kabbalistic approach is that the microcosm (man) parallels
the macrocosm (the universe) in all realms. Using this
idea, we can gain an understanding of the higher levels of
creation by delving into our own individual being.

There is something distinctive in Vital's method. The
general approach of other traditions is that one-pointed
concentration will ultimately lead to expanded awareness.
Vital suggests that although higher realms of consciousness will be enhanced through efforts of concentration,
the topmost level of God-consciousness will not come on
its own. He maintains there is another factor needed to
trigger the flow of divine inspiration, and that this is done
through utilizing the power of imagination. In essence,
Vital teaches us to seed the imagination through visualization, thus giving us access to the highest levels attainable by human consciousness.

Up to a certain point, Vital's method parallels traditional Eastern meditation. There is a period of purification. There is a concentrated meditation to reach a state of
mind where the "imaginative faculty, which usually
works on material supplied by the senses, is now free to
imagine and contemplate more spiritual things."[76]

Then Vital changes direction. He consciously uses the
imagination, allowing images to develop as if one were

having an illuminating experience. In a way, he pretends that he is having a profound enlightenment. This self-guided imagination, once initiated, begins to flow freely, having its own particular magic, and it brings about a mystical, alchemical transformation.

The alchemy works in this way: Just as there is a relationship between micro and macro, this "meditative ascent, though taking place in the imagination only, thus makes the same real impact on the higher worlds and has the same effects on the soul as would a real ascent through the heavens in which the soul ecstatically left the body."[77]

This is an astonishing idea. Most teachings emphasize that we must wait for our supreme moment of mysterious grace. Vital's method is to push ourselves to higher planes through imagination. Obviously, if we have not done the preliminary work of purification, these efforts will meet immediate resistance. As purification increases and concentration becomes stronger, this practice should become more effective.

In the end, there may not be a great deal of difference between this method and just sitting passively. In subtle realms, it is hard to differentiate what or who is doing the motivating. Nonetheless, the idea of using the power of imagination as an active meditative technique provides us with an extremely valuable tool.

The teachings of Chaim Vital regarding meditative practices are thoroughly impregnated with the experiences and wisdom of Isaac Luria, his main teacher. Luria, born in Jerusalem in 1534, made what many Jewish scholars consider the most important contribution to kabbalistic thought in the last five hundred years. He is widely known as "the Ari," which is derived from the first letters of his Hebrew nickname, "the divine Rabbi Isaac" (haElohi Rav Yitzhak).[78] It is additionally a play on words as *Ari* in Hebrew means "lion." His contemporaries felt that he possessed the "holy spirit" and that he was given the "revelation of Elijah."[79] Even today, in traditional circles, Isaac Luria is viewed with awe. Luria is reputed to have practiced solitude and meditation extensively. He left no autobiographical notes, but his students reported that while in his twenties he spent seven years alone engaged in esoteric study on the island Jazirat al-Rawda on the Nile, near Cairo.[80] During these years he spent six days a week in silence and solitude, coming out only on the seventh, the Sabbath.

Despite the fact that he taught for only a few years in the town of Safed in Palestine—he died of plague at the age of thirty-eight—Luria changed the face of Judaism. He introduced a complex system of kabbalistic insight that completely altered the Jewish mystical approach. Our perspective of the visualization techniques of Chaim Vital gives us an insight into the meditative life of Isaac Luria.

Joseph Karo (1477–1575), another in the Safed circle, is famous today as the author of the most authoritative Jewish code of law known as the *Shulhan Arukh* (Arranged Table), which remains a primary source for scholars. He is also known as one who recorded, at length and in significant detail, regular, ongoing interaction with his *maggid* (an inner guide who directs, warns, or encourages its host on a wide variety of spiritual matters). Many well-known mystics in Judaism, including Isaac Luria, Moses Cordovero, Moses Alsheikh, and Moses Hayyim Luzzatto had visits from *maggidim*. However, none of these men chronicled the relationship in such detail as Joseph Karo.

Although Karo was a mystic, he was not considered part of Luria's inner circle in Safed. There were two distinct paths of meditation. On the one side, Luria,

Vital, and Luria's disciples contemplated the unknown dimensions of the *sefirot* (in Kabbalah, the lights and vessels through which the universe was created) and the secret levels of Talmudic exegesis; on the other side, Karo was urged by his *maggid* to cleave to the law, to study constantly, and to meditate on the law whenever the physical engagement in its study was somehow prevented. In the end, both paths had a distinct impact on modern Judaism.

Another teacher who transformed Jewish practice was the Baal Shem Tov, also known as "the Besht," an acronym from the initial letters of this Hebrew nickname, which means "the Master of the Good Name." His given name was Israel ben Eliezer and he was born at the beginning of the eighteenth century in Podolia, a province of Russia. The life of the Baal Shem Tov is shrouded in legend, stories of miracles abound, yet everyone agrees that this man marked the beginning of the modern Hasidic movement. It is said that he and his wife went into seclusion in the Carpathian Mountains during his twenties.[81]

> During his seven years of seclusion, he would meditate in the mountains, as well as in a special cave. When he studied together with the son of Rabbi Adam, he did so in a separate "Meditation Room" and it was in this room that they engaged in unusual practices in an attempt to commune with the Angel of the Torah. Later, when he was a famed leader, he would also spend much time in such a Meditation Room.[82]

From this experience and his propensity to wander alone in the woods, came his insight that joy and devotion in prayer were as important, if not more so for the practicing Jew, than the study of the law. In fact, the study itself needed to have built in to it a sense of intimacy with God; it needed to be uplifted as if it were a form of praying.[83]

One of the early Hasidic rebbes (spiritual leaders who are on a different level than ordinary rabbis) was also critical of rote practice, not only of the opposing scholarly faction, but of his own followers. Reb Menahem Mendl of Kotzk (1787–1859), known as the Kotzker Rebbe, could not tolerate religious observance performed without mindfulness. It was not the law he challenged, for he accepted the traditional tenets as essential to the practice of Judaism, but "he dared to teach that the preparation for prayer surpassed prayer itself. . . ."[84] He also felt that "God loves novelty"; there should not be mere repetition, but rather the creativity of individual intention.

In the time of the Kotzker, only a few generations after the Baal Shem Tov: "Hasidism had become a mass trend, threatened with spiritual enfeeblement, even trivialization. The only possibility of renewal, thought the Kotzker, lay in the reinstatement of the individual's role. The movement that had come into being through stress on the personal aspect of Judaism could be reborn only by an emphasis on individualism."[85]

The Kotzker was one of those rare individuals who so passionately integrated his convictions that he was driven to do what lesser men consider unthinkable. In 1840, when he realized that his message was falling on deaf ears, he decided on a life of complete solitude. This lasted until his death twenty years later. Some scholars believe this seclusion was a resignation, a defeat, perhaps even the result of a nervous breakdown. Yet, although he stopped seeing people, the effect of his silence touched his followers in more profound ways than would have been possible if he had remained accessible. This is not to say that his solitude should be romanticized or that he intended to use his self-exile as a statement. It is clear that he did what he did out of spiritual necessity. He saw hypocrisy, triviality, emptiness, and spiritual corruption all around him. This was almost unbearable for him and so he became, as one of his biographers, A. J. Heschel, said, "a thunderbolt in solitude."

Mainstream Jewish teaching is generally opposed to isolation. There is the view expressed by Hillel, a sage who lived two thousand years ago and whose legal opinions dominate Jewish law, "Do not sever yourself from the community,"[86] and the teaching of Rabbi Chanina ben Dosa, another ancient sage, who appears in the Talmud, "Anyone who is liked by his fellow men is liked by God; anyone who is not liked by his fellow men is not liked by God."[87] Still we find that "solitude was a common practice among mystically inclined Jews. Even the non-mystical Jewish writers of the Middle Ages seem to agree that solitary living was indispensable to the attainment of spiritual purity. This view may be found in the writings of Abraham Ibn Ezra, Maimonides, Badarshi, Falaquera, Gersonides, Albo, Crecas, and Abravanel among others."[88]

Rebbe Nachman of Breslov (1772–1810), the great-grandson of the Baal Shem Tov, is another powerful figure who spent large amounts of time in solitude. He recommended that his disciples spend at least one hour a day alone in communion with God. As a young boy, Nachman had ascetic tendencies, and he was known for going out of his way to avoid the pleasures of food, either by eating without chewing or by fasting. In later years, he would often abstain from food during the week, breaking his fast only on the Sabbath. It should be noted, however, that at the end of his life he admonished his students not to be excessive in austerities and admitted that he should have taken better care of his body.

One of the main disciplines Rebbe Nachman passed on to his followers, which is still practiced today, is *hitbodedut*, a method of going out alone, preferably at night in a forest, and talking to God in a common language rather than structured prayer. We may do this practice in a quiet room, but Rebbe Nachman preferred to be in natural surroundings. *Hitbodedut* is an unrestricted, free-form method of prayer, where a devotee can pour out his heart to God. Nachman, who throughout his life suffered from severe physical problems, deaths in the family, mental anguish, and constant conflict with other religious figures, refused to succumb to sadness or angst. He said over and over, "Never despair," for the only way to commune with God is through joy.

One of the best-known Jewish mystics of the twentieth century is Rabbi Abraham Isaac Kook (1865–1935), who was the chief rabbi of Palestine before the founding of the state of Israel. Rav Kook was a universalist, as most mystics tend to be. He was known for his open-arms approach to Jews and non-Jews alike. From his perspective, thoughts of division and separation strengthen individual egos, and this is the antithesis of enlightenment.

The firmer a person's vision of universality, the greater the joy he will experience, and the more he will merit the grace of divine illumination. The reality of God's providence is discernible when the world is seen in its totality. God's presence is not manifest in anything defective. Since He does not abide where there is a deficiency, how can He abide where everything is lacking, where all we have is the weak and puny entity, only the particularity of the ego?[89]

Rav Kook also respected silence and spiritual retreat, and he often wrote of it as if it were an imperative. "The person with a radiant soul must withdraw into privacy frequently. The constant company of other people, who are, for the most part, crude in comparison with him, even in their spirituality, dims the clear light of his higher soul."[90]

Seclusion, however, is not the end, but the means. It provides for spiritual renewal, but community demands play an even higher role for the spiritual aspirant. Rav Kook taught:

> It is very difficult to suffer the company of people, the encounter with persons who are totally immersed in a different world with which a person who is given to spiritually sensitive concerns, to lofty moral aspiration, has no contact. Nevertheless, it is this very sufferance that ennobles a person and elevates him. The spiritual influence that a person of higher stature exerts on the environment, which comes about through the constant encounter, purifies the environment. It lends the graces of holiness and freedom on all who come in contact with him. And this nobility of a holy grace returns after a while with stronger force and acts on the person himself who exerted the influence, and he becomes sociable, abounding in spirituality and holiness. This is a higher attribute than the holiness in a state of withdrawal, which is the normal fate of the person to whom the higher spiritual concerns are the foundation of his life.[91]

At another point, Rav Kook teaches about the person with spiritual longing:

> Let him not be troubled by any impediments in the world, whether physical or spiritual, from hastening after what is the essence of his life and his true perfection. He may assume that it is not only his own perfection and deliverance that hinges on the improvement of his character, but also the deliverance of the community and the perfection of the world. Every soul that has reached fulfillment always perfects the general character of the world. All life is blessed through the truly enlightened ones, when

they press on resolutely on their course, without being restrained by life's obstacles.[92]

In true kabbalistic form, Rav Kook gives us a balance between inward and outward. He recognizes the need for solitude in refining the soul, but he does not walk away from the community, seeing its power as a mode of purification. He considers that the individual drive toward enlightenment has its necessary impact on the whole of humanity, the microcosm being a reflection of the macrocosm, and vice versa. He appreciates the universality, while not denying the role of particularity within a universalistic model. Although clearly a traditionalist, he seems as modern as any contemporary author. Indeed, for twentieth-century Judaism he remains a brilliant light of inspiration.

Jewish mysticism follows a number of paths, which are not necessarily mutually exclusive. There is the traditional approach that requires immersion in Talmudic study, a Hasidic approach that emphasizes prayer and service, and a kabbalistic approach that has unique aspects while overlapping the traditional and Hasidic worlds.

Recently there has been a popularization of Kabbalah in the West. A number of "schools" purport to teach the esoteric secrets of the Kabbalah, exclusive of the basic studies of the Bible, the Talmud, and Jewish law. This is similar to reading a handbook on relativity, knowing that $e = mc^2$, and believing that we therefore understand Einstein's General Theory of Relativity. Yet, Jewish mysticism, including Kabbalah, is accessible for one who is determined. It takes steady patience and extensive study, but the rewards more than compensate for the effort involved.

THE UNIVERSAL NATURE
OF MYSTICISM

We have briefly explored the mystical side of five major spiritual traditions. As we examine the language of the mystics, we soon discover themes that are not limited to a single tradition—and indeed, studies have revealed cross-fertilization. Medieval Kabbalism and Sufism in some cases have identical reference points. Christian mystics understood a clear kabbalistic content in the teachings of Jesus. Hindus and Buddhists, while at odds in doctrine, show commonality in many principles.

The mystical experience is like a great symphony. Each listener filters the music through his own ears and sits in his own space. Thus, he reports in his own special way. Moreover, one who plays a stringed instrument may be more attuned to the string section than one who plays percussion.

Anyone with a ticket can get into the concert hall. Each will appreciate the music according to her or his level. And, whether Kabbalist, Sufi, Buddhist, Hindu, or Christian, no one is going anywhere else since there is no other symphony in town. It is the same for the reports of mystical experiences; if the names are missing, we will have trouble identifying the different traditions. A Sufi may sound like a Kabbalist, a Hindu like a Christian. This is the lovely universality of the "mystical fragrance."

THE UNIVERSAL NATURE OF MYSTICISM

There are certain basic spiritual practices that enhance the mystical experience. Clearly we increase our sensitivities through silence, simplicity, and solitude. From that starting point, almost any activity in which we are engaged will be intensified. When this happens, our potential for deeper experiences increases, our inner worlds become brighter. The clarity and truth of this inner vision will often lead us to deeper practice.

When we meditate alone for a long enough period, visions, illuminations—some would say hallucinations—are commonplace. We experience voices, colors, apparitions, shapes of people, faces both recognizable or unknown, demons, angels—a vast array of experiences. It is therefore helpful to have a guide or teacher who will interpret, caution, encourage, calm, redirect, and stabilize us. Meditation experiences are often disturbing. They may produce intense ecstasy or devastating fear.

If we do not have a reliable guide and are undertaking a solitary retreat without any external support system, it is important to develop a relationship with the "inner guide," that part of us that knows when we are pushing against something that is too big. Without this connection, in the beginning retreats should be undertaken with professional practitioners, in groups, with teaching guidance.

Something awakens in us when we take a retreat. After a week or ten days of silence on a group retreat, a special comradeship develops. When retreatants see each other again, at a new retreat, it is like a family reunion, a deep, unspoken connection, a bond of true respect.

When I retreat at home, as I often do, I am alone, in silence. But I am also with thousands of others around the world, sitting quietly, all of us bonded together in our effort, our solitude, and our prayers. Each moment of the day, thousands, perhaps tens of thousands, are sitting in strong concentration, deepening awareness not only for themselves but for everyone. We are opening our hearts, alone but all-one, joining others throughout the centuries in timeless realms. We dwell in unknown realities, hearing the whisper of universal truth, singing a song of the revelation of the divine. My last extended retreat is finished, but for me it never ends. As my previous retreats blended into this one, it too is blending into the next.

We speak of silence, but it is the richest silence in the world. We speak of simplicity, but what is revealed is the bursting profusion of life. We speak of solitude, but a mystic is never alone.

Perhaps you would like to experience a spiritual retreat for yourself. A part within is probably afraid and says no; another part clearly says yes. The rest of this book is written for your affirmative side. It provides information you need to design your own retreat. If you do not have a spiritual guide, you can begin alone. Your teacher will appear at just the right time.

Each conscious step brings us closer to true realization. Every conscious breath is a moment of expanded knowledge. Everything we ever wanted in spiritual growth is within us. It is only a matter of taking one step, drawing one breath, saying one word with genuine awareness.

SETTING UP
A
RETREAT

INTRODUCTION

When we think of spiritual retreat, we usually think of monasteries or nunneries, caves or forests, deserts or mountains; we think about romantic faraway places like India and the Himalayas, the Sinai, or Tibet. Yet all distinguished teachers remind us that enlightenment comes from within. It does not come from traveling, sitting under a magical tree, drinking sacred waters, or being touched by another enlightened being. It always comes from within.

There are indeed some retreat centers located in gorgeous mountains or on remote islands. There are also retreat facilities located in the middle of noisy cities, in private homes, or near busy traffic lanes. The person sitting quietly in deep concentration does not notice any of this. It does not really matter if the meditator is in the middle of nowhere or surrounded by ten million people.

The most common retreat facility is our own home. It has many advantages in terms of convenience, comfort, cost, timing, and a sense of security. Its disadvantages are usually related to the presence of family members, the telephone, and the doorbell. The less obvious disadvantages have to do with patterning and familiarity, falling into the traps of habitual behavior that break concentration.

Basic guidelines for retreats apply whether we are at home or are fortunate enough to have a convenient facility nearby. An organized group retreat may have a format with variations that meet the need of a particular retreat style. The self-guided retreatant, however, must learn, often the hard way, how to organize the retreat in terms of his or her physical, psychological, emotional, and spiritual needs.

The biggest demon we encounter when thinking about taking a retreat is *our sense of lost time*. It is almost as if time is the enemy, time has us in its grasp, running us ragged, constantly pushing while never giving enough of itself. Time slips past us in the stealth of the night and appears abruptly to startle us in the morning. It dominates our lives with reminders everywhere—beside our bed, in our kitchen, and attached to our arm.

"When do I have time for a retreat?" or "Sitting quietly, doing nothing! It seems such a waste of time!" These are the primary weapons of the time demon. When we are in its territory, these arguments seem so logical, so correct, that they usually win us over.

When we are focused on this feeling of lost time, some part of ourselves is expressing itself. It may be the part that constantly pushes us to achieve something, that measures our self-worth by our actions, or that is afraid of being alone. These and other hidden forces within us that compose our sense of identity, indeed our self-image, will come under scrutiny during a spiritual retreat. This can be very threatening. Thus, the time demon becomes a tool of those parts of us that do not want to be examined too closely. When we face the resistance of not having enough time, we must consider whether in fact it is true, or if it is a ruse to avoid the soul-searching that is a natural product of a spiritual retreat.

If we are clear enough to break through this resistance and are able to find a few days, or even a week for a retreat, then we come to realize what we have been missing. We taste the sweetness of silence, and we ask ourselves why we waited so long. We even make a commitment to take retreats on a regular basis to refresh ourselves. We come back into the world feeling wonderful. Our resistance mechanism waits patiently on the sidelines for a while, and then slowly, inexorably, it creeps in and tries to put us back asleep, using the time demon to convince us that we really cannot afford to take a retreat right now.

It is almost always a struggle to designate time for a retreat—much more so than, for example, taking a vacation. Yet most people who go on retreat gain enormous benefit. Hidden in this paradox is a teaching, which has to do with the cosmic battle between good and evil—when we define good as that which brings us closer to the divine and evil as that which separates us.

Rebbe Nachman of Breslov reveals that "All the barriers and obstacles which confront a person have only one purpose: to heighten his yearning for the holy deed which he needs to accomplish. It is part of man's nature that the greater the barriers standing in the way of a certain goal, the more he desires to achieve it."[1]

With great insight, Rebbe Nachman goes on:

There are people who after a whole lifetime of materialism suddenly feel a strong desire to walk in the paths of God. The attribute of Judgment then rises up to accuse them. It tries to prevent them following the way of God by creating barriers. The unintelligent person, when he sees these barriers, starts to back away. But someone with understanding takes this as the very signal that he should draw closer. He understands that God is to be found in the barrier itself—and the truth is that God Himself is indeed hidden in this barrier.[2]

Our resistance mechanism also uses a more insidious tactic than the time demon. We notice it especially when planning a retreat of more than two weeks. Invariably before such a retreat things will come up—temptations out of the blue, business opportunities, or family crises—things that seem important enough to draw us away from our objective. We need to be very clear and strongly directed to succeed in initiating a retreat.

Getting started is a major defeat to our resistance to self-inspection, and that alone has enormous rewards. If we are able to do nothing more than maintain a regular annual retreat schedule, a few days here and there, perhaps an occasional week or ten days, without considering other gains in terms of spiritual growth, our resistance is weakened. This helps to keep us more sensitized to the elements that drive us, thus resulting in a more balanced approach to life. When we know how to take time for ourselves and learn to appreciate the value of inner silence, everyday pressures do not overwhelm us as much.

After a few years of experience, a committed retreatant knows what to expect from, and how to deal with, the time demon. When time does not dominate us, it becomes a companion, a friend. Time on a retreat is precious, often delicious—a marvelous luxury. Whereas most people point to the benefits of their daily work in terms of possessions, the retreatant realizes that the greatest commodity is not money or what it can buy, it is time and what it can offer. When we are in a state of wakefulness—what is often called "remembering"—every moment is filled with delight.

Most traditions address the constant battle between "remembering" and "falling asleep." In this context, remembering is related to the idea that our primal state is one of full awareness, while in normal consciousness our awareness is blanketed. This buried awareness is called sleep. In Zen, for example, the experience of insight we can attain through practice is called *kenshō,* which literally means "seeing into our true nature." Most of us are asleep. Every so often we remember, then we fall back asleep. Enlightenment is the process of remembering, and a high level of enlightenment is a constantly "remembering" state of being.

A retreat is in itself an environment conducive to remembering. Our initial problem, however, is to awaken enough from sleep to remember and arouse our awareness. When we have enough experience, our awareness remains fresh enough to keep us in our practice. Without experience, we must be brought out of a deep slumber, and that often unfortunately requires considerable shaking and disruption in our lives to help us realize that we are spiritually asleep.

SILENCE

Eliahu (Elijah) "went a day's journey into the wilderness, and came and sat down under a broom tree: and he requested for himself that he might die; and said, it is enough; now, O Lord, take away my life; for I am not better than my fathers." After he slept under the tree, an angel awoke him, and made him eat, two times. After the second time, he "went in the strength of that meal forty days and forty nights to Horev the mountain of God. And he came there to a cave, and lodged there. . . ." He talked with God, and was told, "Go out, and stand upon the mountain before the Lord."

> *And behold, the Lord passed by, and a great and strong wind rent the mountains, and broke the rocks in pieces before the Lord; but the Lord was not in the wind: and after the wind an earthquake; but the Lord was not in the earthquake: and after the earthquake a fire; but the Lord was not in the fire: and after the fire a still small voice. And when Eliahu heard it, he wrapped his face in his mantle, and went out. . . .*[3]

For a retreatant, silence is the environment in which we may hear the "still small voice." One way to reach this inner silence is to stop making noise on the outside—to stop speaking and to stop listening. This is the first level, but it is not sufficient to assure inner silence.

SILENCE

There is a story about an experienced retreatant who decided that he was going to arrange a perfect retreat environment and then sit as long as necessary to attain enlightenment. He found a cabin in the woods, stocked it with provisions, and began his retreat. After a couple of days, however, he noticed noisy music outside. It was constantly distracting him with all kinds of familiar tunes. Finally he realized that it was the bubbling stream running past his cabin!

The music, of course, was in the retreatant's busy mind. Just as fear can bring to life all the shadows on a dark night, so a busy mind can amplify and be irritated by innocuous sound, whether it be insects, rain, or wind. Anyone living in the country is familiar with the racket crickets make at night, or the early morning cacophony of roosters, donkeys, or chirping birds.

Racket? Cacophony? What words are these to describe nature? Yet this is how it might sound to someone seeking perfect silence. If we believe that outward silence is a necessity, then indeed there is hardly a place in the world that will meet our needs. Every sound for us becomes a disturbance.

Some very disturbing sounds certainly exist. These are the sounds that engage the intellect—the sounds of logic, argument, debate, analysis, and commentary; these sounds disrupt inner tranquillity. The usual cause of this type of sound is the human voice, speaking in a familiar language; it may also be the "sound" that jumps off a written page, making a racket in our minds.

The fact that some sounds are disturbing helps us rule out certain sounds for a retreat. Conversation is out, as is television, radio, newspapers, magazines, most books, letters, and business papers. All of this is out. The retreat environment should be arranged to avoid verbal communication, preferably completely, except with a teacher or guide. If we are in a noisy neighborhood and are disturbed by these sounds, we should consider wearing earplugs (the silicone variety is very effective). The retreat space should be cleared of all distracting print material except perhaps one or two works that are inspirational. There should be no letter-writing materials, but a small notebook or journal may be useful.

Some group retreat facilities provide a bulletin board for absolutely necessary communications. After many days on retreat, we begin to glance at the board more frequently, thirsting for some contact with the world, secretly hoping that our name will appear on a note. It would even be nice to read someone else's note! Anything! Then it happens that there is a note for us or somebody writes an open letter to the group, and we get a rush of energy as we read and ingest the words. Then, dear friends, we spend the entire day, perhaps the next day or two, with the mind revolving around the words we read. We begin to be sorry we ever looked at the bulletin board in the first place. Finally the mind gets quiet again, and in its perverse way begins to feel a bit lonely, and we sneak looks at the bulletin board once again. So the cycle goes.

The ingredients of silence on a retreat are one-half preparation, logistics, and design, and one-half determination, integrity, and letting go. It is not natural for us to cut out all outer stimulation. We will fight it with all we have. The mind is extremely ingenious, so we must find a way to build determination. One method we sometimes use is to trick the mind into letting go. We tell ourselves that the retreat is scheduled for a fixed time; we calm ourselves by setting parameters of a few days, a week, a month, whatever. When the retreat is over, we can do as we wish; during the retreat, however, we will accept self-discipline.

We can undertake discipline with strong resolve if we know it is not an indefinite commitment. At the beginning of a retreat, we promise to stick by the rules we have set for this fixed period of time. Once the commitment is made, we try not to think about it again during the retreat, apart from acknowledging it. There are some retreatants who torture themselves by noting the calendar: "Only six days left to go!" or "Just three more days of this!" Then it becomes a self-imposed jail sentence and the mind is not freed at all; it is caught in the trap of expectations and this can be very painful.

If it is so unnatural and so difficult to maintain silence, to eliminate stimulating input, why do it? Sri Ramana Maharshi suggested an answer: "The pure state . . . devoid of any attachment, alone is one's own state of silence. . . . That silence, having experienced it as it is, alone is true mental worship. . . . The performance of the unceasing, true and natural worship . . . is silence, the best of all forms of worship. Silence, which is devoid of the assertive ego, alone is liberation."[4] He went on to say: "Silence is the most potent form of work. . . . The highest form of grace is silence. It is also the highest *upadesa* [teaching]. . . . Silence is never-ending speech. Vocal speech obstructs the other speech of silence. In silence one is in intimate contact with the surroundings."[5]

One of the factors that makes silence so difficult is that the mind is usually completely out of control. To a considerable extent, the communications we have—our daily activities, our continual engagements—provide a smokescreen that makes us unable to recognize the unbridled mind. Once we introduce silence, the spinning mind begins to make itself known. Only when we see it for what it is can we begin to harness it, quiet it, bring it into line. Although it may take a long time to gain real control over the mind, even a partial success results in enormous benefit.

It is often hard to convince ourselves that we might benefit by living in an environment of silence for a few days or more. However, although the retreat process is likely to be demanding, at the end of the period we will appreciate it in a way that defies all logical explanation.

There are some exceptions to the rule of silence on retreat. Brief communication is acceptable with a guide or teacher when it is specific to the retreat itself. Working together with other retreatants in a communal task may require communication, but this should be terse and to the point. We may use sounds, like mantras or sacred music, as part of our practice. On occasion we may, again briefly, read passages from inspiring works or record short notes in a journal.

Wherever there is a limitation, there is a leniency. Leniency is up to the retreatant, and there are times when it is a good idea to break the rules altogether. In this way we often discover how useful the rules are and how much breaking them interferes with the quieting process. Through this experience of confronting the constraints of a disciplined retreat, we realize that the rules are not so much a burden as a framework which has proven effective over thousands of years of experience.

The work on inner silence is accomplished through spiritual practices, which are discussed in the next chapter. The simple truth is that we would benefit without doing any special practices other than sitting in silence. In silence insight develops spontaneously, for that is the nature of the mind.

It has been pointed out in this chapter that hardly any

absolutely silent places exist in the natural world. However, experiments have been done using isolation chambers to simulate environments of complete sensory deprivation. One of the most innovative experimenters with isolation techniques is Dr. John Lilly: "Lilly has probably gone further than anyone else in creating a limited environment. He immerses himself in a bath at the temperature of 96° F, has himself fastened into a harness so that he can hardly move, breathes only through a snorkel so that even his face is covered with water and there is no differentiation of sensation on any part of his body, and within three or four hours he is having tremendous visionary experiences."[6]

If the purpose of a spiritual retreat were to have "tremendous visionary experiences," complete silence in isolation would be the order of the day. A number of other methods would also produce various visions, even ecstasy. The orientation of a retreat, however, is much more profound, much longer lasting—the goal is to develop strength in will, concentration, and self-purification. In so doing, we move continuously in the process of growing awareness, the path of enlightenment.

Inner silence is an essential element of this path. In the works of *Chuang Tzu,* we read: "Men do not mirror themselves in running water—they mirror themselves in still water. Only what is still can still the stillness of other things."[7]

SOLITUDE

The definition of retreat is solitude, a place of separation from our normal world. Usually we think of a cabin in the woods, a hut on a mountain, or perhaps a boat at sea. Arranging for such a place can take time and money, or involve travel. Most people consider a place of solitude a luxury they cannot afford.

Our own residence, however, might be a perfect place for solitude. Even people with large families have been successful in cordoning off a "sacred" space for a period of time. Actually most households have such a space—it is called the bathroom! It is the one place many people can relax in undisturbed peace, to relieve themselves or soak in the bathtub. What a state of affairs it is that for some the bathroom is the only haven in the world!

The first step toward making a place of solitude in our home is believing it is possible. At first glance, most people reject the idea out of hand, thinking there is not enough room, the family is too big or would think it strange, nobody would be willing to cooperate, and moreover, what would the neighbors think?

We need to engage this internal resistance and test its basis. It is true that solitude is much more easily attainable by leaving a family home for a period of time. This may be the most reasonable solution for the person who yearns for time alone. It is particularly useful for an inexperienced meditator who has not built a solid foundation of practice. Nevertheless, if the option of going off for a period to be alone or to join a group retreat is not available, then we should give careful consideration to working out a "sacred" haven within the home.

The likelihood of finding solitude in our own home has to do with priorities. In the beginning it may be difficult. We have not yet savored the delights that come from solitude; thus it remains an ideal instead of a true motivation. At this early stage, the objections stated above seem much more relevant and the idea of retreat may be rejected because of lack of time or space.

After some experience on retreat, ways are found to overcome most barriers and spiritual growth becomes a high priority. A spare room is often available or even part of a room can be screened off. At times it is impossible to consider retreating with a family around, especially with preteen children; at other times family cooperation can be surprising.

If we begin the retreat process with one or two days, it can become part of a life-style for the family to have periods of meditation and periods of relative quiet while a family member retreats. In places like Burma, some retreats are like family outings in the same way that picnics are for Americans; it is simply a matter of priorities.

When one person goes into solitude, everyone in the family is affected. Not only is that person missing from daily activities, but the entire family is naturally brought into a new state of self-reflection. A family is a bonded unit; we cannot undertake a serious spiritual practice without affecting everyone else in the household.

A retreat at home will also have an impact on our

neighbors. More often than not, once they are satisfied that this is not a sickness or depression, they will admit that they too would like to take time to themselves alone. Of course, then they will list the reasons why they think they cannot do it!

This busy life we lead, our calendar filled with business obligations, social activities, or family interaction seven days a week, is a relatively new phenomenon for humankind. It is true that people still find time to relax—evenings in front of a television set, weekends watching or engaging in sports and games. But even this kind of relaxing is still a form of engagement. Missing for most people in today's world is the weekly period of solitude and reflection that was an integral part of life for thousands of years.

In Western tradition it begins with the fourth commandment: "Remember the Sabbath day, to keep it holy."[8] Throughout the Bible there are many instructions concerning the Sabbath. In the Jewish tradition, the Sabbath is a time separate from the six days of the week, a special time for reflection upon the creation. It is a retreat from worldly influence, filled with prayer and study of the Torah. All details of everyday life are excluded from Sabbath conversation; all activities of business or future planning are unacceptable.

Western religions have accepted the idea of the Sabbath as an integral part of the week. For Jews the Sabbath day is Saturday; most Christians have chosen Sunday as their Sabbath; Muslims have chosen Friday. In earlier days, the Sabbath was a time of reflection, inner work, and spiritual revitalization.

The Sabbath provides a different perspective on what is meant by spiritual solitude. In its normal, everyday use, solitude means to be alone, to be physically separated from others. This is not the definition of spiritual solitude. We can experience spiritual solitude in the midst of dozens, hundreds, even thousands of people. Spiritual solitude means separation not from people, but from that which is part of the manifest, physical aspect of creation.

We have all had the feeling of aloneness in the midst of a large crowd of people. This is more a sense of alienation, not being like the rest of those around us, not having enough in common. In spiritual solitude the opposite happens. We feel commonality and universality with all creation and we dwell in the timeless and spaceless realms, where the soul is at home and the heart is at peace.

There is a definite correlation between spiritual solitude and physical solitude. Both exclude activities of everyday life. Silence—both inner and outer—is a criterion for spiritual solitude, although not so much for physical solitude. On the other hand, whereas physical solitude means being alone, spiritual solitude allows us to be among others—under one of two conditions: 1) the others are simultaneously engaged in the practice, as in a group retreat; or 2) the others are sensitized to and protective of the needs of the practitioner.

A third way to achieve spiritual solitude among others, which is available to exceptional meditators and retreatants, occurs when we have developed enough light within us to bring it into the world, to be here and yet not caught up by the world. Some accomplish this by continuous internal repetition of a mantra, some observe their breath, and others have advanced practices that keep them in a state of constant awareness. This is difficult to do, but the more experienced the meditator or retreatant, the easier it becomes.

The celebrated Jewish philosopher Maimonides (1135–1204) considered this type of spiritual solitude "the highest perfection wise men can attain." He taught,

> When we are with our heart constantly near God, even while our body is in the society of men, when we are in that state which the Song [of Songs] on the relationship between God and man poetically describes in the following words: "I sleep, but my heart wakes; it is the voice of my beloved that knocks."[9]—then we have attained not only the height of ordinary prophets, but of Moses, our Teacher. . . .[10]

The Sufis also believed spiritual solitude in the world to be an exceptional state. "The true saint goes in and out amongst the people and eats and sleeps with them and buys and sells in the market and takes part in social intercourse, and never forgets God for a single moment."[11] The Naqshbandi mystics of the fourteenth century defined this as "*khalwat dar anjuman*, complete absorption in proximity to God in the midst of a crowd; the perfect mystic's concentration can no longer be disturbed or altered by any external event or occupation."[12]

In Buddhism, Zen master Eihei Dōgen admonishes us,

> Do not think that this silence is useless and empty. Entering the monastery and doing zazen in silence, or leaving the monastery and going all about are both the form of the continuous practice. . . . Do not sit and wait for enlightenment, for great enlightenment is to be found in everyday activities such as eating or drinking tea.[13]

It is very nice to be able to go off to a cabin in the woods or an established retreat facility, but a good, solid, fulfilling retreat can be accomplished in our own home. After realizing that it is possible to work out a place for solitude at home, the next task is to acclimatize anyone else who lives with us to the idea that we are going to take some time to ourselves. Usually, the fewer the people involved, the easier this is. Anyone who lives alone may have to do nothing more than post a note on the door and turn on the telephone answering machine. It is also relatively easy when there is only one other person, a spouse, or a roommate. It gives the other person a chance for quiet as well.

If we live in a family, a retreat takes a bit more planning and preparation. Everyone needs to know what is going on and what is expected in terms of cooperative behavior. Everyone needs to be reassured that their physical needs will be met, and, more important, they must feel psychologically and emotionally comfortable with the situation and understand that they are not dealing with a strange sickness or mental illness.

It is unusual for people to be given time and space to be alone in their own homes. Today we think of it as bizarre behavior; years ago the newspapers made Greta Garbo seem weird because she said, "I want to be alone." Also, people are often uncomfortable when someone in the same dwelling does not speak. They may think it is something personal, and insecurity and paranoia can arise.

When we are accomplished meditators, we can recognize when the mind is caught in fear, anger, paranoia, or other negative frames of reference. Unfortunately, a person who does not meditate often becomes identified with these states and can make life difficult for anyone who simply wants to be alone.

Just as spiritual solitude does not mean that a person has to be physically alone, conversely, being alone does not mean we will have spiritual solitude. When those closest to us are agitated about us, our minds may also become agitated. So it does not help to seal the door to our private room if we have left emotional baggage with others in the living room. The door is not thick enough to guarantee our solitude. Leaving an unprepared family and going to a cabin in the woods will not grant us the solitude we are seeking.

It becomes a delicate issue when our impulse for spiritual solitude is not appreciated by the rest of the family. Everyone does not need to concur, but there does have to be some degree of understanding. The keys here are timing, compassion, and beginning slowly. We must realize that the spiritual imperative for others may not be as pressing as it is for ourselves. Adequate groundwork with plenty of time for reflection will slowly accustom others to the idea. Beginning with a very short retreat of between one and three days is usually not too threatening.

There are many solutions. We can go to a friend's house or to a local hotel; it is obviously easier without the kids. It is a rare family with preteen children that can provide a protected space for a family member. The kids can be farmed out for a few days to friends or family. When the children are beyond the early teens, however, other arrangements can be worked out.

It is usually just as good, if not better, to have one other person around than to be completely alone. This person can be the guardian of the retreat space, intercepting messages, dealing with necessities, answering the door, and at times even preparing food. My wife plays an invaluable role in protecting my solitude when I retreat at home, which is often. In return, I always enjoy being the guardian of her retreats.

If at least one other person is around, the rules of solitude are fairly simple. A basic physical space should be available where the retreatant can sit and lie down. This space needs to be completely private. There should be no need for anyone else to enter it. The family should be asked to minimize frivolous noise, but everyday activities and conversation do not have to stop. Preferably the location of the private space will be away from most conversation; if not, the family can be asked to speak more softly. It would be good, if possible, to set a moratorium on the use of television, radio, and stereo. Everyone, in some way, will be participating in this retreat.

The retreatant will need to go to the bathroom. Family members must understand that chance encounters will not be met with a greeting, perhaps not even with a silent glance. This is often very difficult for others. Most of us tend to be uncomfortable when not acknowledged. We need the reassurance of brief conversation, or simply a grunt or slight gesture. Even when warned in advance, a person encountering a silent family member may experience the feeling that something is wrong, which can trigger doubts and fears. The retreatant should therefore try, whenever possible, to avoid contact with others.

This private space within the home becomes the retreatant's domain for the entire period. The rest of the house should be considered the outside world. A retreatant often wishes to step out a moment for a change of scenery or a breath of fresh air, but he or she must be wary of a chance encounter with family or neighbors. The solitude can be easily disrupted. A brief exchange, even if the subject matter is trivial, can affect hours or days of our inner silence.

Azikri (sixteenth century) says:

> It is written, "and Noah walked with God."[14] This signifies that he secluded himself with his Creator and avoided human company. Or else it may signify that he was so advanced in the practice of solitude that even when he was among men these did not distract

him, for they were as nonexistent in his eyes. . . . A man in the company of others is like unto one who has fallen into the sea—unless he swims well he will be drowned; but if he flees society and secludes himself with his Creator, then he is like one in a boat, saved and in communion with God.[15]

SIMPLICITY

"Simplify, simplify, simplify," Henry David Thoreau advised us from his own life experiences and his famous retreats near Walden Pond. Most of us have heard this sage counsel but very few have followed it or begun to understand the sublime impact simplicity could have on our lives.

We live in a consumer society. This means that our environment is saturated with consumerism: buying and selling, creating believable needs, production and marketing. Some real estate promotions even try to convince us that the air we breathe is something we need to buy. As factory production proliferates, it appears more and more true that our air, our water, our forests, our natural resources will become consumer goods that all have a price.

Simplification is another word for the conservation of life's most precious commodity: time. Whether we are on retreat for one day, a weekend, or three months, every minute is precious. We learn as part of the retreat training to approach every task as a meditation; there is really no way to waste time when we are properly concentrated. Nevertheless, we simplify life because some activities are difficult to undertake, some draw off considerable physical or mental energy, and some are just outright distractions.

As our minds become quieter, we are able to turn up the power of the inner microscope on our thought processes. Thoughts move at lightning speed, so the microscope must be very high-powered. At a certain point in quieting, we have access to an even more powerful magnification, like a mental electron microscope. With this we can actually see thoughts as they arise; we can see what caused them, what molds them as they take shape. We can watch them flow, observing how our mind state affects them, how they affect our mind state, how they blossom into ideas and concepts. We can watch them being confronted by other thoughts and beliefs, and we can watch them fade away, as they always do.

All of this normally happens in a few seconds, but it can seem like hours, days, or weeks. It is as if each thought-stream creates its own universe. During the time we live in this universe, we believe it to be real. When we snap out of it, it disappears, and we often cannot remember it even existed. Think of the mental universes you were in yesterday. There were thousands, but you can hardly remember any. Try to remember even five minutes ago.

Every activity that makes up our day, each wandering thought, every movement of the body, is the catalyst for an entire array of thinking which will give birth to one or more inner universes. Each of these thought universes has its birth, life, and death; throughout the day they pile on top of one another in rapid succession.

Each bubble in this effervescent mind process leaves a residual effect. Our state of being, our mood, our interactions, our coping, our alertness, everything is related to the mind flow. Moreover, from a meditative perspective, our ability to tune in to the more subtle realms, the finer levels of consciousness, is directly dependent upon our ability to minimize this free-flowing thought process.

Almost all meditation technique is directed to the simplification of the mental process. (In the next section we will discuss many methods for accomplishing this.) Meditation practices can be enhanced if we structure the external process of living in simple terms. This of course not only applies to the preparation for a retreat, but is a significant element in daily life. The more simply we organize our lives, the more rewarding we will find our inner work.

Part of the reason we do not try to simplify our lives is because we have come to believe that we need things that are in fact unnecessary. Often we have become so accustomed to a particular way of living that we cannot conceive of any change. This again is not something that can be explained. It can only be experienced. When we appreciate the deep satisfaction of simple existence, as for example during a long retreat, we gain a new perspective on what in life are true benefits and what are actually liabilities that weigh heavily on our consciousness.

The extent to which we are able to simplify is a matter of individuality. People have had different life experiences, and they will begin from different points. One person needs to be outdoors more, another cannot tolerate the bugs. One person needs plenty of heat, another prefers a cooler climate. One person cannot begin the day without a large breakfast, another does not eat until afternoon. The individual retreatant must decide which of his or her particular needs are important.

The retreat space should have in it only the things that are needed for the retreat. Extra items can be distractions or temptations. Books or magazines, newspapers, a tape recorder, photo albums, old letters, a television set— things like these do not need to be in a retreat space.

A worthwhile act of preparation is to clean a space for ourselves. As we sweep away the dust, we can also put away memories, burdens, stale thoughts; we can set aside temptations, we can open a place of optimism within, a place of hope.

A large percentage of the waking hours on retreat are spent "sitting." As will be discussed, there are many different practices that we can do sitting, but the sitting itself is usually the major activity. Comfort therefore becomes a key consideration for a retreatant. Experienced meditators have a wide range of sitting paraphernalia: cushions of all designs, foam lifts for knees, folding chairs, kneeling benches, and normal full-sized chairs.

Although we may have meditated an hour a day for a long time before attempting a first retreat, it is not uncommon to discover that the intensity of sitting on retreat puts more physical demands on the body than expected and new sitting arrangements must be explored. No matter what sitting arrangement we finally use, invariably there will be periods of discomfort and pain.

Some meditation disciplines are very strict concerning the number and kind of cushions used. My own tendency is to be lenient, to use whatever I need in the quest for comfort. My retreat space has plenty of cushions, pillows, foam, and whatever else is necessary to find a configuration that will work for me. It often changes from one retreat to the next, but the vital thing is always to keep the back straight.

I once sat with a friend, a Zen monk, who wryly commented on my "throne" of foam. One morning someone suggested we all do a two-hour sit. Two hours

SIMPLICITY

is not unusual for me, as a *Vipassanā* practitioner, but most Zen meditation sits, because of strictness and formality, last under an hour. In fact, dedicated Zen students call a double sit, which lasts about an hour and twenty minutes, "killer" sits.

Ninety minutes into our meditation, I heard the quiet rustle of my friend's robes, as he tried to adjust his position without being noticed. Trying to adjust position, one learns, is usually a terrible mistake. It only makes things worse. Sure enough, in a few minutes, he was moving without caring about the noise. Moving! For a Zen monk this is cause for *seppuku*. He made it to the end of the sit, moving a number of times, grand beads of sweat pouring onto his beautiful Japanese robes.

At breakfast he asked if I had felt any pain. I said that I had; it had been a rough sit. He looked a bit relieved, admitting he wanted to throw all the eggs against the wall and the frying pan through the window. Some Zen monk! Nonetheless, we laughed at our frail egos, and he has never again commented on my foam "throne."

We need very few clothes, even on a long retreat. I have a preference for clothes that are loose, baggy, warm, soft, in white or innocuous colors. I do not like to feel constricted, and flashy colors do not appeal. It feels very good to wrap myself in a blanket cocoon, if the weather is not too warm. There is no need for jewelry; anything hanging or dangling is a nuisance. I did not wear a watch for a long time and still prefer to be without one, but some kind of timer, preferably with a gentle alarm is important for a retreat.

Food is always a major source of distraction for a retreatant. When to eat, what to eat, the concern of eating too much, the fear of eating too little, thinking about eating, preparing to eat, tasting the food, desires, aversions, comparisons, cleaning up after the meal, feeling the digestive system, regretting, thinking about next time— all of this goes on in our daily lives. On retreat, food becomes even more central to our thoughts because in relative terms it is one of the main components of activity, a time of relaxation that is often the sensual highlight of the day.

At an organized group retreat, food is a problem. Even if we are not involved in the kitchen tasks, a great deal of attention and anticipation is focused on meals. It becomes humorous standing in line, watching our thoughts, feeling the greed arise, judging others as they take their shares, picking and selecting choice morsels, observing all this mind activity around food.

During an individual retreat, food should be simple and modest. It is useful to prepare things in advance so that minimal effort is required. Basic foods with careful combining will minimize bloating and flatulence. Juices are often a good, quick snack. Our need for food often diminishes during retreat. Meals can be cut down to one or two a day and portions can be reduced. It is usually better to feel a little hungry (hunger quickly goes away) than to feel stuffed (a condition that often puts us to sleep).

Some retreatants turn to food as an escape and use it to break their concentration. This can be very challenging in the beginning, but a retreatant soon learns the difference between hunger that is a call for nourishment and hunger that is merely a habitual indulgence.

After a while, food can become a burden for a retreatant. A stage of mental energy is reached at which food seems dense. The food brings us down into a more physical realm. Very simple and light, quick-to-eat and easy-to-digest foods are important throughout a retreat, but particularly at these times. Fasting is sometimes used as a practice, but it should be minimized. A number of traditional practices require extensive fasting, but when practicing alone this is a difficult and often dangerous practice. A main problem is that once we begin a fast and enter an altered mind state, we do not always know when to stop. We keep thinking that in just one more day we are going to see God. Any fast that lasts more than a day or two must be attended by a guide or teacher who can judge when things are going too far.

A retreat is enhanced when sleep is kept to a minimum. This is one of the reasons for setting up a new, simple bed—a foam mat and enough blankets to keep warm. If you use your own luxurious innerspring mattress, the tendency will be to sleep more. But remember, every individual has his or her own needs. If you must sleep in your own bed, do it.

There are times when a retreatant will begin a retreat in an exhausted state, either physically or spiritually. It is not uncommon to feel very tired for the first few days. At this time, more sleep is required and should be taken. This is another advantage for having a foam mat in the retreat space; we can catnap often throughout the first few days, without breaking a whole retreat pattern by constantly going to the bedroom.

It is also useful, for those who are not accustomed to it, to sleep close to the ground. It changes our frame of reference; it is more basic; it helps bring us into a more "primitive" state of mind. It also affects dreams, which are strongly influenced by the retreat, and can become very intense.

Personal grooming and hygienic requirements should also be simplified. On many formal Buddhist retreats, makeup and perfumes are prohibited. Bathing, when used as a form of purification, can be helpful to a retreatant's state of mind. When used for self-indulgence, bathing can be excessive.

On retreat, one sits, walks, eats, sleeps, dresses, and takes care of personal hygiene. These are the basic physical needs. Keep it as simple as possible—clean, light, uncomplicated, spacious, empty—and use this pristine external form as a vehicle for and reflection of what we want for our inner being.

SECURITY

One of the primary universal laws is that all matter is in motion, nothing is static in absolute terms. On the most microscopic level in the subatomic universe existence is based on movement. A definition of movement is that something is constantly changing its position. This constant change means that nothing is ever the same from one moment to the next.

The constancy of change is a principle in every religious tradition. In the West, we are all familiar with the cycles of life described in Ecclesiastes—the constant spiral of events that is repeated from one generation to another. In Hinduism there is the idea of *līlā,* an endless cycle of One becoming many and many becoming One. In Buddhism we find the fundamental idea of *anicca,* impermanence, the constant, ever-changing nature of all matter. The *I Ching,* the Book of Changes, once again reveals a continuous revolving wheel.

Still, despite all this tradition and wisdom over thousands of years, we continue to confront the idea of change. The Greek philosophers tried to describe eternal things, the basic building blocks. The "atom" is something that cannot be divided. Today we view the atom as a mysterious mixture of waves and particles, a shimmering, intangible nothing that seems to be something. All we know for certain is that there is a continuous aspect of change, even in the atom.

Our intellect continually attempts to solidify the ephemeral. We believe that to know something, we must somehow grasp it. It must be accessible, scientifically ascertainable, repeatable, something that we can define, which will always remain the same. Our spiritual teachers say otherwise. They have experienced the realms where there is nothing tangible, nothing permanent, nothing truly repeatable, nothing ultimately definable.

One of the processes of enlightenment is the full realization and integration of this idea of continuous change. If accepted as an inherent truth of life, it can profoundly transform our perspective. Until this happens, we are grasping at things every moment, trying to gain a sense of existence or identity by holding on to something. It keeps slipping through our fingers like a fistful of water, but, in ignorance, we reach out again and again in a futile effort to substantiate our existence by holding something constant.

As a result, except for the relatively few beings who have attained high levels of realization, almost all of us suffer from insecurity. This insecurity manifests itself most often as a form of primeval fear. It may be the heart-stopping fear of facing a physical threat like a mugger or a wild animal or the more insidious fear that can direct our lives: the fear of not being loved or accepted, the fear of failure, rejection, acting foolishly, or saying the wrong thing. There is additionally the ultimate fear of death in its many variations. The list of ways we are motivated by fear is quite long.

In setting up a retreat, we need to acknowledge that fear plays a significant role in our lives. As we know, a fear mechanism is part of our built-in survival gear. For example, it is usually a good idea to freeze before stepping on a rattlesnake or to hold back from touching a red-hot iron. Most fear, however, is of the inappropriate variety, such as when we freeze at a shadow we imagine to be a snake, or when we refuse to touch something out of concern that it might be dangerous. In preparing for a retreat, we must accommodate both kinds of fear—appropriate and inappropriate.

A retreatant needs to feel as secure as possible, so that the distractions caused by fear will be minimized. As human beings tend to be insecure, these distractions can dominate a meditation and play havoc if not controlled. There is no way to eliminate fear; in fact, it is an intrinsic part of the retreat process to investigate our fears. In some instances, we actually need to invite in fear, to have a major encounter, to realize our own inner strength. In the beginning, however, it is best to minimize the potential for fearful situations, as they can be traumatic for an inexperienced meditator.

A retreatant's sense of security can be strengthened by arranging human protection, a bodyguard, sometimes called the "retreat guardian." This is a person living nearby, or in the same dwelling, who is able to participate indirectly in the retreat. It is useful, but not necessary, that this person be an experienced retreatant. It is important only that he or she is responsible and capable of being sensitive to the needs of the retreatant.

The retreat guardian's main job is to be a liaison with the world. Conversation is usually avoided, including nonverbal communication, but it is often useful to arrange a time when a note might be passed, usually from the retreatant to the guardian, to request something needed—forgotten toothpaste, special food, whatever. The guardian, on the other hand, should be more reluctant to send notes. Unless it is something the retreatant absolutely needs to know, it should not be communicated until after the retreat. The guardian must realize that any communication can, and probably will, send the retreatant's mind spinning. Often an entire retreat will pass without notes or other communications.

The guardian manages the ordinary daily details such as mail, bills, phone messages, shopping, family, and friends. The guardian must be capable of making judgment calls as if the retreatant were totally inaccessible, halfway around the world. In truth, on an extended retreat the retreatant *is* in another world. At that stage, mundane details seem like a foreign language.

This first level of security is very important to the retreatant. We may conduct a solitary retreat without a guardian, especially when experienced, but it remains useful and emotionally nourishing to know there is always someone who has us in mind. This helps avoid a sense of total isolation, which can be terrifying.

One last point—the guardian should realize that this, in a way, is also his or her retreat. As a guardian, there is a karmic connection to the retreatant; the deeper the retreatant enters other realms, the more the guardian's consciousness will be affected. The guardian often merits unusual benefits without having to undertake the enormous effort of the retreatant.

Another consideration in the physical setup for a retreat is the dwelling itself. Some people are very comfortable in the woods—a tent is fine for them. Others need sound walls, a solid roof, screens on the windows, and a door that locks. Any natural sense of vulnerability becomes more acute as sensitivities increase. Our state of mind in an extended retreat has been described as having the same proclivities as when in a powerful psychedelic drug experience; vast feelings of unconditional love may manifest or there can be considerable paranoia. It is useful for the retreatant to have a place of safe refuge, a totally protected space.

Another major consideration is that a retreatant's personal space must be sacred, in the sense that it is inaccessible to any intrusion. A retreat can be completely disrupted, if not ruined, by a passerby who happens to drop in. This is why it is often more secure to be in our own home with a guardian living in the same dwelling who can intercept all possible interruptions.

A cabin deep in the woods is usually fairly secure, but even here sometimes a sign needs to be posted. At times, a retreatant working intensely in a lonely cabin draws people, in a curious way. The psychic realms can attract energy. Many of us have experienced being in places where we did not think there was another human being for miles around, when suddenly someone appears out of nowhere. It is a good idea, even in "nowhere," to post a notice suggesting people return at another time.

In a regular retreat facility, there are resident guardians, the physical setup is secure, and the space is sacred. On an individual retreat it is not difficult to arrange something like this, once the need is clearly understood.

Despite the best security to allay physical fears, there is still the potential problem of inappropriate fear. A substantial amount of this kind of fear is connected with relationships, which are virtually excluded while on retreat. We worry about our loved ones, memories of innocuous conversations arise that now seem monumental, we have fantasies that people are in danger without us or we begin imagining what life would be like without them, feeling panic when we visualize the loss of someone dear. Conversely, we may feel miserable and afraid because an imagined loss does not cause any apparent remorse. Fear can go in any direction.

In addition, some fears are primal: things that creep may make us nervous, the dark may feel ominous, strange sounds may give us the shivers, aloneness may strike terror in our hearts. Some fears are transcendental: strange beings arise in visions, we may see a kaleidoscope of unknown faces, we may imagine events coming to a terrible end.

Inappropriate fear works like a bad dream. If we are identified with the dream, thinking it is a reflection of our character or our essential being, then the experience becomes terrifying. The dream is something about which we believe we must be concerned, a definite sign of mental aberration or deterioration. On the other hand, when we are not identified with the dream, rather view it as source material for exploration or a vehicle for uncovering hidden truth, then we do not make a value judgment about the dream as being "good" or "bad." It is merely another instrument for gaining insight.

This is how we need to approach any of our experiences on retreat. In the same way that we may experience sublime bliss and ecstasy or commune with the angelic realms, so too may we enter realms of primitive or transcendental fear, finding ourselves thrust into the demonic arena. Strengthening our "observer," minimizing our identification, is one way of building protection and a sense of security. It is reassuring to know that this happens to many people; it is nothing special.

When considering a solo retreat we should ask ourselves how we have dealt in the past with nightmares. After waking in a cold sweat, do we dwell for days and weeks in this experience? Is it cause to seek professional help? Does it disrupt our lives? If the answer is yes to any of these questions, then we should seriously consider doing the initial retreat with a professional retreat guide or teacher to get the added support we may need. If, however, a nightmare results in a day of reflection and then is for the most part forgotten, perhaps cropping up now and then in momentary flashbacks, this is exactly the way a retreatant will deal with dark visions. If a person is afraid to go to sleep at night, for fear of bad dreams, then this person should have guidance on retreats.

Another effective way of developing a sense of protection while on retreat is to invoke our "inner guide." We can call on God's help; we can invite into our imagination personal spiritual teachers or a guardian angel. We can even use imaginary paint to cover the entire mental field in a healing, protective hue. There are a multitude of worthwhile ways to invoke psychic assistance in difficult transitions. Some traditions frown on this practice as a crutch that perpetuates the ignorance of a deluded mind. Other traditions, particularly in the West, find the practice a natural access to internal power realms that are an intrinsic part of creation.

The idea of undertaking a personal retreat always has a little anxiety around the edges, even for the most experienced retreatants. There are many familiar mental arenas that we revisit and many scenes that replay like old videotapes, but every retreat has its own flavor and there is no predicting how it will proceed. It is a challenge, an adventure, a step into the unknown. It can be scary.

Security is a major element of a retreat. When we attain certain states of mind, the sense of security helps keep us on track, adding to the courage we need, offering us a haven for stability. This is very important for both beginners and advanced retreatants. However, in every tradition there is a point of release where all security needs become unimportant. At this point the mind state is inclusive, universal, liberated. There is nothing to protect, nothing to "secure," and we are in a continuous state of being that does not differentiate between everyday life and retreat.

WILLPOWER

Various motivations inspire a spiritual retreat—many of them, unfortunately, wrong-headed. Some people undertake a retreat because they are tense and would like to relax, believing it is a good way to get away from things. Some people seek enlightenment. Some people are willing to try anything new to add to a long list of adventures, like a merit badge to show their friends. Then there are those people who recognize within themselves a deep yearning to be connected with the source of life.

It is good to remember that the Buddha himself said, "The purpose of my teaching of the holy life of the Dharma is not for merit, nor good deeds, nor rapture, nor concentration, nor insight, but the sure heart's release."[16] In many ways, any desire to reach a goal will lead to dissatisfaction—except, perhaps, the continuing process of liberation and freedom that comes from direct experience, the insight that results from serious meditation.

If this liberation of the heart were so easily attained, the world would long ago have been enlightened. It is not an easy process—our mind patterns often seem fixed, our emotions vacillate in wide arcs. Moreover, since a fundamental principle of the life process is continuous change, there is no "steady state" that is in itself a lasting freedom. Liberation does not eliminate potentially negative thought bubbles; it is rather a realization, a perception of the nature of things.

There are two main levels of suffering: the considerable suffering that is part of the natural cycle of birth, sickness, aging, and death and the suffering that we generate through our attachment or aversion to things. Freedom of the heart does not end all pain, only that which is self-generated. However, this comprises a large proportion of the suffering most of us experience.

G. I. Gurdjieff pointed out that we are basically mechanical, often acting like conditioned robots. It is sad, and frightening, to realize that most of us do not exercise the free will we think we have. Upon deeper analysis, many of our actions and thoughts are generally predictable if enough information is provided to assess our patterning.

The truth remains that we do intrinsically possess free will, but in order to express it fully, we must first encounter the conditioned part of ourselves. We must find a way to break this conditioning, to rebuild ourselves in a way that enhances the expression of our free will.

Without a strong will, a person is likely to leave a retreat early. It does not take long for the initial excitement to wear off, the doubts to begin, and the wondering about what we are doing. Pain and boredom soon follow, along with any combination of anxiety, fear, anger, frustration, criticism, or other negative mind states.

The early stages of a retreat are often the most difficult. The first three or four days, most retreatants agree, are physically demanding; the body must adjust to sitting still and walking consciously. This is true for experienced meditators as well as beginners. As time goes on, we become accustomed to the physical demands, and the physical part becomes easier. This does not mean that all the pain disappears. It can come and go for a long time. We also experience cycles of moods, of busy mind or negative-mind states. One sit may be exquisite, the meditator thinking some new level has been attained; the next sit may be filled with doubt, fear, or anger. Things can go splendidly for a week and then one day everything falls apart.

This shifting and changing demands enormous persistence. Obviously, in the beginning it is easier to take the positive states, the ecstasy and sublime bliss, than the experiences of mind chatter or boredom. After a long while, even the positive states begin to be a bit ho-hum, a place we have visited so often that our mind naturally wonders, is this all there is? Or worse, things are going well, but we know that just around the corner is another low point. Sure enough, when it appears things seem in many ways no different from the first day we began meditating.

This can all be very discouraging. The secret taught time and time again by masters over the centuries is the need to persist, to overrule the internal resistance, to be constant in our effort, not to waver.

The mystic understands that there is a cosmic battle taking place between the forces of unification and the forces of separation. In some traditions, the forces of unification are called "good," while the forces of separation are called "evil." The mystic appreciates that each individual is a warrior in the battle, that each of us plays a significant role. The greater the effort we make toward unification, the more we will encounter tactics from the side of confusion and delusion.

It is a common experience for a retreatant to discover a battlefield in his or her own mind. One of the most important literary works in religion, the *Bhagavad Gītā,* is staged on a battlefield. The warrior is Arjuna and his predicament is the ultimate spiritual battle of man—to shed ignorance and gain the wisdom of enlightenment.

Insight is acquired through discovering the different kinds of weapons and learning how to deal with them. The central source of power for the side of unification is the will, while the power of the Other Side, the side of ignorance, rests in doubt, anger, or any negative mind state. All negativity is intrinsically separating and weakens our resolve for unification.

Carlos Castaneda, in his tales about the sorcerer Don Juan, offered two key concepts for the warrior engaged in the cosmic battle. A warrior is a hunter and acts with impeccability. The quality of being a hunter is related to concentration, while impeccability is related to willpower. "Impeccability" means a flawless integrity and a sense of meticulous attention, an attitude of high perfection regarding our acts.

Willpower is something we often consider in terms of strength. We have a "strong" will or a "weak" will. We often believe "I have a strong will when it comes to not killing helpless creatures, but I have a weak will when it comes to chocolate." Will in this context has something to do with action or withholding action.

As has been pointed out, there is a theory that most of our action is mechanical, conditioned; therefore, most of the things we do cannot be considered expressions of will. We are conditioned not to kill helpless creatures, and our chocolate cravings are also conditioned. If this is so, where does the will come in? According to P. D. Ouspensky, who gives us the teachings of Gurdjieff, "Will is absent in ordinary mechanical man, he has desires only;

and a greater or lesser permanence of desires and wishes is called a strong or a weak will."[17]

At another point Gurdjieff is quoted as saying: "A man has not sufficient will *to do* [anything], that is, to control himself and all his actions, but he has sufficient will to obey another person. And only in this way can he escape from the *law of accident*. There is no other way."[18]

We may not agree with Gurdjieff about our capacity to evoke will, but his observations offer considerable insight. If we were in a spiritual vacuum, without guidance, mentors, or role models, we would not have any idea how to proceed on the path of self-liberation, nor would we even realize that there was such a path. There would be a yearning but no vehicle for expression.

With something or someone external that can function as a guide, there is an outside source of vitality which feeds an emptiness within us. This gives us strength to repeat a process, over and over, until we build a new pattern. In essence, this constancy of effort strengthens the will. As we continue the nourishment in this way, a transformation can take place whereby mechanical action is no longer the habitual response; a new being evolves, a being with a vital new force called the power of will.

It is fascinating that Gurdjieff used an exercise he called "stopping" to help break the old mechanical routine. With this method, students were stopped at random points in the midst of their activities and were instructed to observe their actions and thoughts. This offered a moment of insight into one's thought process. Gurdjieff was of the opinion that this "stopping" could be accomplished only by an outsider and not by oneself—that one does not have the necessary power when in the ordinary state of mind. It would seem, however, that there are many ways to introduce random stopping points, one of the easiest being a watch that beeps regularly.

The entire purpose of a spiritual retreat is this process of stopping. We physically interrupt our normal life activity and begin an unusual mode of behavior. Additionally, our work while on retreat is continuously directed to heightening and sensitizing our moment-to-moment awareness. We come to know what we are doing or thinking and we observe those functions that are apparently mechanical.

In this way, we discover that our old patterns are constantly trying to reassert themselves. When we slip into them, we fall "asleep" almost instantly. When sitting in meditation, it is very common to discover ourselves drifting in thought. The thought can capture us for seconds, minutes, even hours. Our minds are wandering in a never-never land; it never existed in the first place and will never be seen again. But when we are in its clutches, it is the only universe of which we are aware.

This is where impeccability becomes the watchword of the retreatant. We must develop a sense of integrity. When not on retreat, when the morning alarm goes off, we often try to catch another few minutes of sleep, rationalizing a thousand reasons why the extra rest is needed. On retreat, we try to be impeccable, pushing ourselves a bit, responding quickly when we hear the alarm. This does not mean we need to become fanatical— the hard edges of fanaticism are self-defeating. Quite simply, when we hear the alarm, we get up—no big deal, no battles. This surrender is part of our impeccability; it is a major component of our ultimate realization.

In the teachings of Hazrat Inayat Khan, who founded the Sufi Order of the West in the early twentieth century, will and concentration are powers that can be improved through consistency. If we make a commitment to do something, the process of following through, in spite of real or imagined obstacles, automatically builds willpower. On the other hand, neglecting even a casual commitment, putting it off for another day, weakens the will.

Impeccability is a quality that builds willpower. It works in everyday life and is especially apparent on retreat, when we are constantly confronting ourselves. Approaching a retreat in this way, duly cautioned about exerting ourselves too hard, is the best way to minimize the pain and struggle and maximize the beneficial results. The way to maintain impeccability without excessive strain is to begin slowly, not promise ourselves too much at first, set reasonable goals. The important point is to follow through once obligations have been undertaken.

There is a Talmudic teaching that a person who does a good deed because he wants to do it does not receive as much merit as the person who does a good deed because he has been commanded to do it. At first this seems illogical; we would think that a person doing something from his heart should be rewarded more than someone who does something out of obligation. The sages say no.

The person doing a good deed out of obligation first of all is in a higher state of transcending his own ego, he does not think he is doing this because *he* wants to, he is doing it because it is the thing to do. A time will come for the person operating simply from the heart that he may not feel like doing the good deed, whereas the person motivated by obligation will be much more consistent.

Also important in the reasoning of the sages is the esoteric principle of surrendering our will to the will of God. A teaching in the ancient Jewish ethical treatise *Pirke Avot* (Chapters of the Fathers), says, "Treat His will as if it were your own will, so that He will treat your will as if it were His Will. Nullify your will before His will, so that He will nullify the will of others before your will."[19]

In this teaching is the paradox regarding will to which all major traditions allude. In order to build the power of will, we must let go of ourselves, surrender by actually nullifying our own will, thereby allowing the divine will to flow through. The way to surrender is to accept a discipline, preferably one established and proven over time, and follow its tenets with full obedience.

Eventually this may become a lifetime commitment. For now, we are contemplating a retreat, which is a concentrated spiritual event. Thus we need to find a guide or a discipline, use good reference material, prepare ourselves mentally and physically, and decide in advance on a basic schedule and practice. Then we try to be faithful to this program for the duration of the retreat.

Faithfulness, integrity, and impeccability are the qualities that bring steadiness to a retreat experience; when these qualities are weak, the process will be irregular. Whereas steady practice minimizes the normal flow of doubt and negative mind states, irregular practice increases our vulnerability to these experiences. Without firmness of commitment, a retreat may be ended early or may somehow transform itself into a troubled rest period or a guilt-ridden vacation.

On the other hand, honest, gentle effort, clarity of purpose and program, tenacity in the face of a rebelling inner child, and solid, steady practice will reap a certain harvest. It will provide nourishment not only for the retreat itself, but will also benefit our daily activities for some time to come. There will be more willpower, more concentration, and a more directed, centered approach to even the simplest activities.

TEACHERS

All traditions emphasize the need for a good teacher. Many hold that it is impossible to make progress without one. Judaism, for example, is structured with two basic streams of transmission that began over three thousand years ago: the written tradition and the oral tradition. The written tradition includes the five books of Moses, known as the Torah, and extends through the books of the Prophets and what are known as the Holy Writings, such as the Psalms, Proverbs, Lamentations, Ecclesiastes, and Chronicles.

The oral tradition, which had continued from father to son for dozens of generations, was compiled in written form almost two thousand years ago when it appeared that the oral transmission was being lost. This was called the Mishnah. However, it was created in such a cryptic fashion that it was impossible to understand without a teacher. From the beginning, commentaries on the Mishnah have been gathered into the Gemara, the basic text of the Talmud. More commentaries were then added to this basic text, followed by a vast literature of new interpretations. Today the oral tradition is composed of a body of writing that is many times greater than the written tradition. All of this does not change the simple fact that it remains impossible to learn the oral tradition without a teacher.

All established spiritual teachings have an oral tradition, wisdom that has passed from parent to child, from spiritual teacher to disciple. In the transmission, this teaching is partially factual, but the bulk of it is inexpressible. A famous Hasidic story tells of the disciple who went to sit by his rebbe, not so much to hear what he had to say, but to watch how he tied his shoelaces.

Often in mystical tradition, the sole act of sitting in the presence of the teacher brings about internal changes. In India this is called *darshan* (holy sight). For example, concerning Sri Ramana Maharshi it was written: "Instead of giving out verbal instructions he constantly emanated a silent force or power which stilled the minds of those who were attuned to it and occasionally even gave them a direct experience of the state that he himself was perpetually immersed in. In later years he became more willing to give out verbal teachings, but even then, the silent teachings were always available to those who were able to make good use of them. Throughout his life Sri Ramana insisted that this silent flow of power represented his teachings in their most direct and concentrated form. The importance he attached to this is indicated by his frequent statements to the effect that his verbal teachings were only given out to those who were unable to understand his silence."[20]

Teachers have additional qualities: keeping students on track, helping them avoid pitfalls, encouraging and supporting them so that they can proceed at the right pace, providing counsel—all well-known qualities of good teaching.

The major problem we encounter when seeking spiritual teachers is related to our expectations. We have conditioned ourselves to believe that the spiritual path offers training that will ultimately imbue us with awesome capabilities. This belief is perpetuated by the tall tales, miracle stories, and hero myths that surround well-known spiritual leaders.

The briefest glance into any tradition reveals feats of superhuman character, powers beyond the imagination, voyages into the unknown. For strongly rational people the tendency is to doubt the veracity of such stories, to write them off as folklore or overworked imagination. Intellectuals usually try to find an explanation for miracles, proving that they are no more than natural events or, at the very least, exaggerations.

The person on the spiritual quest, however, is not operating from the intellect alone. This person is being drawn by an unknown aspect within themselves, something that cannot be quantified, takes up no space, and is timeless. Without time and space, paradox reigns supreme, and nothing can be pinned down. In this realm, human limitations do not exist, miracles are a matter of course, and the interplay of macro- and microcosm is an exquisite dance that transcends all perceptions of reality as we know it.

Thus, part of our nature relates to the traditional tales with a certain respect and does not concern itself with rational analysis. It understands on a different level of knowing. These are potent tales, wisdom tales, and they release psychic energy which can empower us in fascinating ways.

Viktor Frankl spent three years in a Nazi concentration camp and survived. He writes:

In spite of all the enforced physical and mental primitiveness of the life in a concentration camp, it was possible for spiritual life to deepen. Sensitive people . . . were able to retreat from their terrible surroundings to a life of inner riches and spiritual freedom. Only in this way can one explain the apparent paradox that some prisoners of a less hardy make-up often seemed to survive camp life better than did those of a robust nature.[21]

Anyone who made it out of a death camp would consider survival a miracle—and it was. There is no method to assess and determine who had the best chance for survival, for it depended as much on a spiritual connection as on physical strength. Frankl's book is filled with the horror and terror of that experience, yet consider another tale:

One evening, when we were already resting on the floor of our hut, dead tired, soup bowls in hand, a fellow prisoner rushed in and asked us to run out to the assembly grounds and see the wonderful sunset. Standing outside we saw sinister clouds glowing in the west and the whole sky alive with clouds of ever-changing shapes and colors, from steel blue to blood red. The desolate gray mud huts provided a sharp contrast, while the puddles on the muddy ground reflected the glowing sky. Then, after minutes of moving silence, one prisoner said to another, "How beautiful the world could be!"[22]

It is hard to imagine that inmates of a concentration camp, facing daily acts of the most deadly brutality, were able to view the world as beautiful. The depth of spiritual power extends beyond all rationality. I know of a highly regarded woman in Israel, a teacher of teachers, who is a survivor of Auschwitz. She not only suffered daily deprivations but was also a candidate for medical experimentation. She came out sterile. When asked about camp days, she replied: "It was not so bad. I was able to serve HaShem [God] in so many ways."

This level of faith boggles our minds. In this kind of

belief is a power that transcends most measurable limits. This is the power that is tapped in each of us when we relate to the charisma of our spiritual heroes.

And herein lies a problem. That which may nourish us spiritually as we reflect upon the legends surrounding outstanding teachers of the past becomes a liability when it translates into expectations regarding living teachers. We want our teachers to be special beings, with extraordinary powers. Plainly put, we want our teachers to be trans-human—people who excel beyond human limitations.

As we saw in the first section, there are indeed some teachers who seem to have these qualities, who can perform amazing feats of endurance and arouse an enlightenment experience in disciples with a glance or a word. It is important to notice, however, that even those rare individuals are able to transmit the light to only a handful of disciples, perhaps only one or two, and in some cases not any. In other words, placing ourselves in the presence or under the training of one of these special beings does not guarantee anything.

Unfortunately there are many teachers who would like to think they are special or whose disciples have put them on a pedestal. They may have excellent skills, and may have developed their spiritual power through years of arduous practice, but they will sometimes manipulate students with intimidation, power plays, and even sexual abuse. This is not a rare event. It is all too common, even among the most austere traditions.

The search for the trans-human teacher often leads to the serious problem of a student's willingness, and sometimes perverse desire, to be exploited. We expect teachers to be spiritually attained beings, who should not be affected by our adulation. But teachers are only human and they can be worn down. Just as power corrupts in business and politics, so too does adulation and idealization corrupt many spiritual guides and teachers. This applies not only to the little-known teachers but to the brightest luminaries in the spiritual world. It has been particularly prevalent in the last twenty years in the burgeoning population of nouveau-spirituality in the West.

How, then, do we go about finding a spiritual guide? The first point is to assess our own expectations. If we want a teacher to walk on water, we should be prepared for a long search. If our quest is for someone to teach or give us the kind of enlightenment that will bring peace and tranquillity into our lives, we will probably be disappointed, despite the promises.

But if we are looking for someone who can transmit a method or skill to enhance our spiritual development, the world abounds with excellent spiritual teachers. The principle is to avoid seeking "specialness"—either the special teacher or the special results we hope to gain. Rather than something special, we need to seek only the quiet wisdom of a spiritual practice that works for us.

Through the process of experimentation, we will find a practice that is suitable, and this will become our personal practice. Once the practice is found and a commitment made to it, then it will naturally evolve that a particular teacher or teachers will be in closer harmony with us than others.

It sometimes occurs that we discover a teacher before settling on a spiritual practice, and the teacher thereby defines the practice. More often we are attracted to a practice that is compatible. The best approach, then, is to work on the practice with various teachers and the one most in harmony with us will naturally manifest. It is an axiom of true spiritual development that the student does not find the teacher, the teacher finds the student.

Often there is one main teacher encountered somewhere along the path. On the way, however, are many teachers. In this, the student needs to become a child once again. Children accept teachings from all sources. They do not ask for qualifications when being shown how to tie their shoelaces. They are interested in the new thing, what it is they are learning, rather than the personality of the teacher.

So too on the spiritual path. We must undo the ingrained assumption that somehow studying with a teacher puts us in jeopardy, that we might surrender our personality to this teacher. This notion is partially due to our primary relationship with parents, who were our early teachers as well as authority figures and disciplinarians. Our school teachers were also authority figures who graded us. The relationship between teachers and authority often affects our relationship to spiritual teachers.

When doing spiritual work, the relationship to authority becomes a major question. An essential element of spiritual development is the ability to surrender, to let go of self-identity, to accept the authority of a teacher. But we must remain tuned to the guide within, the inner voice that assesses balance and harmony, which knows whether an action or path is correct for us. Often this creates conflict and tension, as the messages are not completely clear. This is part of the spiritual journey— working our way through the thicket of ideas, practices, and other people's "trips" until we find our own clearing, our own open, light-filled pasture of truth in the midst of a forest of delusion.

We must approach our spiritual work with childlike

curiosity and openness, taking teachings one at a time, trusting our inner guides. We will feel the confusion of tugs and pulls in different directions. All of this is the natural process of spiritual development. Our life choices and growth are usually based on rejecting what does not work for us. We cannot select what will work for certain, we can only discard what we know for certain does not apply to us. In so doing, by a process of elimination, we naturally evolve our spiritual paths.

This does not mean that something rejected is necessarily eliminated for life. Often we are born into a religious family but reject the tradition of our inheritance and set off to find our own path. After years of exploration, we may discover roots not appreciated in earlier years and thereby return to a tradition once rejected. We grow, we learn; the spiritual path is a lifetime process. The more we let go of our self-identities, the more surprises we encounter. We are not who we think we are; the path of truth is not what we thought it would be.

In the end, everyone is our teacher, on one level or another. The child is our teacher, our friends, our family, the stranger on the street. Every experience is a challenge; a teaching is always hidden in it. Every thought that bubbles up in our minds can teach us things about ourselves, if we are able to listen.

The search for a teacher is really more a necessity to develop a "listener" within us. Potential teachers abound. Are we being taught? Without a listener working within, the search for a teacher is often fruitless. Even major teachers, surrounded by large numbers of students, have felt that their words were falling on deaf ears. Krishnamurti felt that not a single person understood what was being taught. After all those years of teaching tens of thousands of people, he openly said that nobody understood his message.

There are meditators who can share their experiences; there are meditation teachers who can outline principles. There are spiritual guides who can illuminate traditions, and there are teachers who themselves have inspirational practices. Bookstores are filled with information on spiritual practices. A wealth of teaching is available. Our work is not so much to find a teacher as to improve our own receptivity and sharpen our ability to hear the teachings all around us.

It is fairly safe to be eclectic in our approach, to be open to all possibilities. We must, however, begin to deepen our practice sooner or later. Otherwise we will continue swimming on the surface of a vast ocean. The more we refine our practice, the easier it is to dive—at the same time diving requires more skills in this ever-narrowing world.

This is a little tricky because increasing commitment and practice tends to constrict our perspective. Out of this can come corrupted beliefs and limited values that mark radical and fanatical views. Such views are often associated with so-called fundamentalists, but also apply to New Age libertarians who have no tolerance for beliefs that stray too far from their own.

Thus, another paradox looms. It is generally agreed that we must choose a practice, a teacher, and be consistent in effort to grow spiritually. At the same time, this concentrated effort often leads to less, rather than more, awareness, and can be self-defeating. We cannot resolve this dilemma. We can only try to stay attuned as much as possible to avoid the traps.

Nonetheless, some guidelines can help us in our

decision-making process. When we are taking on a practice, we should inquire: "How long has this practice been around? How many people over time have devoted themselves to it? How well do I relate to people who are students of this practice? Is this a practice that comes out of my own culture, and if not, does the other culture have values compatible with my own—in other words, would I be able or would I want to live in that culture? Where does this practice touch me—am I drawn to it because it is exotic, others are doing it, it seems to have worked for friends, or is there something in it that really calls to me, that touches my soul?"

Although it has been pointed out that everything can be our teacher when our listening side is open and that there are a large number of people who can help guide us, there remains "The Teacher," the one to whom we are drawn and who will provide major input into our spiritual growth. The criteria we may examine here are: "How well do I relate to the disciples—do I feel a genuine connection with them? How accessible is the teacher? Does the teacher live according to the teachings? How much am I affected by the teacher's reputation or fame and how much am I genuinely touched by what the teacher does or says when I am in his or her presence? Do I ever feel that this teacher is manipulating or exploiting his or her disciples? Do I feel comfortable emulating this teacher's personal habits?"

Often our spiritual teacher is more important to us than our biological parents. We tend to model ourselves on the teacher, whether consciously or not. Our entire perspective of spiritual reality is affected by this teacher. Hidden doors may be opened, but a danger exists that passages may be closed forever if the teaching is on a low level. This is especially true with regard to power trips and sexuality. A student is well advised to avoid, at all costs, involvement in such a situation. It may leave scars that cannot be mended in this lifetime.

Finally, there are many who are not drawn to one particular teacher, but who still make their way on the spiritual path. Perhaps they stumble more often, but they are steady and consistent in effort. Most of these people would surely like a helping hand, but they do not leave the path in search of this help. Their main objective is the path; should a teacher appear so much the better.

This is perhaps the healthiest approach. Stay focused on the primary objective—the path itself. Do not sit at the bottom of the mountain waiting for the teacher to arrive in a magic helicopter to give a lift to the top. Just move along, finding a way around the boulders, perhaps slipping now and then. Signposts are usually along the way to help us, but it is worthwhile to have the attitude that we may have to make most of the climb without a teacher.

We are rarely alone on the spiritual path. Even when there is no clear guide, there are almost always fellow travelers. A group of aspirants on a particular path is called a *sangha* in Buddhism. The *sangha* is self-supporting, and it is inspiring to know others are struggling along with us. The mere presence of others will often strengthen our meditation and add to our courage. The *sangha* works powerfully on a group retreat, but it can influence even the lone retreatant from the knowledge that others are wishing him well. Although we may appear to be struggling mightily on our own, we almost always have support on many levels.

Invariably, guides will come along when we need them the most. There is a wonderful, almost magical quality when a new guide appears—at just the right moment. It is then we realize that we are never alone on this quest. We must simply have faith. In the end, who knows, it may be our task to make it to the top without the help of spiritual energy from other realms or we may meet a teacher who is a high-altitude guide. It does not matter; either way we must remain on the path, maintain our faith, and always move toward spiritual evolvement. This is the essence of the spiritual quest.

GROUP PRACTICE

A vital element of spiritual retreat is solitude, which, as explained earlier, does not necessarily mean being alone. A retreat taken by oneself has an aspect of isolation and severity conducive to intense self-inquiry. A somewhat different experience occurs on a group retreat, where there is a security in the comradeship of fellow retreatants working individually but together. In some group retreats, individuals take advantage of both processes, sitting for long periods alone in their rooms and occasionally joining the group.

Most of the instructions given up to this point apply whether we are alone or in a group. Clearly, it is possible to initiate a retreat by ourselves, but it is sometimes easier to go to an arranged retreat so that we do not have to be concerned about logistical details.

In North America many retreats are offered by Buddhist groups: Zen, Tibetan, or Vipassanā. There are also a great many Christian retreat facilities both for the individual retreatant and for groups. Some Hindu-oriented ashrams also offer group retreats, and there are a handful of Sufi- or Jewish-oriented retreats.

Additional advantages of working in a group besides an increased sense of security are greater incentive and motivation, the accessibility of teachers and guides, a formal schedule, and an uplifting sense of community.

The drawbacks are a tendency to be more socially involved (which affects practice), greater opportunity for distractions, a schedule that may not be compatible with our rhythms, participation in community activities like food preparation and clean-up, and the requirements of the specific practice of the group itself. It is often uncomfortable to attempt a different practice from that followed by the rest of the group.

Something can be said for both individual and group retreats. It is often easier for a beginner to get a sense of what retreats are like by experiencing a group retreat. Yet this can also be a disadvantage because a *zazen* experience is not exactly like a *Vipassanā* experience; a Sufi retreat is not like a Christian retreat. What we experience in a group for a week is likely to be completely different from sitting alone at home for the same period.

The advantages of an individual retreat are that we can set one up fairly quickly and spontaneously, it costs virtually nothing extra, and we can tailor the schedule to our individual needs. The problems, of course, are that there is no teacher, it may be threatening to be alone for extended periods, and finding a quiet, protected space may not be so easy.

When considering joining a group practice, the same cautions noted in the previous chapter concerning teachers apply. Most groups have a certain amount of clarity as to their purpose; this is also a function of the person guiding the group. Occasionally, a group may be confused about the relationship between the emphasis on spiritual development and the social interaction that occurs naturally when people get together. A serious aspirant should establish beforehand whether an event has strong social overtones or if it is primarily devoted to practice.

If possible, it is useful to sit (meditate) with a group or its teacher a few times before deciding to join a retreat. At the very least, it is useful to sit with any other group following the same spiritual discipline to get an idea of how the practice works. There is no assurance, however, that the two groups are practicing in the same way, even if the name of the practice is identical.

Groups have their own power. They quite often influence a spiritual practice as much as it influences them. There is very little consistency—we would say "quality control"—from one group to another. In *Vipassanā* meditation, for example, each teacher leading a retreat has his or her own method, and consequently the experience may be different.

This is equally true in Zen, Tibetan Buddhist, Sufi, Jewish, Christian, and Hindu practice—do not assume that inner compatibility exists in one tradition any more than the similarities between traditions. The lack of consistency is a major problem for the serious retreatant who wants to follow a fixed method. There are only two solutions: always retreat alone, or always retreat with the same group and the same teacher. Even then, every retreat will have its own personality, but at least we do not have to deal with extenuating factors.

Some people prefer the challenge of changing retreat environments every time. Just as life is constantly in motion, why not experience different retreat styles? When people become steady enough in their practice, they are less influenced by the surroundings, and it matters less and less that each group and each teacher has a distinct personality. In fact, it may add a little zest to an otherwise repetitive process.

However, we need to be warned about the major pitfalls of group practice to save us considerable emotional strain. When we start meditating as beginners, the primal energy centers of the body are the first to be stimulated. The less experience we have, the more primitive the energy aroused. Two of the most fundamental centers are sexuality and power.

It is common for a meditator on a silent retreat to enter into a fantasy romance with a person across the room. In the days of silence, if we do not yet have the strength of concentration to inhibit thought processes, this romance may become a full-blown universe, complete with journeys to the South Seas, a grand home filled with riches, beautiful laughing children, incredible sensual relations—the sky is the limit. This can continue for many days, perhaps weeks, with an absolute sense of certainty that the other person must be having the same feelings.

Then one day the bubble bursts and the result can be devastating. An enormous amount of time has gone into our fantasy. The other person has been entirely unaware of what was going on and even of our existence. This can cost us the whole retreat. Beware!

The same is true for power experiences. It can start when a fellow retreatant squirms too much, breathes too hard, coughs in the wrong way, blows his nose strangely, takes too much food, moves through the line too slowly, walks too fast, walks too slowly, smells strange, always makes that same stupid gesture—the list goes on forever. We want to control everyone else, make them do it right, teach them the proper way to exist. Our days can be filled with criticism and comparison, watching everyone, annoyed by everything they do. Nobody seems to know how to do anything. This can also be an expensive way to spend our days. After a while the realization dawns that we are projecting all of these critical thoughts, but it can be a long time coming for the inexperienced retreatant.

It is true, of course, that we can have romantic fantasies and invent enemies while sitting all alone since everything takes place in our minds. But the presence of others can spark our imagination in extraordinarily distracting ways and lend more strength to our illusions.

In the end, groups have both value and risk. Since a retreat is for a fixed period, even if the group does not work out well, it will be over in a short time. Make the most of it. Every experience is a teaching; every retreat has a valuable lesson for future retreats.

If the retreat really becomes unbearable, we can always decide to leave. We are free agents. Nonetheless, it is usually worthwhile to stay the course even if it is difficult, for the best lessons come out of the toughest experiences.

The general experience working with groups is positive. There is a unifying aspect to the common effort; a sense of sisterhood and brotherhood comes out of mutual hardship. A wonderful sharing occurs in the unspoken realms. Often, a bonding takes place and people become dharma buddies for life, even though they may not see or talk with each other for years at a time.

It is a good idea to try to arrange a group retreat of a week to ten days at least once a year. It improves individual practice, strengthens resolve for future individual retreats, and maintains a gentle connection with other retreatants—people working in their own way on the same path—giving us a sense of spiritual community that is mutually supportive and revitalizing.

SCHEDULING

The schedule is the framework upon which a retreat is built. It not only sets the discipline, defining what is to be done and when, but is an important link with everyday reality. There are well-known experiments of placing people in caves where not a glimmer of daylight can enter. The subjects are not given any timepieces and must estimate when it is day or night. Invariably the biological clock runs differently from the actual time and within a few weeks they have switched day and night.

When we enter into deep concentration, time becomes much less significant, as does our sense of the physical world. There is a tendency to neglect our own physical needs. Also, conflict arises—the idea of "just a bit longer" constantly presses, or its opposite, "it must be time to quit." When on solo retreat without a schedule, we are in our own psychic cave, separated from reality, and quickly become disoriented.

This disorientation may be accentuated if we do not have an anchor in the world. The easiest anchor to use is time. The mystical realms are timeless, whereas the physical world operates completely in time dependency. We learn to deal with this dependency the more we become liberated. On retreat, however, it keeps us from drifting too far and minimizes the chance of getting lost in a stormy sea of emotional upheaval, or becoming shipwrecked in a frustrated early termination.

Some advanced retreatants prefer unscheduled days. They want to be guided by impulse. This can be a valuable lesson in understanding our natural process of choice: where we tend to make stronger effort and where we ease off. It is a method that can be used to advantage by experienced meditators. However, even those retreatants who are more advanced work within the context of time constraints. Beginning meditators are definitely advised to use a schedule.

The schedule is arbitrary. It can have a wide degree of latitude or be filled with detail and relative precision. At times, a retreatant will begin with one schedule and after a few days adjust to another. It might be a planned change, so that the schedule becomes more rigorous as time goes on; it might be a spontaneous change, when we discover that we cannot live up to the schedule we had planned. The point is that some form of scheduling should be maintained during the course of the retreat, even though it may change a number of times.

Just as there are no hard and fast rules as to the overall timetable, there needs to be flexibility in the daily schedule as well. A retreat is a very demanding process. The retreatant needs to be careful to maintain a balance between the hardness of pushing oneself and the softness of self-indulgence. It is a fine line and requires continual adjustment.

There are times when we want or even need to sit beyond the end of the sitting period and there are times when we clearly need to end early. Perhaps a meditation period should be skipped altogether and replaced by a nap or some fresh air. There are frequent opportunities for a schedule change; on occasion we surrender, usually we do not.

The gray area here is vast, and there are no set rules. Yet experience does provide us with one basic rule of thumb: most of the time it is detrimental to break the schedule. The schedule is the "authority"—even though it is arbitrary and we made it ourselves, still, it has become the authority.

An arbitrary authority is by definition the enemy of self-expression. Most of our complaints, most of our desires that conflict with the schedule are insidious power plays to assert self-expression, to defeat the authority. When we give in, the idea of "self" is strengthened.

Spiritual unfolding, on the other hand, requires a certain degree of surrender, an elimination of this identity of self. Thus the schedule, as an authority, provides a tension, constantly demanding a surrender. We find that throughout the day we gladly enter scheduled periods such as eating and resting. Then there are those activities that arouse resistance, usually having to do with the practice we have undertaken. This requires surrender. Some retreatants are very meticulous in this process, making sure to be seated on their meditation cushions at the proper moment; others are more relaxed, allowing many minutes to tick away as they amble to their seats. Each type of personality offers new insight when challenged by a schedule.

One of the advantages of being with a group is that the schedule is set by someone else. It is hardly likely we would have made up the same schedule ourselves, but now we are surrendered into group process. Although we might consider the schedule too rigorous, we see our companions struggling along and this gives us incentive to push our limits. Alone, we are more likely to make adjustments, since there are no others to encourage us.

For inexperienced retreatants, it is best to make a gentle, broad, and flexible retreat schedule with shorter practice periods, more time for quiet reflection, and more hours for sleep. As we gain experience, the tendency is to make the schedule more demanding. If we have attended a group retreat, often that schedule becomes our prototype. There are many types of retreat schedules—some samples of commonly used schedules are given in an appendix at the end of the book.

The earmark of a good schedule is that it is structured to maximize practice time as it balances our physical needs for rest, personal care, and nourishment. After a while, everything we do on retreat is our practice. Still, the schedule paces us in the specific discipline we are using for that retreat, whether it be a sitting and walking meditation, yoga, prayer, or prostrations.

A good schedule also stretches our physical limits. We can sleep less, eat less frequently, moderate all our normal daily activities so that time is not simply passing but each possible moment is being utilized. One of the things we learn on retreat is that many of our imagined limits are self-imposed. There is a tremendous feeling of liberation in breaking these artificial barriers. A characteristic in the enlightenment process that brings true freedom is the appreciation that we set unnecessary limits and then think we are trapped and bound by them.

A schedule applies throughout a retreat but has a different purpose during each phase. A short retreat of one to three days has a single phase, but retreats of one week or longer have three distinct periods. The first few days are a time of acclimation and integration. This period is often marked by physical discomfort as our bodies readjust to new patterns and by apparent fatigue, as we are still working with stress and tension carried in from everyday life. At this stage the schedule is very important to acclimatize us quickly to a new living pattern, to shock us into rapid adjustment. A slow, lingering repatterning is much more difficult than a quick jump into the cool waters of retreat.

The middle phase is usually the bulk of a long retreat. This is the period of settling in. There is usually less physical discomfort since the patterns of the retreat are flowing. At this stage the main work is accomplished; we have arrived at the battlefield. Here the schedule is the rhythm of the retreat. Like a strong heartbeat, it is constant, regular, steady. It minimizes our decisions. We do not decide when to sit, when to walk, or when to eat. It tells us. As people in spiritual disciplines have learned over thousands of years, expansion comes through constriction; the structure of the constraints is a step toward spiritual freedom. The schedule is one of the most important tools of a retreat as it supports and encourages a deepening awareness of steady practice.

The third phase is the ending period, the time of reintegration with the world. Often, on long formal retreats, this is actually built into the schedule. By this time we are completely in our own universe. Even though we may feel no different from usual, the truth is that reentry will be experienced as a great shock. The retreat guides know this and therefore set aside a day or two—in some situations a few days—on which the silence is broken. As the normal schedule is relaxed, each retreatant has a chance to become reoriented to social skills and verbal communication.

The solitary retreatant usually anticipates the culmination of the retreat in a natural way. As the final day approaches, we discover that we are making adjustments to the schedule, softening on self-discipline. We notice that our minds are turning more and more to details, planning, and fantasy regarding personal interaction with family and friends. We begin to lose a grip on the retreat during the ending period, which is a healthy, natural part of the retreat process.

It is actually a difficult period as well once we begin to let go, because the retreat becomes more and more of a burden. On the one hand we may yearn to be free of the discipline; on the other, we may never want to leave the peace and quiet, and the prospect of reentry can become disturbing. It is important to keep the final period of retreat short, not allowing it to appear too early. A strict adherence to the schedule will keep it at bay until the last couple of days.

During these last days, although the schedule begins to disintegrate, it still retains useful elements. It is usually comforting to follow parts of the schedule as it is now an old friend. We feel it so clearly at this time, we often make commitments that our everyday life will include a healthy dose of spiritual practice. We also tend to plan future retreats, perhaps every few months. More often than not, this commitment is too ambitious, but in itself it is a sign of the progress and growth we have accomplished during retreat.

Although we often cannot live up to our aspirations while engaged in the whirl of daily life, we retain a glowing ember within that regularly tugs us, reminding us that it may be time for another retreat. Often we forget the detail of experiences of a profound retreat, while the ephemeral feelings of the experience remain. The general tendency is to push away the idea of another retreat, with the excuse that we do not have enough time, the family has more pressing needs, and so forth. Still the ember burns, calling us. When we acknowledge it and take another retreat, we quickly remember the place of silence, the beauty within, the sense of being alive.

Retreat is not for everyone. Some of us, however, despite the ups and downs, the hard work, the pain, and the constant challenge, approach retreat as an elixir, a taste of nectar, a doorway to unimaginable worlds. It is a place of cleansing and purification, of hope and loving kindness, a place that offers moments of exquisite peace. Those of us who feel this way embrace the spiritual retreat as our major practice, a practice without dogma, offering us opportunity for growth and realization as we continue on the ultimate path, to understand the Truth, to be free.

SPIRITUAL
PRACTICE

INTRODUCTION

There are a great number of spiritual practices, including breathing methods, yogic *āsanas* (postures), rites of purification, and various forms of meditation such as mantras and visualizations. There are in addition many practices that do not fit into a traditional mold. Some people make a practice of walking daily in the woods, writing poetry, or working with music or dance.

We need to understand the concept of practice and what makes it spiritual. Practice is an activity that is regularly performed and is an open-ended process, never reaching a point of perfection. We can develop skills or even mastery with practice, but there always remains a quality of something new to learn.

If approached with a dull mind, even the most exotic practice becomes a rote expression. A person could spend a lifetime in practice this way and accomplish no more than a perfunctory exterior form without any spiritual substance. Unfortunately, many people find themselves following a traditional practice for the wrong reasons. They make all the right moves, but there is no heart in it.

We should approach the most mundane practice with a bright, open beginner's mind and regularly discover new insights, whether brushing our teeth, washing the dishes, or making the bed. Tying our shoes is something most of us do unconsciously, yet remember the Hasidic tale of the student who was not as interested in a rebbe's teaching as to observe how he tied his shoes.

At first glance it seems absurd to include making the bed as a potential spiritual practice, compared, for example, with *prāṇāyāma* yoga (breath control). Yet one person can make a bed with full attention, and thereby gain significant benefit, while another may practice *prāṇāyāma* with an uninterested, tight, hard mind and accomplish absolutely nothing at all.

For a master, every detail is part of one's practice. There is a story of a young Zen teacher, Tenno, who studied diligently for ten years. One day Tenno visited a Zen master named Nan-in. "The day happened to be rainy, so Tenno wore wooden clogs and carried an umbrella. After greeting him, Nan-in remarked: 'I suppose you left your wooden clogs in the vestibule. I want to know if your umbrella is on the right or left side of the clogs?' Tenno, confused, had no instant answer. He realized that he was unable to carry his Zen every minute. He became Nan-in's pupil, and studied six more years to accomplish his every-minute Zen."[1]

It is a common myth that certain practices will assure us of outstanding results. This has been particularly abused in the last twenty years by hawkers of hula-hoop spirituality who promise things like instant power, weekend enlightenment intensives, or guaranteed tranquillity.

A practice has no permanent goal and is always introducing new challenges. A golfer never hits a ball the same way twice; the best golf pros in the world still end up in sand traps.

What makes a practice spiritual is a challenging question. Can dishwashing or golf really be practiced as spiritual? Two wonderful books on this have become classics: *Zen in the Art of Archery* and *Zen and the Art of Motorcycle Maintenance*. They answer our question affirmatively: golf or archery can be a spiritual practice, as can dishwashing and motorcycle maintenance.

The spiritual ingredient has to do with the practitioner's frame of mind. It is sometimes described as a mind that is soft, open, expansive, observing, fresh—all the qualities of a beginner's mind. In this state the spiritual significance of any action is accentuated; almost any activity has a distinctive quality when accomplished with the beginner's mind.

If the mind is awake and more aware than usual, a simple body movement may produce remarkable perceptions. We may experience a flood of impressions in each millimeter of movement. Every breath, every physical interaction, every thought holds infinite implications.

The spiritual ingredient has two aspects. One, as noted, is the state of the practitioner's mind. The other is the quality of the practice itself. Even though we can discover the spiritual aspect of making beds, there is far more inherent quality in engaging spiritual disciplines that have been with us for thousands of years. When we have a combination of spiritual practices that have withstood the test of time and a practitioner who is able to approach the practice with a soft mind, a chemistry results that opens new gates of awareness.

One perspective of this combination raises a fascinating question: how is it that each of us has an affinity with some practices and not others? Some find sitting quietly a perfect mode of deepening spiritual connections; others must be more physically engaged, moving in t'ai chi chuan or yoga. Some love to pray; others need absolute silence. Individuals resonate with distinctive mantras. Each of us is drawn by some unknown voice to particular practices, yet we are not attracted to others.

To add to the complexity of individual preference, there are many teachers who maintain that the very resistance we feel to a practice indicates the need to familiarize ourselves with it, thus confronting the resistance and gaining insight into it. They would add that spiritual growth does not come from gliding along with what is comfortable; it is more involved in making breakthroughs, struggling, overcoming those parts of ourselves that need to be changed.

This leaves the spiritual seeker in a quandary. How do we go about choosing a practice? There may be a practice that is reputed to be good for the purpose of gaining insight, but is it in harmony with our needs? There are a vast number of practices and no certain way of knowing if it is a good idea to try one that seems compatible or if it would be better to take on a practice toward which we feel resistance.

We approach these questions by exploring the elements that constitute our frame of mind. Our mind state is conditioned by our environment, our experiences, to some extent by our genealogy, and by the fact that the universe is constantly changing. The process of reconditioning this mind state has been investigated through spiritual inquiry for thousands of years.

Some basic principles have been defined. As long as we follow old patterns, our previous conditioning remains strong. If we do a task by rote, without external input, we are likely to perform it in this way for the rest of our lives. As long as we repeat activities that keep the mind spiritually asleep, it will remain so until something comes along or an effort is made to awaken it; it will not awaken by itself.

The process of awakening is usually slow in the beginning. We use trial and error to discover the things that work. While we are still asleep, it is difficult to know what is working and what is not working. This is why it is very helpful to have a teacher, but we need not wait for a teacher before beginning. Unfortunately, one of the excuses people use to stay asleep is that they do not have a teacher. With patience and careful observation, however, we can gradually make progress in awakening. The teacher will find the student when the time is right.

Certain methods will improve the chances of awakening. Silence, simplicity, and solitude are time-tested and proven processes that encourage wakefulness. Additionally, there are four indispensable elements fundamental to every practice: purification, concentration, effort, and mastery.

All spiritual discipline is based on the belief that our original nature is pure. Our existence in the material world, however, contaminates this purity in many ways, and thus we lose contact with our true essence because of layers of desire, aversion, and other qualities that distort our perceptions. Purification is the process of correcting these distortions in order to gain a clear inner perspective.

Purification, in Buddhist terminology, has to do with things like right action, right thought, and right livelihood. Purification qualities are also developed by helping others, making sacrifices, avoiding harmful acts, and generally being conscious of our relationship to everything around us. One of the main principles of purification is to bring a new awareness to everything we do or think. This awareness, coupled with practices to guide our thoughts and activities so that they do not add new veils of separation, helps us to clear the way for deeper insight into the truth of our original nature. There are many guidelines for acts of purification and traditions often have hundreds of precepts. As we discover and appreciate the purification qualities in each true spiritual practice, that practice becomes more effective.

Another quality required is concentration. Our normal mind state is scattered as we rapidly sift through fantasies, reactions, planning, ideas, anger, boredom, and anxiety—this continues even in our dreams. The mind has often been described as a team of wild horses with nobody holding the reins. The goal of concentration is to take back the power and get a firm grip on the reins of the mind. This is not easy to do. Every spiritual practice requires using and strengthening concentration for the purpose of quieting the mind.

The quality of effort as an element of spiritual practice is a little more difficult to understand. Most teachers point out that if we try too hard on the path of spiritual attainment, we tend to strengthen our egos rather than gain true clarity. Somehow, we must work on our inner development by making an effort but not becoming attached to the result. This quality is known as "effortless effort." It comes from constant practice, having a regular discipline, and integrating a method until it becomes part of our nature. We must be careful, however, that it does not become rote. This is always the danger of daily practice. Somehow we must assimilate the practice while maintaining a vitality in awareness and intention. All practice requires this kind of effort.

The quality of mastery is also required for sustaining a practice. It is the part of us that refuses to be distracted from the task at hand. While effort brings us to the practice day after day, mastery keeps us there. Effort and mastery work in harmony, one being our drive and motivation, the other our restraint and perseverance. As there is no final moment of spiritual endeavor, no graduation day, and the practice extends without limit, perseverance is always required. Indeed, we discover later in our practice that effort and perseverance arise from an infinite source identical with our center of awareness, and from this we gain a profound insight that effort, perseverance, and awareness are one and the same.

Each of these four qualities—purification, concentration, effort, and mastery—is not only essential in our practice but in every moment of our lives. These elements of spiritual practice are examined in depth in my book, *The Heart of Stillness.*

The practices that follow in this section accentuate one or more of the above qualities. No single practice is a guaranteed, assured path to enlightenment. It is worthwhile to sample a few and experience the different qualities each offers. To do so, we need to approach an experience openly, make a commitment for a few weeks or a month, and then at the end of the commitment reassess the situation.

We need to be wary of extremes. It is not uncommon to experience a powerful rush of bubbling emotion when the barricades begin opening. This will pass. It is unwise to make a lifetime commitment, join a group, or run off to a new community based on these experiences. Feeling good is not necessarily the test of a worthwhile spiritual practice. It helps, but there are many other variables to consider.

It is also not wise·to reject a difficult practice too quickly, since the experience of it is likely to change. Nevertheless, be very slow to accept the idea that if something hurts or is uncomfortable, it must be good for us. This is often the approach of a cult, and is a method used by power manipulators to confuse unwary and inexperienced seekers. It is certainly true that we must confront things that are not pleasant, but we should never cast aside good judgment.

A beginning spiritual practitioner is usually best served by those practices that feel compatible. They do not have to bring "highs," but they certainly do not have to be unpleasant. Another quality we may use as a measuring rod is to ask, "Is there a sense of harmony and balance, a feeling of being touched somewhere inside, a knowing that this is what is needed at this time?" It helps to tune in to the whisper of the inner guide.

As we become more experienced, we will try new practices that may be more strenuous, more demanding. There is plenty of time to face and break through our resistance, which is certain to appear and reappear. We need not go out of our way to seek it in the early stages. In spiritual practice resistance is a close relative who visits frequently, uninvited.

Guard against becoming a dilettante who tastes the entire spiritual smorgasbord, waiting for the "right" or "perfect" path to come along. Almost any technique that has withstood the test of time can be beneficial to our spiritual growth. We will surely be more adaptable to some and will discover this as we continue. Stay with each one for a while, then pick the best and remain with it for a longer time. Once spiritual practice becomes part of our daily routine, we tend to gravitate naturally to the most suitable practice for our current needs.

Practices can be discovered while on retreat. It is best, however, to have some experience with a practice before undertaking a retreat. There is a wide choice of learning

INTRODUCTION

situations, a plethora of books, and plenty of people around who can share experiences.

We must use our best judgment when following through on this search. There are a great many people on personal missions in this world of spiritual inquiry. Warning signs usually flash fairly early. Be on the lookout for power trips or sexual innuendo. Also watch out for high-priced, glitzy, popular, faddish experiences. Usually these are a waste of time and money, and occasionally they can be damaging to the psyche.

We do spiritual work because the process itself is an imperative for deeper understanding. Throughout our lives we will experience a continual tension that pulls us away from our practice. Each time we fall away slumber begins to overtake us. If we are fortunate enough to notice, we begin to practice again and this helps us stay awake.

Volumes of instruction exist for each of the practices described in the following chapters. In addition, many of the practices require guidance from someone with extensive experience. The purpose of presenting these thumbnail descriptions is to give the beginning meditator an idea of the range of options available and to clarify that retreats have numerous thematic possibilities. Although there are many ways to develop concentration and expand awareness, there is a tendency for people to believe only in their own practice, feeling it is the right way or the best way to conduct a retreat. This is simply not so, as we shall see.

An attempt has been made to describe the fundamentals of a practice but not the details. In this way, the reader can get a good idea of the principles involved. It is then a matter of selecting practices for further exploration and seeking out teachers or books for study in depth.

Ultimately all descriptions will fall short of the experience. It is vital to taste the deeper truth of a practice as it touches different levels of awareness that extend far beyond the intellect. The entire spiritual journey involves practice of one form or another. We will not get anywhere through wishful thinking. If we truly want to grow, we must do the work. Here are some possible ways to cultivate awareness of our true nature.

BREATH

In the beginning of the Western tradition's Creation story it says: "And the Lord God formed man of the dust of the ground, and breathed into his nostrils the breath of life; and man became a living soul."[2] The ancient Hebrew in this verse for "breath of" is *nishmat*, which is the same word used in modern Hebrew. The Hebrew used in the Creation story for "soul" is *nefesh*, which Kabbalah teaches is the lowest of three main levels of soul. It is sometimes called the animal soul, the vital aspect of living matter. A higher soul level in Hebrew is the *ruah*, which means spirit and is also the word for "wind"; and a still higher level is the *neshamah*, the soul in direct communion with the Creator. The *neshamah* has the same root as *nishmat*, the word for breath. Thus, in Jewish mysticism, the breath holds within it the secret of the direct link to God.

The Sufi Chishti poet, Khwaja Muhammad Bangash, wrote:

> *Thy every breath is a pearl and coral of inestimable price:*
> *Be careful, therefore, and guard every respiration well!*[3]

In all spiritual traditions we find practices that are related to the breath. Many use breathing as a practice to steady and calm the mind and emotions, while others use the breath as the focus and gateway to higher consciousness. In Buddhist *Vipassanā* practice, for example, the breath is often the primary object of attention, through which the practice of mindfulness develops.

The idea in *Vipassanā* is to observe the breath without artificially extending or shortening it. We do not try to control our breathing and we become one-pointed and precise in noting a particular aspect of it. Here are the simple meditation instructions from a Thai master in the *Vipassanā* tradition, the Venerable Ajahn Chah:

> *When it is balanced, we take the breathing as our meditation object. When we breathe in, the beginning of the breath is at the nose-tip, the middle of the breath at the chest, and the end of the breath at the abdomen. This is the path of the breath. When we breathe out, the beginning of the breath is at the abdomen, the middle at the chest, and the end at the nose-tip. We simply take note of this path of the breath at the nose-tip, the chest, and the abdomen, then at the abdomen, the chest, and the tip of the nose. We take note of these three points in order to make the mind firm, to limit mental activity so that mindfulness and self-awareness can easily arise.*
>
> *When we are adept at noting these three points we can let them go and note the in and out breathing, concentrating solely at the nose-tip or the upper lip where the air passes on its in and out passage. We don't have to follow the breath, we just establish mindfulness in front of us at the nose-tip, and note the breath at this one point—entering, leaving, entering, leaving. There is no need to think of anything special, just concentrate on this simple task for now, having continuous presence of mind. There's nothing more to do, just breathing in and out.*[4]

Many meditation retreats are filled with people who do nothing more than this apparently simple practice of watching the breath. People who have never experienced such a practice believe that this would be boring; but the truth is that a great deal happens when we are sitting quietly, breathing in and out. We quickly discover that it is very difficult to harness the mind and simply observe the breath. No matter how hard we try, the mind keeps slipping off into thoughts, fantasy, and meaningless chatter. It can be quite a shock for beginners to discover that they cannot succeed in the simple assignment of observing the breath.

For many advanced meditators, breathing practice is the baseline for all their meditation. There are variations on the theme. Many meditators concentrate on the abdomen rather than the nose. Some use the air flow at the back of the throat as their primary focus. When we begin breathing practice, it is common to allow our attention to rest on different parts of the body. Most teachers recommend, however, that after this initial period it is best to stay with one point of concentration.

It is also possible to observe every nuance of the breath. This can arouse great interest as the noticed phenomena become ever more subtle. At first we may notice how the temperature of the air changes coming and going, then how each breath is slightly different from the previous one, how the air passages expand and contract around the breath, the movement of hair in the nose, the muscular-skeletal system moving in the chest, the continuous infinitesimal balancing adjustment the body performs to keep from falling over, muscle movements all over the body, the different exterior stimuli impinging on each breath, background sound, light and motion, and the mental process of thought flashes rising and fading away. The diversity of thought that passes in a short sit could easily fill a book. It would not be a book of connected thought and reasoning but more of a picture book—instant snapshots on a wide variety of subjects.

By observing the breath in such detail we soon realize that every breath is unique. Each is like a snowflake; it has similar overall design but no two are alike. An untrained person cannot imagine what could be interesting about the breath; appreciating the uniqueness of each breath seems almost impossible. Yet this practice may be the dominant experience in a retreat that can last for months.

There are many other types of breathing exercises. For example, a broad array of *prānāyāma* (breath control) practices are found in yoga. The *Bhagavad Gītā* says: "Offering the inhaling breath into the exhaling breath and offering the exhaling breath into the inhaling breath, the yogi neutralizes both breaths; thus he releases *prāna* [life force] from the heart and brings [this] life force under his control."[5]

The practice of *prānāyāma* has been developed in India over thousands of years and consists of many different exercises. Some teachers suggest that certain exercises are sufficient in themselves to raise a person to the highest levels of consciousness. Many *prānāyāma* methods have been kept secret and are transmitted orally from teacher to disciple. There are also some well-known forms, a few of which are described below.

SAHITA KUMBHAKA: THE HOLDING BREATH

We breathe through each nostril alternately, pressing the right nostril with the thumb of the right hand to close it and the left nostril with the third or fourth finger of the right hand. There are several variations to this exercise. Usually it is done by counting: inhale through one nostril to a count of four, hold for a count of four, then exhale to a count of eight. Repeat with the other nostril. Count at a regular rhythm, neither speeding up nor slowing down. The intervals should work fairly comfortably but if any count is too much of a strain, reduce it.

It is important to begin with a very easy count. Usually the exhalation is twice the length of the inhalation, but some methods use an equal count. The holding breath can be extended, but should not exceed a comfortable range. Some methods exclude the holding breath altogether. Some require the *mūla bandha,* which is the squeezing of the sphincter muscles while holding the breath.

For beginners, the *sahita kumbhaka* breath can be done for fifteen or twenty minutes, once or twice a day. We should maintain the same rhythm for at least three to four days before gently extending to a new rhythm. Whenever a strain is noticed, drop back to a previous rhythm. Advanced practitioners should not do more than forty-five minutes of practice two or three times a day without guidance.

SŪRYA BHEDANA: THE HEATING BREATH

This breath requires learning the *sanmukhī mudrā,* a method for closing the upper orifices of the body. This is accomplished by placing the thumbs into the ears, the index fingers over the eyes, the middle fingers on either side of the nostrils, and the ring fingers over the mouth. We alternate pressure on the middle fingers to control the air flow in each nostril.

We begin by exhaling all the breath from the left nostril. Then, inhaling through the right nostril, we retain the breath while pressing firmly on ears, eyes, both nostrils, and mouth. Again, work with a count, extending the retention as long as comfortable. A count of 4-8-8 is a good beginning. For this breath, we always exhale gently through the left nostril, and inhale through the right.

This breath increases body heat and should never be done without supervision more than twenty minutes a day in the summer or thirty minutes in the winter. The heating breath is used when we feel physically cold or when we have been diagnosed as having a "cold" condition according to Oriental medicine. It is also sometimes used to warm these cold, contracted feelings.

SITALĪ: THE COOLING BREATH

In this breath the tongue is rolled so that each side touches, thus forming a tube like a pipestem. The breath is sucked in, making a hissing sound. It is retained from four to eight seconds, and then the exhalation passes out both nostrils. The exhalation should be twice the length of the inhalation.

This breath cools the body and is usually not done in the winter. No more than forty breaths should be necessary to accomplish a cooling. This breath is done when we are physically hot, when our minds are agitated, when we have an excess of "heat" according to Oriental medicine, for burning in the gastrointestinal tract such as ulcers, and for cooling angry feelings.

BHRĀMARĪ: THE BEE'S BREATH

We breathe through both nostrils while constricting the throat to produce a high-pitched sound, like the buzzing of a bee. We do not use the vocal chords for this sound. It vibrates in the back of the throat. Hold the breath for the length of the inhalation only; do not extend the retained breath in the *bhrāmarī*. This a good technique for building concentration and is also useful for extending voice range and control.

This breath can be very intoxicating (dizziness is an indication that we should stop immediately). This breath can be used twenty to thirty minutes twice a day. The *sanmukhī mudrā* (see above) can be used with this breath.

KAIVALYA: THE *HAMSA* BREATH

This is an integrated breathing and mantra method which is an advanced practice that should be attempted only after we have reached a degree of proficiency with the *sahita kumbhaka* breath. Breathing is done through both nostrils. The inhalation is accompanied by an internalized, inaudible sound of *ham* (pronounced in our thoughts as "hahm"). On the exhalation we make the subtle, barely audible sound of "sa" by the passage of air in the back of the nostrils, but not with the vocal cords. There is no retention of the breath and no counting. The breathing is done normally, but the internal sound of *hamsa* accompanies each and every breath.

After a few minutes of normal breathing, we hold the breath long enough to repeat *hamsa* mentally three or four times, as if we were breathing. Then breathe normally again with the mantra. Every minute or two, hold the breath but maintain the inner mantra for the length of several breaths.

This practice is best done for short periods, ten to fifteen minutes, four to six times a day. The purpose of the practice is to develop a constant, automatic mental repetition that raises our attention and awareness. It is a practice best done under the direction of a teacher.

This description of *prānāyāma* practices gives just a taste of various techniques. There are a great many more, but most require continuous supervision. These kinds of breathing exercises are a fast track to altered states of consciousness.

Most Buddhist practices do not use controlled breathing. They consider that the breath should be completely natural and that it should be observed rather than manipulated. From the Buddhist perspective, the altered consciousness attained through controlled breathing methods is likely to be deluded, an artificially induced euphoria.

The Sufis work carefully with the breath during the constant repetition of God's name, the *dhikr,* which is a regular practice. Here the breathing is very much a part of the repeated expression, its rhythms inducing exalted states of mind. Different Sufi groups have opposing ideas on how to deal with these mind states. Some excite the ecstasy to the extent that one has no body sensation whatsoever, while others require a clear degree of temperance.

There is a state of concentration in which the meditator's breathing becomes imperceptible. This is called *savikalpa samādhi,* an extremely shallow breath and visibly motionless trance. This state of meditation, according to Paramahansa Yogananda, is a necessary prerequisite to attain the first stages of God perception.[6] He notes that this state was observed in St. Teresa of Avila, who became so motionless in her trances that the other nuns were unable either to move or arouse her.

Thus we see an extraordinary range between breathing states, from the indiscernible to the blindly ecstatic. The practices extend from the simplest observation of the breath to the highest degree of manipulation. Still, with all of this, the breath is life itself and remains a gateway to unknown levels of consciousness.

According to Zen master Taisen Deshimaru, the exhalation is the key to breathing: "*Ānāpānasati* is breathing out, the Buddha's breathing. It was through *ānāpānasati* that he found *satori* under the Bodhi tree."[7] Deshimaru went on to teach that learning how to exhale properly enhances longevity and is essential to the martial arts. He says: "You must overcome your adversary while he is breathing in. . . . Breathing out, on the other hand, you can receive a blow and it doesn't affect you, you don't even move."[8]

Good practices for developing the out-breath are singing, using mantras, and chanting sūtras. We learn to extend breath control this way. Mantras are discussed later in this section.

For beginning meditators, quiet observation of the breath is highly recommended. This method is uncomplicated and does not require supervision. As noted, it is difficult to observe the breath without mental interference, and it remains an ongoing challenge to develop concentration.

The breath is always with us. This is the reason observation of a normal breath can be so powerful a practice. We do not need special conditions. The practice of observing the breath can be done in any waking moment. It constantly brings us back to the present, the in-breath and out-breath. It not only increases awareness and concentration, it brings more calm into our lives. The simple observation of an excited, agitated, or angry breath has a soothing influence, helping us find a better rhythm and thereby calming the mind.

Philip Kapleau discusses breathing in the context of the customary practice of Zen:

The entire nervous system is relaxed and soothed, inner tensions eliminated, and the tone of all organs strengthened. Furthermore,

SPIRITUAL PRACTICE

research involving an electrocardiograph and other devices on subjects who have been practicing zazen for one to two years has demonstrated that zazen brings about a release in psychophysical tension and greater body-mind stability through lowered heart rate, pulse, respiration, and metabolism. In short, by realigning the physical, mental, and psychic energies through proper breathing, concentration, and sitting, zazen establishes a new body-mind equilibrium with its center of gravity in the vital hara *[psychic energy center located in the lower abdomen].*[9]

SITTING

In the world of spiritual practice, the verb "to sit" has become a generic verb meaning "to meditate." Many types of meditation do not require sitting down, as we shall see in later chapters, but the primary mode of meditation is associated with the physical act of being seated. Obviously, as meditation requires a framework, we need to know the difference between the ordinary sense of sitting in a chair and what it means to "sit" in meditation.

Sitting either in meditation or on retreat is related to posture, frame of mind, and an associated spiritual practice. Without these three elements, we are not "sitting." We may be relaxing, daydreaming, or even pretending to be spiritual, but there is no sitting going on. An honest meditator continuously inquires of himself or herself, "Am I sitting now or am I messing around?"

When we sit, the mind keeps falling into fantasy and daydreams. This does not necessarily mean that we are "messing around"; that depends on our intention. When we begin to sit, it is usually with an intention to devote ourselves to the meditation. At this initial point, the work begins.

Once the actual work of the meditation has begun, there is an intermittent tendency to relax. If we give in to this tendency, we begin to float away. When we enter this floating state while sitting, then, by our definition, we are messing around. As long as there is intention, despite the constant activity of a very busy mind, we are still sitting. Therefore, someone might be in a quiet, calm state and be daydreaming, while another might be agitated and confused and still be properly sitting, doing exactly what needs to be done to develop strong meditation skills.

The main rule of correct posture while sitting is that we must sit as straight as possible, but there are many variations on this theme. Some schools of thought are strict on every aspect of the seated position, from the way the legs and hands are folded to the kind of material one sits on. Other schools are much more relaxed, not concerned with how the legs fold under the body or even if one chooses to sit in a chair. The important point for almost all schools is that the spine must be relatively straight.

The straightness of the spine is not meant to be taken literally, as spines are naturally curved; it means that we should be balanced somewhere between slumping that might constrict the flow of energy, and an artificial ramrod erectness, which produces tension not only in the back but in the neck, hips, and legs. We must find a balance, sitting straight up and down, firm but not tight, steady but not locked, in a yielding but upright position.

Many of us will remember the Bozo the clown toy from when we were young. He sat on a round, weighted base. We could punch Bozo and he would roll over, but every time he was pushed, he would bounce right back. No matter how many times we put him down or how hard we punched, Bozo would sit upright. One thing we always remember about Bozo is that he had a huge grin on his face—he always came back smiling.

It is not a bad idea to sit like a Bozo. Many retreatants take themselves and their practice too seriously. A common characteristic of very advanced spiritual practitioners is that they almost all seem to laugh a great deal. Once, on a long retreat, I looked in a mirror and saw this growling, pained creature looking back. My effort was not effortless, I was pushing too hard, and as a result I was in a hard place. I looked at myself and realized that I had to let go. Almost instantly everything improved.

When we sit like a Bozo, strong concentration is still at work even though our faces are passive or slightly smiling. Bozo instantly rights himself when there is a tendency to slump or fall over. We always make minute adjustments when we are sitting; this is the unconscious effort necessary to remain erect. Without this ongoing effort, we would collapse in a flabby heap.

When beginning a sit, it is often a good idea to lean slightly in one direction, then in the opposite direction, left and right, forward and back, gently decreasing the motion until the center point is found. This is exactly how a Bozo would do it, rocking around until an equilibrium is found. Centering gives us a good sense of being in as upright a state as is possible.

Another quality universally recommended for proper sitting is stability. Stability means that the person sitting can hold the same posture for the duration of the sit without external movements. The body, of course, is always moving in a minimal way. In a concentrated breathing practice, this movement related to the breath seems extensive, with surges of expansion and contraction in the chest. In other refined states, we can experience the pulsations of our heartbeat pressing on our skin; we can feel the constant motion of closed eyes shifting this way and that. We are always moving—the more sensitive we become, the more gross the movement feels. So, when teachers advise us not to move, they are directing attention to voluntary movement versus that which is involuntary. The definition of a voluntary movement is that the mind must somehow be engaged, the muscles must be activated through the will.

The reason most meditation teachers are strict about movement is that voluntary body movement reveals movement in the mind. When we are squirming, it indicates that our minds are squirming. The slightest voluntary body adjustment is a cue that the mind is engaged, and it is often evidence of a surrender of intention into the floating state. Moreover, the movement itself reverberates in the mind, causing even more mental stimulation as we adjust to a new position. Thus the meditator is caught in the middle: moving means there was mental activity before the move, and the move itself will cause even more thought.

When we are engaged in normal daily activity, we are oblivious to the nuances within each and every physical move. In the meditative state, things are entirely different. The simplest motion rumbles in our mind. A walking meditation, for example, is full of awareness of the extraordinary detail in taking one simple step. A deep concentration here can almost freeze us with an overload of sensory input revealing what it takes to lift, move, and place a foot on the ground.

In the beginning stages, it is difficult to sit perfectly still. This is because the mind is not at all still. The untrained mind magnifies the boredom or the pain; it is filled with desire and aversion, and the need to move seems overwhelming. When this is combined with postural problems, the situation is unbearable and movement will ensue.

A stable posture helps in the process of quieting the

mind. It also alleviates a good percentage of the discomfort that is part of sitting. The exact position that proves to be stable will differ for each meditator; each will have her or his own way to place and position the legs, feet, and hands as well as the head, jaw, and eyes.

It usually requires considerable experimentation to find a stable posture. Initial discomfort with a sitting position is not the criterion by which we can judge its ultimate value for us—almost all sitting postures are uncomfortable in the early stages. Many experienced meditators have learned that stable posture still involves a degree of pain, which they learn to live with as part of the meditation. It is valuable to have a teacher who can give encouragement and help us past the difficult stages of sitting.

When we take on a discipline that has specific sitting requirements, there is little choice but to adapt to the accepted sitting posture. If the teacher insists that we place the right hand in the left, then we do not sit with our hands on our knees. If the head is to be somewhat lowered with the eyes slightly open, we do not sit with closed eyes. If everyone sits on a single cushion with knees to the ground, we do not sit on three cushions with one extra under each knee.

We have more latitude about sitting requirements when we are unaffiliated with a group or a teacher, but in many ways the situation is more difficult. In a sense, it is easier to have a clearly defined discipline, even though it may be difficult to adjust to its rules. On our own, we can try out many different things, but we are often blown by the winds of our agitated minds. We learn a great deal about ourselves in this situation, discovering how to treat the crybaby inside without pushing past limits in a self-imposed macho motivation.

Most of us need to raise the base of the spine off the ground to attain a straight and stable posture. There are many "official" meditation cushions of different shapes, sizes, textures, and consistencies. There are magazines filled with advertisements for these as well as other sitting paraphernalia such as benches, inflatables, and sundry contraptions. It usually turns out that the simpler items are better.

Once a satisfactory configuration of "equipment" is found for sitting, it is not a good idea to continue experimenting. Find a good setup and stay with it for a while. In the beginning it is all right to be attached to our cushion, carrying it with us to group sessions or other retreats (it is nice to be intimate with one's cushion).

After a while, when we are more experienced and our minds are more balanced, we will have greater flexibility regarding sitting gear. We may prefer our own things, but we will be able to use a wide variety of sitting postures and still maintain stability. Stability, in large measure, has to do with the state of our minds.

Nevertheless, as long as we are in the process of building strength in sitting we should not be concerned about how we compare with others in terms of our physical setup. It is much more important that we do what is necessary so that we can sit very quietly, without voluntarily moving the tiniest muscle.

When working with a teacher, we will obviously follow instructions. If we are on our own, however, we can be quite liberal with ourselves. We place foam where we need it, under knees or ankles, or between our calves. We should try to be relaxed but steady with our head comfortably balanced. Our eyes may be open, closed, or halfway closed. My own experience with beginning meditation is that having eyes closed is usually safer; it avoids distraction. The hands can rest in each other, or just the fingers can touch, or perhaps the hands are placed on our legs or knees.

It is not obligatory to sit on the ground. A chair is fine. Usually we sit on the edge instead of leaning back, in order to keep the back straight. Often, foam is placed under the feet for added comfort. It is important not to have a preconceived notion of what a good meditator should look like—such as a perfect, ideal image of a yogi who sits on bare ground in a full lotus position. If this yogi exists somewhere in India, he or she has nothing to do with us.

I attended a retreat with a large number of advanced practitioners, many of whom were meditation teachers in their own worlds, and I noticed the majority of participants used personal conveniences to add comfort. Many sat in chairs. Even the main teachers of this retreat, committed monks with many years of sitting experience, used small folding beach chairs with canvas backs when they were sitting.

When all is said and done, we examine ourselves when we are sitting. Are we sitting straight? Are we stable? Are we able to sit comfortably without moving even slightly? If so, serious practice can now commence.

In the beginning, sitting can be done for twenty or thirty minutes. Until we reach the point of steadiness, there is no advantage to extending this period of time. If we sit for only ten minutes, on the other hand, there is not enough time to settle down and it is not a true test of stability.

After a while, the length of the sit can be extended, slowly, to forty or forty-five minutes. In many retreats, this is the average length of a sit. Zen meditation often uses shorter sits of between twenty to thirty minutes in the belief that fatigue sets in after the first half hour. Only a few Zen-oriented sits last more than forty-five minutes while other disciplines often sit as long as an hour at a time.

Some meditators believe that the longer they sit, the more tenacity they have and therefore the more progress they will make on the path. This idea is disputed by many teachers and is generally not encouraged. I have had interesting experiences in three-hour sits, but my practice improves more with steadiness and regularity than with flings of virtuosity. There are those whose regular practice is a three-hour sit every morning. It is a question of consistency. If we sit three hours at a time, every day, then this is the normal discipline. But if the longer sit takes place at odd intervals, it might be nothing more than a self-imposed endurance test. Most meditators develop a rhythm of sitting between thirty minutes and one hour.

On a personal retreat there is room for experimentation. It is advisable to follow the schedule, as has been noted, but at times we will be drawn into a deep meditation that simply does not want to stop. By all means, follow through. This is the time to put the schedule away and allow the pull of the meditation to run its own course. It may become so delicious that we feel the sit will never end. It does end, not to worry. And before it does, take the time to enjoy it.

Most sitting involves a certain amount of pain, especially in the beginning. After a while it is possible to distinguish between the pain that is an ordinary complaint and pain that indicates damage is occurring. We need not give in to pain too quickly, but we should also know when to stop. As time goes on in our practice, we push more and more against limits. Many advanced meditators tell stories of pain so excruciating that they thought they would never walk again. Most are still walking perfectly, but a few meditators do in fact damage knees or ankles.

Many books are available with instructions for sitting. One of the best is Philip Kapleau's *The Three Pillars of Zen,* which has a comprehensive chapter on posture with pictures of different sitting positions. It also happens to be one of the most informative books on the practice of Zen.

Sitting is an act that brings us into a more primal relationship with creation. It is interesting to note that one of the anthropomorphic ways in which we relate to God is that He "sits" on his throne. Aryeh Kaplan, a well-known rabbinical scholar who died in 1983, pointed out: "In general, the concept of 'sitting' is that of lowering, and therefore, when we say that God 'sits,' we allegorically are referring to the fact that He 'lowers' Himself to be concerned with the world."[10]

When God is not sitting, He is transcendent; when sitting, He is immanent. Using this metaphor, when we are not sitting, in a sense we transcend the world by living in a world of our own. When we lower ourselves to be concerned with creation rather than being immersed in our own universe, we connect with the divine source in an entirely new way. Indeed, the idea of sitting is this lowering, falling away from ourselves, tuning in to the more elementary levels of creation, thereby communing with the source of creation in a way otherwise inaccessible.

DEVOTION AND PRAYER

All traditions offer a combination of scholarly and devotional practices. Devotional practices are typically emotional expressions of love, admiration, adoration, longing, praise, thanksgiving, or supplication. Each of us has a part that needs to express itself through the emotions, as a counterbalance to the part that seeks to understand the nature of life through the intellect. We also have individual tendencies. Some of us feel most connected performing a *bhakti* (devotional) practice, while others prefer the *jñāna* (wisdom) approach. Although all traditions have mainstream practices in both, in this chapter we will focus only on the devotional side.

In Eastern traditions there is considerable devotional practice. In Hinduism, devotion is expressed to the guru or to an array of deities. This is often done by chanting the various aspects of God in a form known as *kirtan*. The important Hindu scripture the *Bhagavad Gītā* says: "One who is engaged in full devotional service, unfailing in all circumstances, at once transcends the modes of material nature and thus comes to the level of Brahman."[11] This idea is a key tenet in the Hindu tradition. Without devotion to a personalized sense of the divine, a seeker will always be incomplete and thus cannot attain the ultimate truth.

A well-known contemporary Hindu teacher, A. C. Bhaktivedanta, says, "One who cannot elevate himself from the impersonal conception of Brahman to the higher stage of the personal conception of God runs the risk of falling down. In *Srimad-Bhagavatam* it is stated that a person may rise to a stage of impersonal Brahman, but, without going further, with no information of the Supreme Person, his intelligence is not perfectly clear. . . . The servant of the king enjoys on almost an equal level with the king. Therefore imperishable happiness and eternal life accompany devotional service."[12]

Devotion is so much a part of Hindu practice that it becomes an integral part of the everyday experience of the devotee. It is viewed as a major form of purification, as shown in the following comment: "We living entities are contaminated by the material world. *Bhagavad Gita* teaches that we must purify our activities in order to draw our consciousness back from that material engagement. The purification activity is called *bhakti,* or devotional service. This means that although devotees' activities appear to be ordinary, they [the devotees] are actually purified [by doing things with a devotional intention]."[13]

There are often misconceptions about the devotional side of Buddhism, exemplified by the following statement written by a popular Western writer on Buddhism, Christmas Humphreys: "Not by outward shows or priestly ritual, by labels, dogmas, prayers, and creeds is wisdom gained, but rather by deep meditation until the outward appearance is but a mirror to the mind within. In short, nothing will avail in substitution for self-liberation. Always the Buddha taught: 'Buddhas do but

point the way—work out your salvation with dili-
gence.' "[14] Clearly, a major theme in Buddhism focuses
the practitioner inward. Yet this is only one dimension of
Buddhist thought, while many others are devotional.

The entire sect of Pure Land Buddhism, for example,
centers primarily on the devotional practice of calling on
the *bodhisattva* Amitabha (Amida) for salvation. *"Bodhisattva"* means literally "one whose essential being is
Wisdom," but the historical meaning refers to one who
dedicates his or her life to the perfection of all creation.
Thus, the devotee in Pure Land Buddhism employs a
mantra calling on the *bodhisattva* to fulfill his purpose and
thereby raise the practitioner and all beings to an enlightened state.

In Tibetan Buddhism as well, there are widespread
devotional activities in visualizations of deities and repeated prostrations. In other forms of Buddhism the
quality of devotion is expressed in chants and *sūtras*
regarding the pervasive Buddha Mind or the teaching of
Buddha. Christmas Humphreys wrote that in Buddhism
there is "a pantheon of minor 'gods,' many of them
obviously borrowed from Hindu mythology . . . some
being Buddhas, some Bodhisattvas (Buddhas to be), and
some but distant cousins of the Buddhist family. Perhaps
the most famous is Avalokiteshvara (Avalokita-Ishvara,
'the Lord who is seen'), the supreme SELF within, whose
absorption of the individual consciousness is Buddha-
hood. The Chinese version of the term is better known,
the male aspect being kwan shai-yin and the later, female
version, kwan-yin (Jap. kwannon)."[15]

Humphreys goes on: "As J. B. Pratt says, 'The little
lady Kwan-Yin is one of the loveliest forms of Buddhist
mythology. She has not a trait one could wish absent or
altered. In the heart of the Chinese Buddhist she holds the

place which the Madonna holds in that of the pious Catholic.' "[16] Thus, as with all traditions, Buddhism is not monolithic, but multifaceted. As it has penetrated various cultures, we find that there is widespread devotional emphasis among Buddhists, particularly in the Tibetan, Chinese, and Japanese cultures.

In the West, devotional practices are indispensable in Christianity and have played a dominant role in Islam and Judaism. Throughout the history of Judaism, for example, there has been a division of opinion as to whether the wisdom aspect should be emphasized through the constant study of Torah, or whether it was more important to spend time in prayer and communion with God. The original breakaway of the Hasidic groups was to gain more freedom of devotional expression, and there is still an inclination among Hasidic sects toward devotional practice.

Christianity, a tradition centered on love, has always been devotionally oriented. Prayer is directed to God or the Trinity, and in some Christian groups there is a powerful devotional connection with saints. Many of the saints demonstrated utter absorption in their devotions, becoming role models for generations to follow.

Writing about the Desert Fathers of the fourth century, Thomas Merton noted: "Prayer was the very heart of the desert life, and consisted of psalmody (vocal prayer—recitation of the Psalms and other parts of the Scriptures which everyone had to know by heart) and contemplation. What we would call today contemplative prayer is referred to as *quies* or 'rest'. . . . *Quies* is a silent absorption aided by the soft repetition of a lone phrase of the Scriptures."[17]

Merton reveals that prayer includes two additional practices: contemplation and mantra. Although in this book we distinguish between various practices to allow exploration of the elements of each as they apply to meditation and retreat, the reader needs to be aware that many practices overlap. For example, the chapter on mantra, near the end of this section, also includes repetitive prayers.

Devotional practices include not only prayer, contemplation, and mantra but veneration of the sages or saints, visualization of the divine, expressions of loving kindness, and purification rites such as ablution. The diverse nature of devotional practices stimulates fascinating insights into many traditions.

For example, commentary is extensive on the Sufi practice of *dhikr*. It may be done from a purely devotional perspective, but the wisdom teaching adds that the goal is for each and every breath to carry the name of Allah. "True *dhikr* is that you forget your *dhikr*."[18] We reach a point where there is no longer a conscious effort and the entire being is constantly repeating an internalized *dhikr* in remembrance of God. It was said, "Every breath that goes out without remembering Him is dead, but every breath that goes out in recollecting the Lord is alive and is connected with Him."[19] This idea transcends the straightforward devotional aspect of *dhikr;* recollection of God in every moment adds a new dimension to our awareness.

The Sufis describe seven levels of *dhikr*: the spoken repetition, the inaudible *dhikr* consisting of inner movement and feeling, the contemplation of God's beauty and majesty, the perception of the light of God's attributes, the revelation of the divine mysteries, the light-filled vision of unity, and finally, the secret of secrets, the vision of the Reality of Absolute Truth.[20] When understood this way, the *dhikr* is a combination of mantra, visualization, and contemplation.

The *dhikr* is not the only Sufi devotional act. There is the *namāz*, which is prayer in ceremonial worship as required of all Islamic practitioners. Associated with *namāz* is *taharat*, which consists mainly of purification ablutions performed in preparation for prayer. These are devotional practices for all traditional Muslims, but they have a particular intensity for Sufis.

The Sufis, as well as other mystics, believe that every aspect of daily life has potential as a devotional practice. Every bodily movement has its source in the divine. Everything we do, everything seen or heard, tasted or touched, can be undertaken as a devotional practice. This level of devotion brings us into a new relationship with the ongoing creation as we realize that the entire universe is dependent upon the creative energy that vitalizes each and every moment.

We can use devotional practices while on retreat to accentuate this sense of reverence. They are especially useful on short retreats. On long retreats, devotion naturally arises as we become quieter. After a week or two of solitude, a book of scripture becomes alive with previously hidden meaning.

The Baal Shem Tov is famous for bringing devotional emphasis into Judaism. His great grandson, Rebbe Nachman of Breslov, is known for the profundity of his Hasidic tales. Most of his teachings were on prayer and the relationship between the individual and the *tzaddik,* the saintly teacher. Since Rebbe Nachman is one of the great masters of devotional prayer in the Jewish tradition, a few excerpts from his work will enable the reader to savor this spiritual nectar:

A person may have prayed profusely and secluded himself with God day after day for years and years and still feel that he is very far from God. He may even start to think that God is hiding His countenance from him. But it is a mistake if he thinks that God does not hear his prayers. He must believe with perfect faith that God pays attention to each and every word of every single prayer, petition and conversation. Not a single word is lost, God forbid. Each one leaves its mark in the worlds above, however faintly.

As soon as a person stands up to pray, he is immediately surrounded by extraneous thoughts and kelipot, "husks," which leave him in darkness and make it impossible for him to pray. The best remedy for this is to make sure that the words emerge from your lips in truth. Every word which comes from your mouth in truth and sincerity will provide you with an exit from the darkness which is trapping you, and then you will be able to pray properly.

When a person is saying the words of the prayers, he is collecting beautiful flowers and blossoms. He gathers them one after the other and makes them into a first bunch. Then he goes on and gathers more, until he makes a second bunch and puts it together with the first. So he goes on, gathering more and more beautiful garlands.[21]

One of the most effective tools for a Westerner in the repertoire of spiritual practice is prayer. Many of us have problems with a godhead or any entity to which we pray, and others are not accustomed to regular prayer. These do not have to be impediments. In fact, we can use our difficulties as part of the prayer: "Help me believe, help me have faith, help me trust that you exist and even hear this prayer," or simply, "Help me pray." This, in itself, is a strong prayer.

A power is unleashed through prayer and other devotional practices that normally remains untapped when the gates of the heart are closed. It comes from the same source as love. Indeed, we often cannot distinguish between the expressions in religious tradition of love for the divine from the world literature of classical love sonnets and poems.

Christianity, for example, has exceptional works describing the communion and rapture that arise from prayer. St. Teresa of Avila wrote that prayer was the prerequisite for entry into the first level of the seventiered divine castle, which was her metaphor for the soul.

A very learned man told me that souls who do not practice prayer are like people with paralyzed or crippled bodies; even though they have hands and feet they cannot give orders to these hands and feet. Thus there are souls so ill and so accustomed to being involved in external matters that there is no remedy, nor does it seem they can enter within themselves. . . . Insofar as I can understand, the gate of entry to this castle is prayer and reflection.[22]

Let us try to feel the depth of St. Teresa's own devotional practice:

My present manner of prayer is as follows: While praying I am seldom able to reflect with my reason, for the soul immediately begins to concentrate itself and arrive at peacefulness or a trance, so that it cannot use the senses at all, except perhaps for hearing, and even that is useless for hearing anything else. It often happens . . . I am caught up so suddenly by concentration and spiritual exaltation that I cannot preserve myself. . . . My soul merely seems to lose itself. . . . At other times I am attacked so mightily by a dissolving before God that I cannot preserve myself. It seems to me as if my life wants to flow away, and so I feel driven to cry aloud and to call on God. . . . At still other times I am seized by a desire to serve God, which attacks me so violently that I cannot represent it as great enough. . . . Then it seems to me that nothing could happen to me—no hardship, no death, no torture—that I would not bear with ease.[23]

From the records of a convent of the thirteenth and fourteenth centuries in Freiburg, Germany, comes the following report about a nun named Anna von Selden:

It was her custom that whatever she desired of God, she would never stop asking Him for it until He granted it to her. And once she

*came to such union with God in her prayer that God appeared to her
so clearly that for five weeks afterward, whatever she saw, she
thought it was God.*[24]

Another German nun of the fourteenth century, Margareta Ebner, wrote:

*Now when the hallelujah was rung at that time, I began to keep
silence with the greatest joy, and especially in the night before
Shrove Tuesday I was in great grace. And then it happened on
Shrove Tuesday that I was alone in the choir after matins and knelt
before the altar, and a great fear came upon me, and there in the fear
I was surrounded by a grace beyond measure. I call the pure truth of
Jesus Christ to witness for my words. I felt myself grasped by an
inner divine power of God, so that my human heart was taken from
me, and I speak in the truth—who is my Lord Jesus Christ—that
I never again felt the like. An immeasurable sweetness was given to
me then, so that I felt as if my soul was separated from my body.
And the sweetest of all names, the name of Jesus Christ, was given
to me then with such a great fervor of his love, that I could pray
nothing but a continuous saying that was instilled in me by the
divine power of God and that I could not resist and of which I can
write nothing, except that the name Jesus Christ was in it
continually.*[25]

Some traditions as well as individual teachers maintain
that devotional practices, particularly prayer, tend to
mislead aspirants onto paths of bliss and ecstasy that are
not only illusions but spiritual dead ends. We must keep
this potential pitfall in mind, particularly the entrapping
nature of the raptures that often arise in devotional
practice.

One very important point needs to be made—a vast
reservoir of spiritual power does exist in these raptures
and euphoria. Many believe that the source of this power
is identical with the source of spiritual light. Although

there are definite pitfalls and traps, we should not avoid devotional meditation or prayer because of them—the simple truth is that all spiritual practice is laced with obstacles and cul-de-sacs. The path of prayer and devotion has been the root source for Western enlightenment for thousands of years, and it should not be cast off lightly.

On the other hand, people who are devotional will often make criticisms about the wisdom path, complaining that it is too intellectual, too rational, too constricting. Once again a great deal can be said for this view. There is a tendency for the intellect to feed itself until it becomes so grand that all sight is lost of the spiritual core.

In actuality, wisdom and devotion can feed each other. Paramahansa Yogananda writes in his autobiography:

> *My own temperament is principally devotional. It was disconcerting at first to find that my guru, saturated with jñāna but seemingly dry of* bhakti, *expressed himself chiefly in terms of cold spiritual mathematics. But, as I attuned myself to his nature, I discovered no diminution but rather an increase in my devotional approach to God. A Self-realized master is fully able to guide his various disciples along the natural lines of their essential bias.*[26]

Auguste Sabatier, a nineteenth-century French theologian, describes essential prayer as follows:

> *Religion is nothing if it be not the vital act by which the entire mind seeks to save itself by clinging to the principle from which it draws its life. This act is prayer, by which term I understand no vain exercise of words, no mere repetition of certain sacred formulae, but the very movement itself of the soul, putting itself in a personal relation of contact with the mysterious power of which it feels the presence. . . .*[27]

What is this mysterious power that is tapped by prayer? Is it true that everything really happens at random, or is it possible that prayer can influence the flow of events? This question has puzzled philosophers from the earliest times, while religious devotees have no doubts whatsoever. They feel and experience directly the benefits and results of prayer. In religious communities, the "miraculous" nature of prayer is commonplace. Prayers are always being answered.

William James describes the way prayers were answered for a man named George Muller: "Muller's prayers were of the crassest petitional order." In other words, Muller prayed for everything, which is what masters of prayer like Rebbe Nachman advise people to do. Muller's career included the printing and distributing of over one hundred million scriptural books, pamphlets, and tracts, the building of five large orphanages, educating thousands of orphans, and the establishment of schools where over one hundred and twenty thousand adult pupils were taught. How did all of this come about?

"His method was to let his general wants be publicly known, but not to acquaint other people with the details of his temporary necessities. For the relief of the latter, he prayed directly to the Lord. . . . 'When I lose such a thing as a key, I ask the Lord to direct me to it. . . .' " He never went on credit, never bought anything unless it could be paid for, including food and fuel for the orphanages. "Greater and more manifest nearness of the Lord's presence I have never had than when after breakfast there were no means for dinner for more than a hundred persons. . . ."

Muller said that his motive for operating this way was "to have something to point to as a visible proof that our God and Father is the same faithful God that he ever was—as willing as ever to prove himself the living God,

in our day as formerly, to all that put their trust in him."
Muller's unshakable faith is summed up in his comment
on why he would never borrow money or work on
credit.

> *How does it work when we thus anticipate God by going our*
> *own way? We certainly weaken faith instead of increasing it; and*
> *each time we work thus a deliverance of our own we find it more and*
> *more difficult to trust in God, till at last we give way entirely to our*
> *natural fallen reason and unbelief prevails. How different if one is*
> *enabled to wait God's own time, and to look alone to him for help*
> *and deliverance! When at last help comes, after many seasons of*
> *prayer it may be, how sweet it is, and what a . . . recompense!*
> *Dear Christian reader, if you have never walked in this path of*
> *obedience before, do so now, and you will then know the sweetness*
> *of the joy which results from it.*[28]

This degree of affirmation raises something within that
otherwise remains dormant. It is impossible to explain
away as serendipitous all the events that fell into place to
allow Muller to do his work. It does not matter how we
attribute the force of his resolve or the source of the
power that nourished his efforts; we must acknowledge
that something was working here, an unknown resource
that was released through deep faith and prayer.

When on retreat, the practice of devotion and prayer is
accessible to everyone. We can use our own language or
can turn to scripture. Most traditions have a formal set of
prayers, and many additional resources are in religious
texts. Rebbe Nachman recommended talking to God in
our own language and asking for anything we need. If
there is doubt, we pray for clarity; if there is anxiety, for
calmness; if there is anger, for forgiveness.

Prayer can enhance our work on the qualities of loving
kindness, compassion, opening the heart, letting go of

anger, overcoming fear, and becoming generally more kind in our relationships. We do not need to wait for faith or belief in order to pray. We can pray, without regard to "who" is listening, and through direct experience faith will slowly grow.

VISUALIZATION

Many have heard the famous Taoist story of Chuang Tzu, who dreamed he was a butterfly and upon waking could not tell whether he was a man dreaming he was a butterfly or a butterfly dreaming he was a man. When we are in the midst of a dream, it is our reality. The relativity of reality applies not only to our dreams but to our mind state in every moment.

Visualization is a method of disciplined daydreaming. We all experience throughout each day the wandering fantasies of our minds. We are usually willing to follow wherever the inner winds and seas take us, sometimes to the calmness of a deserted island, sometimes into the tumult of a raging typhoon. These fantasies are complete experiences—we actually live them. Even though they are products of our imagination, they have a distinct impact on our mental state and our well-being.

A symbiotic relationship exists between our mental state and our imagination. There is a mistaken belief that imagination is simply a passing phenomenon, rising and falling like waves in the sea that leave no impression behind. The mind is not an isolated sea, however; it absorbs impressions of each wave of thought or imagination. The mind reverberates with each tide of emotion.

One school of psychology holds that we can use our

imagination to induce improved mental health. This phenomenological approach opposes the more traditional analytical one used in classical psychoanalysis. The school of phenomenology uses "psychosynthetic" therapy, based on the idea that "every image has a motor tendency."[29] The therapy is not directed to seeking a cause; it is more concerned with the transformations that can be accomplished by aiming for a goal.

Phenomenology is a modern version of what mystics have used over thousands of years of working with the power of imagination. One of the main ingredients of ancient alchemy was imagination. Our ordinary perspective of alchemy is that its aim was to transform base elements into gold. However, mystics know that the deeper secrets of alchemy are in the internal forms, the transmutation of the lower spirit into its highest aspect.

Mercury, or quicksilver, has always been a primary metaphor in alchemy as it combines rapidly with certain metals, indicating a sense of "desire." In the terminology of alchemy, quicksilver is a kind of spirit within. It is the "quicksilver" quality of the heart that transforms the "lead" quality of the body into "gold." It is also considered to be the quality of soul that transmutes the breath into its most rarified, transcendental state. And it is the quicksilver quality in the blood that raises the dense ("lead") aspect of semen to its highest potential.[30] All of these internal alchemical processes can be accomplished through imagination.

Jung made a major study of alchemy as it applies to spiritual and psychic transformations. His alchemical understanding was part of his analytical repertoire for working with people. More recently, a similar approach to healing has been used by Drs. Carl and Stephanie

Simonton, who have developed a method of visualization for the treatment of cancer.

This power of the imagination has been used by meditators throughout the ages as a catalyst for spiritual transformation. In Kabbalah, visualization is used to attain higher states of awareness. A disciple of Abraham Abulafia (thirteenth century) gave a comprehensive description of what he called the "kabbalistic way"—a complex visualization process that can carry one who is adept to the highest realms.

The secrets of this form of meditation have remained hidden and inaccessible until the last fifty years. Now that they have been revealed by scholars, there are still many difficulties that hamper our full appreciation because of the gap between words and experience. The following quotes offer a glimpse into this world:

This kabbalistic way, or method, consists, first of all, in the cleansing of the body itself, for the body is symbolic of the spiritual. Next in the order of ascent is the cleansing of your bodily disposition and your spiritual propensities, especially that of anger, or your concern for anything whatsoever except the Name [of God] itself, be it even the care for your only beloved son; and this is the secret of the Scripture that "God tried Abraham."

A further step in the order of ascent is the cleansing of one's soul from all other sciences which one has studied. The reason for this is that being naturalistic and limited, they contaminate the soul, and obstruct the passage through it of the divine forms. The forms are extremely subtle; and though even a minor form is something innately great in comparison with the naturalistic and the rational, it is nevertheless an unclean, thick veil in comparison with the subtlety of the spirit. On this account seclusion in a separate house is prescribed, and if this be a house in which no [outside] noise can be heard, the better. At the beginning it is advisable to decorate the house with fresh greens in order to cheer the vegetable soul which a man possesses side by side with his rational soul.[31]

These preliminary stages are in the category of purification, as we find in other enlightenment processes. The similarity ends here, however, and a method unique to Kabbalah begins. It uses the twenty-two letters of the Hebrew alphabet as a concentration focus. One meditates on a word or on a combination of letters, and then one begins to permutate the letters into all their possible combinations. Next comes a process called "skipping," which the Kabbalist describes as follows:

> *It consists of one's meditating, after all operations with the letters are over, on the essence of one's thought, and of abstracting from it every word, be it connected with a notion or not. In the performance of this "skipping" one must put the consonants which one is combining into a swift motion. This motion heats the thinking and so increases joy and desire that craving for food and sleep or anything else is annihilated. In abstracting words from thought during contemplation, you force yourself so that you pass beyond the control of your natural mind and if you desire not to think, you cannot carry out your desire.*[32]

The nullification of desire is one of the linchpins of meditation and is particularly notable in Eastern traditions. Most of these traditions work upon desire by revealing the source. Once we recognize the full implications of our desire function, we are able to inhibit it. The Kabbalist, in this method, uses a different approach. We do not work to understand desire, but instead use the imagination to enter into an altered mind state which automatically transcends desire. There is yet another level of imagination:

> *You then guide your thinking step by step, first by means of script and language and then by means of imagination. When, however,*

you pass beyond the control of your thinking, another exercise becomes necessary which consists in drawing thought gradually forth—during contemplation—from its source until through sheer force that stage is reached where you do not speak nor can you speak. And if sufficient strength remains to force oneself even further and draw it out still farther, then that which is within will manifest itself without, and through the power of sheer imagination will take on the form of a polished mirror.[33]

The writer is describing a state most of us have never attained. We do not have what the Kabbalists call *malbush* (garments), to contain the light of understanding. These garments are qualities upon which the thinking mind can focus. They clothe the essence but are not the essence itself; without garments, essence is inaccessible.

A vital quality within each of us remains inaccessible without some kind of garment. It is vague, we know it is there, but we cannot seem to find it. Without a vessel to contain it, the quality will remain as untapped pure light. Imagination or visualization can provide this vessel.

Whereas the permutation of the letters of the Hebrew alphabet is a unique kabbalistic method, the use of imagination and visualization is found in many traditions. Tibetan Buddhism has a rich practice of visualized images, as does Hinduism and many Christian practices.

Here is a description by John Blofeld, well-known Buddhist scholar, of the tantric visualizations done as part of Tibetan Buddhist practice: "Besides reciting mantras or combining their recitation with yogic breathing exercises, it is usual to visualize their component syllables in colour. For use in this way there are *bijā*-mantras [seed-syllables] and *dhāranīs* [written mantras]. A *bijā* . . . is visualized as springing from a void 'spotless as a turquoise autumn sky' and magically transforming itself into a lotus. This unfolds to disclose a second *bijā*-syllable which instantly assumes the form of a deity. In the deity's heart shines yet another *bija.* . . . This is the essence within the essence that connects the manifestation with the void."[34]

Blofeld continues, "*Dhāranīs* . . . are often visualized in the form of a circle. At times, one of them is seen whirling round in the deity's heart; or, if adept and deity have merged, in the heart of both of them. Their whirling produces the perfect, limitless stillness of the void. Like *bijās, dhāranīs* glow with colour—whether white, blue, yellow, red or green will depend on the part of the mandala to which the deities belong."[35]

These visualizations may have a profound effect on the practitioner: "As soon as the visualization begins, the adept is transported into a magical world which defies description. . . . While he is in that magical state, the most ordinary object—say a door knob—gives him as much joy as the loveliest form imaginable."[36]

Imagination and visualizations may be used to overcome desire, as we saw earlier, yet they may also be a source of desire. The experience of a visualization may be so awe-inspiring or sensual that we immediately find ourselves wanting more. This kind of desire is a treadmill for the mind. It will never be satisfied and ultimately will leave us feeling empty.

The imagination that provides garments and unlocks the spiritual mysteries is not born out of mundane desire; rather it is a function of curiosity, investigation, or exploration. Whenever anything is attached to imagination as an expression of a desire, it is destined to lead to frustration. The desire itself pushes the imagination along a narrow course of conditioned and predefined sets of association, and this will always fall short of fulfillment. A "free" imagination is, of course, not free of conditioning, but it is free of desire, and thereby has a much broader scope. The driving force of desire actually imposes limits on imagination.

The term *visualization* can be a misnomer. Some people do see things with their imagination. They can visualize as though watching a movie; sometimes in color, sometimes in black and white. Other people do not visualize in this way. They have less capability for making images, but it in no way minimizes the effect of their visualizations. They may "think" the scene without seeing an image, or may "feel" the experiences, or they may hear the dialogue without having precise words flowing through their consciousness.

We should not have preconceived notions of what it means to visualize. The imagination works differently for each of us. Indeed, there is no way we can fully appreciate another's imagination. We can get only glimpses and then imagine what we think it might have been like.

Our visualizations are also very individual. Some people like to be guided in visualization; they prefer to have someone else set the tone. Others like the spontaneity of their own imagination, flowing and unbounded. In either situation, the key is to remain open to whatever presents itself in the moment, not to shut out any "unpleasant" images or grasp for the ones that feel good. It is important to let go, to feel that anything is possible. The world of imagination is filled with magic. We can move forward or backward in time faster than the speed of light. It is the world of everything we once thought impossible.

Dwelling in this world empowers us in a special way. The results may be quite subtle. Over a period of time, especially when a strong emotional image touches our imagination, we find ourselves coming back to it often in spare moments. We experience flashbacks or even begin seeing it in our dreams. It works on the subconscious level, slowly bringing about a spiritual transformation.

Begin by experimenting with a few simple visualizations. To visualize with concentration, sit quietly in meditation, calming the mind, minimizing distractions. Then try something like the following:

1) Imagine yourself in the presence of someone you consider a great spiritual being. How does it feel? Speak to this person as if you were good friends. Don't be shy. Say the words out loud, voicing both sides of the dialogue—what you are saying and how the other person responds. Don't let your doubts interfere. Just allow the words to flow even if it feels silly. Speak spontaneously without mental editing. As soon as you have finished, try to write down what you remember. Repeat this process until you are comfortable with it and proficient in carrying on an internal dialogue.

2) Visualize standing in the heavenly court. You must discover why you are there. There is a prosecuting attorney and a defending attorney. Which side are you on? What does the presiding judge look like? Who else is in attendance? Who do you recognize in the court? Ask somebody what case is being tried and what you are doing there. Let the responses flow. Then let the case proceed. All the time, say out loud what the attorneys say and what the witnesses respond. Write down the important things you remember after the visualization is over.

3) Imagine you are walking in a beautiful field. The weather is perfect. You are alone but you know there is a special presence ahead. The closer you get, the better you feel. You know this person you are about to meet is extraordinary. You get close enough to see what the person looks like. Describe her or him. Then you get close enough to talk. Engage in a conversation. As if it

were happening right at this moment. It is useful to record these conversations. Keep them on file for future reference. Even though they may not make much sense today, someday they may.

4) Imagine you are sailing on a boat. You see an island ahead. You land there and look around the island. Allow yourself to explore it very thoroughly. Carry with you a magical protection device. Should you run into danger, face it knowing that you can always escape if you must. Whatever you encounter, beauty and grace or danger and fear, try to go to its heart, try to speak to it and discover its source.

5) Visualize yourself floating in the hands of God—comfortable, protected, calm. Experience the feeling of God's presence. Imagine what it would be like to be in the same room with the Messiah.

There is nothing to achieve in these visualizations. There is no measure of success. They are just experiences with a part of us that rarely has a chance to express itself. This part often sounds simplistic or silly, yet sometimes it expresses a deep wisdom.

Another kind of visualization that has a strong effect was developed in the sixties by Sam Lewis, known as Sufi Sam to his followers, who were part of the Flower Generation. His visualizations are known as the "Walks." The idea is to experience the presence of a great sage, saint, or prophet and begin to move as you imagine that person moved, walk in the spirit of that being. Walk like Moses, Mary, Muhammad, Jesus, Buddha, St. Francis, Abraham, or any other spiritual leader, whether biblical or historical.

The "Walks" are not limited to beings. They can also be used to represent different types of energy. For those who are astrologically involved one can learn to walk like

Saturn, Jupiter, Venus, Pluto, the Sun, the Moon, and so forth. In Kabbalah, one can walk like the energy of the *sefirot* (emanations) of the Tree of Life, walking as though one were *hesed* (loving kindness), *gevurah* (judgment), *tiferet* (beauty), and so forth.

We see here that visualization is not limited to sitting quietly and conjuring up mental images. We can actually "walk" or act out our visualizations. We can "feel" or think a visualization with imagery or without explicit mental pictures. This expression of our active imagination opens broad vistas for meditation practice.

A recent innovation in visualization practice is called "process"-oriented meditation. The meditator consciously switches attentiveness, one moment using visual imagery, at another working with movement, still another dropping into feelings and accentuating them to gain insight. This kind of meditation has a greater psychological component and is well suited for individuals who want a freer form of meditation.

Arnold Mindell has described an uninhibited meditation practice he calls "process immersion." He writes:

> Once you feel at home with your process, walking breaks won't be necessary in meditation because movement awareness makes it possible to remain in a place the size of a yoga mat for hours at a time without the need to get up and stretch. During these hours, you may allow your process to switch channels, first listening to voices, then seeing dream figures, having insights, writing them down on paper, going back to sitting, then swaying, standing, shaking, lying down, and even sleeping. When this is done over the course of several days, you get more and more deeply involved in your process until it becomes a part of life itself.[37]

It may seem like a game to do these visualizations, yet on a much deeper level it taps into new energy resources. When we are not on retreat, in our more complex mental state we barely feel the arousal of these buried forces. On retreat, however, as we purify our systems and become more sensitive, such visualizations can touch us in a strong and permanent way, unblocking and opening passages long concealed.

The garment of visualization is a powerful tool. It has its dark side and must be used prudently to be effective. As with all practices, a good teacher/guide is of enormous value. Nonetheless, we can be independent and explore on our own, within reason. Remember, it is simply imagination. If we find it too troubling, we do not continue but search out someone to work with us. On the other hand, if we enjoy the limitless possibilities of a free-floating imagination, then we give ourselves plenty of rein and begin to enjoy dwelling in the realms of the angels, speaking with the divine, and understanding that our soul has found its home.

CONTEMPLATION

The idea of contemplation is often synonymous with religion. We frequently hear that someone wishes to live a life of contemplation or a person may be called a contemplative. The practice of contemplation has many facets, however, and is related to such diverse practices as prayer, visualization, stillness, observation, remembering, and ablution.

The basic act of contemplation is to let our minds dwell on something, allowing an unimpeded flow of thought to open new vistas and thus expand our awareness. A significant part of our lives is filled with contemplation, which often arises spontaneously. Something catches our attention—a flower, a child, a word, the sky, a sound—anything can draw us for a few moments or longer, and while we contemplate it, we have the experience of complete absorption.

There is a distinction between spiritual contemplation and that which is mundane. The latter is part of our daily experience as we consider the recent past or plan for the immediate future. We may ruminate on how to impose control over the way our lives are unfolding or try to uncover the lessons of recent encounters. We may regret how something happened or think wishfully about an upcoming event. All of this is temporal (mundane) contemplation.

As worldly thought, contemplation is nothing more than "monkey mind." While engaged in this kind of cerebral activity our thoughts and feelings jump about like a nervous monkey, now here, now there, never stopping and constantly chattering in the process.

Our tendency in meditation is to drop frequently into mundane contemplation. This leads to many unhealthy states of mind and an exhausting thought process that seems to rumble forever through our inner stillness. Obviously, the purpose of spiritual contemplation is to move this process to a different arena.

There are opposing viewpoints on what is meant by spiritual contemplation. The underlying principle of one perspective is in the question, "What does this mean to me?" or "How may I learn from this?" We contemplate for a reason, to be able to do something, to build our willpower. There is a tendency toward this orientation in Western practice. The other approach to contemplation is that it must be devoid of ego involvement. There should never be an appearance of "I/me," because this sustains a separation, while the truth lies in unification. Following this egoless approach, contemplation may lead to an end result, but there is no desire on our part.

The adherents of both viewpoints generally agree that the primary subject matter of spiritual contemplation should be universal, with no sense of past and future. We may contemplate noble ideas, eternal questions, inexplicable events, classical tales, and wisdom teachings. As one Christian writer put it: "Meditation [contemplation] is the deliberate, and usually systematic, reflection on some truth or passage of Scripture. It has a threefold purpose: to instruct the mind, to move the will, and to warm the heart for prayer."[38] We should note here that in Christianity, the words contemplation and meditation are often synonymous.

The approach that suggests that the purpose of contemplation is ultimately revealed in an action is based on a theological idea that we have a job to do in this lifetime. It is a predominant doctrine in Judaism and Christianity that all of our spiritual practices should work toward perfecting ourselves and the universe through our actions. This is spoken about in Jewish wisdom teachings: "[Rabbi Elazar ben Azaria, a Talmudic sage in the first century of the common era] used to say: Anyone whose wisdom exceeds his good deeds, to what is he likened?—to a tree whose branches are numerous but whose roots are few; then the wind comes and uproots it and turns it upside down. . . . But one whose good deeds exceed his wisdom, to what is he likened?—to a tree whose branches are few but whose roots are numerous; even if all the winds in the world were to come and blow against it, they could not budge it from its place. . . ."[39] A parallel teaching comes from the wisdom of the Christian Desert Fathers of the fourth century: "Abbot Pastor said: If you have a chest full of clothing, and leave it for a long time, the clothing will rot inside it. It is the same with the thoughts in our heart. If we do not carry them out by physical action, after a long while they will spoil and turn bad."[40]

The egoless approach is somewhat different. When engaged in a pure level of contemplation, there is the feeling that we do not exist and are nothing but a vehicle for the Contemplator within us. This follows a mystical idea that the Divine uses the creation to contemplate itself. A tenth-century theoretical writer, Kalabadi, who was intimate with Sufi practices, said: "The willer [a technical term for the mystical novice—in this instance, one who contemplates] is in reality a willed one, and the willed one (i.e., God) is the willer; for he who strives toward God has this striving only by virtue of a previous striving of God toward him. . . . Thus God's striving toward them (the mystics) is the cause of their striving toward Him; for His act is the cause behind all things, but this act itself has no cause."[41] Another way to understand this is through the Sufi idea "that the end of *dhikr* without words is contemplation (*mushāhada*), in which subject and object are, eventually, indiscernible."[42]

The debate concerning where individual consciousness fits into spiritual practice is a cutting edge about which much has been written. It in itself is a wonderful source for contemplation as understanding what is behind the sense of "I/me" and is one of the main gates into the castle of wisdom.

Spiritual contemplation is especially useful for people who have not had a great deal of training in meditative discipline. As it is an effortless natural process, the only guidance necessary is to have a clear differentiation between the kind of contemplation that is likely to be uplifting and the kind that will lead to monkey mind.

The subject of spiritual contemplation can be as expansive as the heavens, the rolling sea, or the multitudinous forms of nature. Or it can take the form of something as specific as gazing at a name of God, reading Scripture or other spiritual literature, or watching flies buzzing on a window.

The possibilities for the focus of contemplation are unlimited, yet we must be careful to avoid subjects that excite desire, greed, lust, aversion, judging, comparison, or fear—any of which may arise when we become identified with our contemplation. This can be perplexing because the mind is cunning; all of a sudden a true spiritual contemplation can become a full-blown fantasy. It usually takes a while to discover we are caught in a fantasy. The power of imagination is such that it makes us lose sense of ourselves. This is valuable when we use imagination for a practice such as visualization, but when the imagination runs out of control and becomes fantasy, we can be in another world for a long time.

One of the main aspects of spiritual practice, especially important in contemplation, is developing the awareness to recognize thoughts as close to their inception as possible. When we are exceptionally skilled, we can observe thoughts as they arise. Most of us, however, become aware long after we have been captured by it. Our work then is to let go of the fantasy without self-criticism or judgment and take up the practice once again. This process of continually coming back to the practice is basic to all meditation. Each time we slip, we coax ourselves back, knowing that we will slip again. Each time we strengthen our resolve and our concentration.

There are many levels of contemplation. We may begin by trying to understand the deeper meaning of something. As we continue in our practice, we will reach new levels and may even reach a gnosis, a "knowing" that transcends discursive thought. Eventually we may subdue thought altogether and experience a state in which we are no longer separate from the object of our contemplation.

The eleventh-century Sufi Hujwiri said: "There is a difference between one who meditates upon the Divine acts and one who is amazed at the Divine Majesty: the one is a follower of friendship, the other is a companion of love."[43] At one point the contemplator is the friend of the Divine, meditating on the wonders of the universe. At another point, after a rush of profound awareness, the contemplator is consumed in the fire of inexpressible amazement and then becomes the lover of the Divine. Christian contemplatives often choose New Testament stories as a starting point. The account of Christ offers a rich scenario for this kind of practice, whether in the stories of the miracles, the struggles, or the teachings. As parables are a major form through which Christian teachings are expressed, the meditator is offered a perfect vehicle for contemplative exploration. Each parable is a garden in which many varieties of plants may be found growing.

The difference between contemplation and visualization is that a visualization of the Sermon on the Mount would draw us into the experience as if we were actually there at the moment it was being given, bathed in all-pervasive love, whereas a contemplation would be oriented to discovering the deeper meanings of the message of charity and brotherhood. Visualizing the Buddha sitting under the Bo tree, we may experience tranquillity and equanimity, while a contemplation would penetrate what the Buddha meant when he said, "All things must pass." We can visualize Moses coming down the mountain with engraved tablets of stone, experiencing awe and fear when we see the light emanating from his face, whereas a contemplation would inquire what it meant for him to break the tablets when he saw the golden calf being prepared for idol worship.

In addition to the two views of contemplation, some meditative disciplines oppose it in *any* form because it utilizes thought and thereby strengthens the power of our cognitive process. In many Eastern practices, for example, there is a rejection of all contemplation, visualization, and petitional prayer. We must be alert and observant, therefore, to notice when the process is enhancing our overall practice and when it might be introducing barriers.

Those who suggest contemplation should result in action point out that the strengthened thought process may lead to endless cognitive gymnastics, and any practical application may be lost forever. We must always be careful to remain grounded in the reality of the human predicament so as not to be carried away in the reverie of thought for its own sake.

From the other perspective, an impediment arises when the ego is present: there is a separation and a tendency to be trapped in mundane contemplation. We must be vigilant in any cognitive meditation to catch the earliest sign of "I/me" in our thoughts and as soon as we become aware of its presence, return to a neutral starting point.

There is no resolution to this dispute. However, wisdom may arise in the recognition that there is truth on both sides and that a balance must be established between the two. If we are too committed to finding a reason for action, we may lose sight of the relinquishment of ego, which is clearly necessary for the highest unification. If we are too concentrated on practice without concomitant deeds, we may slip into the snare that occurs so often: practice without content, form without substance, spirituality in name only. Thus each side of the argument has its wisdom; it is up to us to listen to and use both as we refine our continuing practice.

The Kabbalah offers a fascinating perspective that integrates both sides. In kabbalistic terms, contemplation carries the divine sparks of the world of action (*asiyah*) and raises them to a higher world. They may be raised to the world of formation (*yetzirah*) or the world of creation (*briah*). If one attains a true revelation, the sparks reach the highest world, the world of emanation (*atzilut*). In everyday language, this means that anything in existence can be contemplated, and the contemplation itself actually adds light to the divine sparks contained within the subject, thereby helping to raise it to higher worlds of creation.

This is an important idea for the meditator and is a source of profound reflection. It is not possible to engage in true spiritual contemplation without engaging in a cosmic aspect of universal healing. Each pure contemplation can raise the subject matter from its level of density to a realm of greater light, thus bringing the universe closer to perfection.

A similar Christian perspective on this point is expressed in a book known as *The Cloud of Unknowing*, a fourteenth-century anonymous work subtitled *A Book on Contemplation:*

> *Lift up your heart to God with humble love. . . . Indeed, hate to think of anything by God himself, so that nothing occupies your mind or will but only God. . . . It is the work of the soul that pleases God the most. All saints and angels rejoice over it. . . . Moreover, the whole of mankind is wonderfully helped by what you are doing, in ways you do not understand. Yes, the very souls in purgatory find their pain eased by virtue of your work.*[44]

Obviously, when we improve things through our good deeds, the consequences are immediate and usually recognizable. The power of speech to help make things better is also often observable. However, we learn from this teaching that although the results are subtle, sitting in deep contemplation can have an impact upon the physical world and the spiritual world without our "doing" anything more than the contemplative act itself.

We are told, however, that we should not perform contemplation with this in mind. This would put our contemplative effort into the realm of desire; there would be an attachment, and the pure nature of the contemplation would be affected. True realization manifests only when our motivations are pure, so we must always be careful to know why we are doing things. If we are trying to improve the world through our contemplations, this can only add a kind of stickiness to our practice. If our spiritual work is an end in itself, without expectations or goals, then it will do whatever it has potential to do. We see here the delicate balance of our practice having a significant purpose as long as we do not attach significance to it.

Contemplation is an excellent practice for integrating our meditations into everyday life; it can extend the effects of a retreat for a long time. Once we learn the discipline required for spiritual contemplation, it becomes an easy daily practice. Simply reading one line of something inspirational each morning can provide excellent material for contemplation if we design a practice that helps to encourage contemplative moments throughout the day. Some people set their watches to beep every so often, or on the hour, as a reminder to return briefly to the daily thought.

The power of the practice is that with the right kind of subject, and the right frame of mind, we can dwell for extended periods in thought forms that revitalize the essence of our being. We can allow ourselves to be absorbed by a contemplation, to be drawn away from the temporal world, and this alone brings us into a deeper relationship with unknown realms.

We can tap many resources to continue this process. For people in a busy, active environment, it is perhaps the

CONTEMPLATION

most accessible spiritual practice. A few moments of contemplation can be accomplished even in the middle of a business meeting. This experience is not like a passing daydream but affects the quality of life, deepening our spiritual connections, drawing us into reflection and constant realization of the soul's quest to be at one with its divine source at all times and in all places.

MINDFULNESS

Whereas in visualization and contemplation an element of discursive thought weaves images into ideas and concepts, the practice of mindfulness slices all thought into its essential components. The awareness of these components help us to comprehend the insubstantial nature of creation, the constant rising and falling of phenomena, the true meaning of impermanence. The insight that results from mindfulness is that the element of discursive thought does not rest on a firm foundation, nor does it provide a solid basis upon which other thoughts may be placed. In other words, as a teacher of mindfulness meditation puts it, "There is no thought worth thinking."

This meditation is based on a major Buddhist teaching called the *Mahā Satipatthāna Sutta*. The word *satipatthāna* is difficult to translate, but is related to Right Mindfulness, the seventh step of the Buddha's Eightfold Path. In this practice, the student is taught to be aware of her or his mind state in every moment.

The Venerable Ajahn Chah describes the word *sati* as "that which 'looks over' the various factors which arise . . ."[45] It has the quality of what we in the West sometimes call the "observer." In the practice itself, however, a paradox will arise if we ask, "Who is observing?" because the premise of the practice is the principle that there is no observer, there is simply observation.

In Buddhism there are two general types of meditation: *Samatha*, or tranquillity, and *Vipassanā*, or insight meditation. *Samatha* is usually based on one-pointed concentration that leads to a state of absorption. *Samatha* purifies, increases the power of concentration, and is often associated with a sense of peace and happiness. Traditionally it has been the prerequisite for *Vipassanā*.

Deep states of absorption still have the quality of impermanence. Many meditators have experienced marvelous states of mind, yet shortly thereafter they are caught in the web of an internal drama, struggling with delusions and desires. In other words, even the benefits of the various concentration practices are ephemeral. A transformation is always taking place in the subtle realms, but our daily consciousness may continue to vacillate. As we become more skilled and experienced we clearly benefit from the meditative work, but the change is a long, slow process.

According to the teaching of *Satipatthāna*, true liberation comes only through wisdom that is derived through insight meditation (*Vipassanā.*) This mindfulness penetrates to the essence of delusions and desires. The purpose is not to exclude them from our consciousness, but to be so aware that we observe elementary thoughts as they arise in consciousness and thereby avoid becoming attached or identified with them. By noticing things as they arise, we are able to eliminate them at the source before they become full-blown associations. Desire, delusion, or aversion arise and quickly fall away; they are nothing but ordinary phenomena, like the sound of the wind or the chirping of birds.

SPIRITUAL PRACTICE

Some Buddhist disciplines describe *Vipassanā* as the insight that arises out of *Samatha,* which is the traditional meditation process. Current teachings suggest, however, that meditators can integrate the practice of mindfulness into their concentration so that the process need not be linear but more holistic. This leads to a meditation technique designed specifically to arouse insight.

The fundamental principles in Buddhist teaching are that everything is impermanent, everything is unsatisfactory, and there is no "self." The *Vipassanā* meditation focuses on impermanence. As we probe more deeply into this phenomenon, we gain increasing insight with regard to the nature of our "selves" and of the unsatisfactory nature of life, which is often called suffering.

Vipassanā teachers talk about "seeing things the way they are" or "seeing the true nature of things." At first we may think that the idea of true nature is dependent upon the observer's frame of reference. The physicist has an idea of true nature somewhat different from the chemist's. The mathematician approaches reality from a different viewpoint than the musician. In the end, all disciplines interlock in what Hermann Hesse called the Great Glass Bead Game in his novel *Magister Ludi.* Hesse used glass beads to represent a primordial abstraction that could be applied to each discipline of knowledge in its own way. Each year a game master would arrange the beads in a new game form, and everyone would learn something as they saw how it applied to their own field of knowledge.

The *Vipassanā* idea of true nature is on the level of these glass beads; it is based on primordial elements. Each moment a game master following some cosmic design rearranges the beads, and this is the basis of our reality, filtered through our individual limitations and clothed in our own delusions.

Throughout history attempts have been made to find the common denominators of primordial nature. Even today, science is engaged in the ongoing search for a Unified Field Theory, in which the essence of creation can be quantified. The Chinese system of Five Elements shows the entire world to be interrelated in some way to earth, fire, water, metal, and wood. In Kabbalah, it is composed of the ten original emanations, upon which the universe is founded. The Greeks proposed earth, air, fire, and water. And the Hindu teachings of the Vedas and Upanishads speak of the same four elements plus ether, the space in which transformation takes place.

For the meditator, the principle is to enter a kind of primitive mind, to view things in as simple a way as possible. We can, for example, notice the qualities of stimuli in terms of dichotomies: hot or cold, soft or hard, narrow or wide, sharp or dull, heavy or light, bright or dark, straight or round, full or empty, and so forth. We see or touch something that is bright, hard, cold, sharp, and straight, and we find ourselves calling it a knife. In this practice it becomes clear that we identified the concept of "knife," although our information was simply a combination of different degrees of the qualities of bright, hard, cold, sharp, and straight. From this we realize that everything we relate to in the world is a combination of elementary qualities around which we have wrapped a concept.

This leads to the understanding that our reactions to everything are conditioned by the way we have clothed them in concepts. A multitude of emotions are attached to seeing, feeling, and even thinking about "knife." At this very moment we are reacting to the idea of knife; we cannot read the word without it evoking, if only for an instant, some response. Knives can cut. Most of us have experienced this. They can also seriously hurt or kill.

As a reader you are reacting to a word on a page, although it is nothing but shaped darkness on a light background. When we actually see or touch a knife, we are encountering a combination of its properties of bright, hard, cold, sharp and straight. If our minds were primitive, if we had no concept of knife, we would simply experience these elemental qualities. If we did not conceptualize at all, we would be seeing the "true nature" of the knife.

The next step is understanding that our own self-image is a composition of concepts along with the dynamic interaction of qualities such as desire and aversion. In Buddhism, the sense of self is a composite of five groupings, called *skandhas:* the material level, or physical body; the emotions, or feelings of pain and pleasure; our memories and perceptions; our impulses and mental states; and the conscious awareness of all this.[46]

If a sharp knife moves across the skin of a finger and cuts it, we say, "My finger hurts." The physical part of the image is "finger"; the emotional level is "ouch" or "hurt"; the perception is the experience of pain as the knife cuts; the impulse and mental state is aversion, not-liking, wanting to avoid; and finally the consciousness is the identification with "me." Once we have the identification that "My finger hurts," we usually take off in some direction, such as "That was stupid of me," or "Who was the idiot who left this sharp knife out?" or "Darn, I just bled on my dress"—any number of scenarios.

However, what actually took place was that something

MINDFULNESS

sharp penetrated something soft, which is the nature of things. This body has pain receptors that respond when activated. The natural response of the body is to avoid pain. Memories of painful experiences add to our conditioning. All of this is how nature works. We can observe processes like this with equanimity or we can identify with the "me" part and then get angry, sad, self-abusive, or emotionally overwrought. When we get attached, we build a personal drama that runs its course, usually making things much more complicated than they are.

The deeper the insight, the more we come to realize that there are not only external stimuli that drive our lives, there is a cyclical internal process with which we interact and identify. This process makes up the bulk of our daily experience. It is not the basic stimuli that cause the trouble; it is our constant grasping or avoidance, the continuing associations and identifications that fill our lives with universes of thought and delusion so that we miss seeing the world "as it really is."

The intention of mindfulness meditation is fundamentally different from ordinary one-pointed meditation. For example, one-pointed meditation might focus on the general experience of breathing, the widening and narrowing of the nostrils, the expanding and contracting of the chest, or some other aspect of breathing. It does not attempt to use as the object of meditation the constant rising and dissolving of momentary sensations, as this can be distracting from total absorption.

On the other hand, "In *Vipassanā,* one may take precisely the actual momentary sensations which are constantly arising and passing away in each instant as the primary object. Further, one may include in awareness whatever other physical and mental phenomena become predominant, rather than excluding them as in tranquillity meditation.''[47] The object is not so much to be one-pointed as it is to notice everything in its most embryonic state, instantly recognizing it for what it is, and observing it pass away.

There is a practice in *Vipassanā* called "bare attention" which accurately portrays and sums up the underlying principle of insight medita tion. Joseph Goldstein, a well-known American teacher of *Vipassanā* writes:

> *There is one quality of mind which is the basis and foundation of spiritual discovery, and that quality of mind is called bare attention. Bare attention means observing things as they are, without choosing, without comparing, without evaluating, without laying our projections and expectations on what is happening; cultivating instead a choiceless and non-interfering awareness.*[48]

This kind of awareness is typified in haiku poetry. Goldstein quotes one of his favorites as an example of bare attention:

> *The old pond.*
> *A frog jumps in.*
> *Plop!*

Bare attention is an essential practice of mindfulness. It is pristine, direct, pithy, without frills. It goes right to the point, adds nothing, subtracts nothing, and leaves without a trace. Despite its simplicity, it is a demanding practice.

In a retreat format, *Vipassanā* is more rigorous than most other disciplines. Any phenomenon has potential for being the primary object of the meditation. Everything on a *Vipassanā* retreat is grist for the mill. Any activity that lures us into a habitual thought process in which our observer is asleep is discouraged. The *Vipassanā* retreat is designed to keep things very simple, which is the only way we can begin to get to "true nature."

A *Vipassanā* schedule is usually highly structured. We either do a sitting meditation, a walking meditation, or an eating meditation. We move carefully from one place to another, trying to maintain mindfulness throughout. We never relax this attention, even when using the toilet, brushing our teeth, or preparing for bed. There is no time for drifting, contemplating, visualizing, or any other distracting activity.

In the sitting, we normally meditate on the rising and falling of the breath. In the beginning, students learn to observe the breath in a *Samatha* form, practicing concentration and one-pointedness. As soon as possible, the instructions change into a *Vipassanā* mode, and the meditation opens into a continuing process of mindfulness.

The same is true for walking meditation. We move slowly on a path that leads nowhere. Any goal orientation is avoided. Walking is usually in a limited space, fifteen or twenty paces in one direction and then the same number returning. There are different approaches to the pace we take—some move infinitesimally slowly; some walk at a normal speed. An outsider might think that these people, particularly the ultra-slow walkers, belong in a mental institution.

Walkers are intently focused on the legs and feet. The overall mental observation may be on lifting-moving-placing. The mindfulness part of the practice is in being aware of the flood of impulses necessary to get that foot from one place to another. There is a physical, emotional, and mental dimension, right down to the minute observation of when the initial impulse arises to begin to think about moving the foot in the first place.

Eating meditation is enlightening as we observe our

enormous urges and needs regarding food. Here we sit, slowly moving, carefully observing the intricate motion of the arm and hand lifting the food to our mouths, placing the spoon gently between the lips, slowly removing the food from the spoon, savoring it for some time, feeling the juices flowing, beginning slowly to chew, finally swallowing—and all the while our minds incessantly press us forward, wanting to gobble the food down and get on with things.

It takes some time to build this kind of discipline and it is usually worthwhile to experience it on a group retreat before attempting to structure our own insight meditation. A wide range of teaching is available in this practice, from strictly orthodox to highly egalitarian, liberal, psychologically oriented approaches. Some *Vipassanā* meditation centers are limited to a standard approach while others encourage a more eclectic program.

Vipassanā is not for everybody, but those who are attracted to it find it enormously beneficial. Standard retreats are a week to ten days, but they can often extend for a month or longer. An annual three-month retreat is held at the Insight Meditation Society in Barre, Massachusetts, and a large number of the participants return year after year. Except perhaps for living full-time in a spiritual community, this retreat is one of the most intense commitments one can make on the spiritual path, and its rewards for most participants richly compensate the effort involved.

Mindfulness practice is not limited to a Buddhist format. In Hinduism, many disciplines require the constant awareness of mindfulness. One of the most common forms is the practice of being continuously aware of the guru's presence. This has its devotional aspect, but also has a distinct quality of mindfulness in that every act is under the scrutiny of magnified awareness—just as we always see things with more critical observation when we are accompanied by a friend or loved one.

In the Western traditions, mindfulness is associated with devotional practices in which the Divine is a constant companion within us. In Sufism, a highly refined practice requires our awareness of the presence of Allah in every breath. In Christianity, the practice is having Jesus by our side at all times. In Judaism, the kabbalistic idea that creation is taking place in each and every moment brings an acute sensitivity to everything. All of these ideas can be practiced to raise our level of awareness and induce an entirely new perspective of seeing things "as they really are."

VISION QUESTS

The spiritual search is an exploration into the inner dimension, working with primitive substances such as fear, anger, love, and survival. In the areas between spiritual consciousness and psychology or psychotherapy there is a distinct overlap. Organized retreats generally have a disproportionate representation of people who are engaged in the healing arts; many are social workers, psychologists, psychotherapists, psychiatrists, or psychiatric nurses.

Many meditators approach retreats as a form of therapy, working not only on their spiritual advancement but on their problems in relation to the world. Some believe that the obsession among Westerners to be involved in their own therapeutic and analytical inner work is the very reason so few attain the degree of liberation that Easterners realize. Much can be said for this observation. Often we hear Western students probing for reasons, while the approach of many Eastern teachers ignores all "why" questions and deals only with "how."

The description of practices up to this point has assumed that the work is done in a safe, quiet place, a protected environment that allows for extensive reflection or complete absorption. This is the archetypal retreat environment, which allows a great deal of space for spiritual inquiry. It can also open the gates for psychological exploration.

Another retreat process bypasses opportunities for reflection or one-pointedness and thrusts us directly into confrontation with primal nature. In this situation there is little time for analysis because the retreatant is engaged in survival and fear as a stark reality. He or she is forced to draw on personal resources and reserves that may have lain dormant throughout his or her entire life.

The vision quest is a rite of initiation used by diverse societies, from American Indians to Aborigines. The literature of anthropology is full of accounts of initiation rites and vision quests that mark the transformation from childhood to adulthood or from spiritual darkness into light. The metaphor is one of birthing or rebirthing. The experience is usually traumatic, intended to touch the most primitive vibratory chord so that the individual is never again the same.

One of the main themes of initiation is death. Mircea Eliade writes:

> Everywhere we encounter the symbolism of death as the foundation of all spiritual birth, that is, of regeneration. In all these contexts, death signifies the transcending of the profane, unsanctified condition, the condition of the "natural man," ignorant of religiosity, blind to the spirit. The mystery of initiation gradually discloses to the neophyte the true dimensions of existence; by introducing him to the idea of the holy, the mystery obliges him to assume a man's responsibility. Let us remember this, for it is important: for all archaic peoples, access to spirituality is translated by a symbolism of death.[49]

Eliade describes mysteries and secret societies, both male and female, all of which have death symbolism built into the process of spiritual unfolding. Because of the power released in this process, most traditions display a natural separation of the sexes in the initiation procedure. A few, like the Bektashi Sufis, included men and women as equals in the initiation rites, which also involved symbolic death by hanging.[50]

Each society is inclined to symbolic expressions of its own. Many initiation rites involved physical mutilation that would be repugnant to twentieth-century Westerners. Some tests of survival we would be unequipped to handle. Yet the outward form of the initiation is only as important as the degree to which our essential being is engaged in the process of realization and transformation.

Sophisticated urban professionals who know their way through the treacherous concrete jungle, keep a wary eye out for muggers, and can spot a con artist a block away often melt into shivering, terrified kittens when placed alone in a forest at night, when all they have to do is sit quietly in the dark. Most of us are scared half out of our wits in a natural setting, where there is nothing between us and the wilderness. Even the sound of a mouse is frightening when we are sitting in a vulnerable place thinking about mountain lions.

A vision quest ultimately implies revelation. This revelation comes from confronting our anxieties, dwelling in the realms of primal fear, and finally suffering a symbolic death that signals the transition to a new awareness.

The need for security has been emphasized as indispensable in setting up a retreat. On an intense retreat, we naturally encounter deep fears and mini-deaths as an aspect of spiritual development. A large number of accounts testify to dying and rebirthing experiences at critical points in one's inner growth.

In a vision quest, we throw away the element of security and go directly into a confrontation with our primary inner survival gear. For most people this involves coping with fear. For some, it is more an issue of self-image, of weakness versus strength, the ability to stand on our own and function independently. It may be a test of character, maintaining an equilibrium in an arduous, uncomfortable situation. For a few, there is a unique personal challenge that must be met and overcome.

Some organized vision quests or survival schools are very helpful in providing a supportive framework for individuals to gain a sense of self-sufficiency. They also have a large social component and active comradeship that inhibits, to some degree, extensive self-reflection. Nonetheless, it can be a deeply spiritual experience scaling a sheer wall with a potential fall of fifty or one hundred meters, even though there are good, strong people at the other end of the rope.

Some vision quests are oriented to self-reflection and fit more the model of spiritual retreats. Survival in these experiences emphasizes living by our wits with minimal resources and spending time alone. This induces a heightened state of sensory awareness, which is a form of meditation. Often the schedule will include a number of days of silence and solitude, which help us break through our own sense of limitation.

Guided vision quests usually encourage self-empowerment practices. They may be methods of moving, visualization, or breathing control—practices that bring calm, focus, and a sense of protection. For some, especially those who take solitary vision quests, the practice is simply to be there, doing what is necessary to meet basic survival needs.

If we have had experience in the wilderness and know how to camp, have good equipment and a good background in survival technique, there is nothing to hold us back from a solo vision quest. There is a difference, however, between a solo camping trip and a vision quest in the wilderness. It is similar to the difference between a retreat and a vacation. It has to do with intention and how we utilize our time.

If we do not have wilderness experience and the idea of a vision quest is appealing, it is not a good idea to go out alone. Even for those with experience, a guided event will often open new vistas and suggest techniques that can enhance the power of the journey within.

The vision quest has been a spiritual regimen for centuries. Our civilized life has distanced us somewhat from the world of nature, but our primitive nature can be rapidly aroused in the right circumstances. This is a "fast" method for transformation; the encounter is often dramatic and overwhelming.

At times retreatants in a rural setting will use the practice of a vision quest as part of the retreat schedule. During a long retreat, it is sometimes beneficial to go on an overnight hike into the countryside or perhaps spend a couple of days away from "home" in the retreat hut. This change of pace can add insight and provides a great deal of material for processing.

It is important, however, to be well equipped experientially to manage alone. Our altered frame of mind in the midst of an intensive retreat may not have the same coping mechanism as when we normally engage the world. In addition, a departure from a retreat environment will dramatically affect the flow of our meditation, and there is the possibility that a chance encounter may completely disrupt the retreat.

The vision quest is usually best undertaken with guidance. Usually, the teachers have a background in a psychological discipline, or their field experience has given them the deep wisdom of common sense. Our security is the knowledge that we are in good hands. Almost anyone can do a vision quest with guidance. It does not require advance practice or particular mastery of skills and has an impact on almost everybody at some level. The vision quest is not an ongoing practice for most individuals, but it can provide a significant boost for those who are seriously engaged on the spiritual path.

ABLUTIONS

Everything we do affects our daily lives and influences our spiritual development and so it is important to establish purification as a continuing process.

Each practice we undertake while on retreat has its purification characteristics; each works on a different part of the whole being. Some practices emphasize the physical dimension, some are more emotional, some go straight to the intellect, and some work in unfathomable ways.

Although ablutions have a physical dimension of cleanliness, they have a greater effect on inner cleansing than the exterior body. A well-known example of this is baptism, which is one of the most mystical expressions in Christianity and a ritual purification of the soul.

Ablutions involve a ritual act in the material world with one of the primary forms of matter: water. Water has always been perceived with a mixture of awe and fear in the mythology of various cultures. Even modern science is amazed at the properties of water. Scientists call water the "mother of life" and the "queen of all solvents." One of its qualities is that it is more dense as a liquid than as a solid, which is a unique property among known matter. It means more than the fact that ice cubes float. Life, as we know it, could not exist if it were not for this property of water.

Water is also said to be endowed with an even more unusual quality, that of purification. This is true of each major element. Air, with its life force *prāna,* is the element that the practice of *prānāyāma* uses for transformation. Fire has obvious purification properties in the way that it transforms matter. So too the earth, which embraces, absorbs, and transmutes all that it gathers throughout the cycle of life.

The ancient practice of using ablutions as a preliminary to meditation and prayer, or as a meditation in itself, leaves a potent impression in the meditator's mind. We find a high percentage of ancient cultures used ablution as a mode of purification. It is still practiced today in the East among some Buddhists, Hindus, Shintoists, and others, while in the West it is found in Judaism, Christianity, and Islam. Ablution also extends far beyond these traditions and can be found in aboriginal practices throughout the world.

When we recognize a practice so widespread, the implications of primordial collective unconsciousness are indisputable. Obviously there is a common point in humankind that resonates within a conceptual framework of purity and impurity. This has nothing to do with ethical and philosophical principles and is not necessarily connected with the exalted ideals of humankind. It is a cognizance of our divine substance, which is pure and pristine, compared with our material substance, which is distinct from the divine.

Unfortunately a tendency to confuse the idea of profane or impure with something dirty or disgusting leads to serious misunderstandings regarding purification practices or the situation of being in a ritual state of impurity. It is easy to fall into the mistaken belief that an impure individual is somehow in a lower caste, like an untouch-

able, who is shunned by society. Yet, a simple act of
ablution or other form of purification cleanses such a
person.

The problem arises in the language. The idea of impurity is associated with something diseased or infectious.
From the mystical perspective, however, every person
goes through states of impurity as a natural part of living,
and thus acts of purification are natural reflections of our
continuing attunement to our spiritual station. There is
nothing disgusting about being in an impure state—no
more than an exhalation is dirtier than an inhalation because it has a higher degree of carbon dioxide.

The breath is a good metaphor for the process of
purification. If the gums are diseased and the breath is
"bad," this has nothing to do with spiritual impurity. A
person can be in a state of purity and still have awful
breath. On the other hand, good hygiene and eating
habits may give the mouth a glow and the scent of
ambrosia and the person may still be spiritually impure.
The saints all experienced times of spiritual impurity. It is
not a condition to arouse repulsion.

Whenever the concept of pure versus impure is discussed in spiritual terms, it is on the abstract level, like the
relationship between holy and profane or divine and
manifest. It has nothing to do with any substance that is
measurable or scientifically verifiable. The procedures of
purification all work on this abstract plane.

In the modern world, our sophistication and knowledge of primitive beliefs tend to pull us away from many
of these rituals. We have more confidence in rationality
and scientific methodology than in voodoo and witch
doctors. There is a solid empirical basis for this, notwithstanding the awareness that in some situations the witch
doctor can accomplish more than a modern medical

professional. Still, the progress of humankind is dependent upon our rational, intellectual approach.

This does not mean, however, that we lose all connection with certain essential experience that can be derived through ritual. The most intellectual and sophisticated person must still confront primitive thought forms, whether in dreams or in daily life. We can often also experience a primal response when undergoing rituals, such as ablutions.

In the West, considerable emphasis is placed on ablution. In Christianity, baptism is mandatory for some denominations. In the traditional practice of Islam and Judaism, ablutions are part of daily life. The practice is similar in both traditions, including its name—*taharat* in Islam and *tahor* in Hebrew.

In Islam, prayers are offered five times a day. Whenever a Muslim becomes impure, a ritual purification must be performed before the next prayer. This involves the use of water on the face, hands, and feet in a special way. It is said of the Sufis that "some would become enraptured at the very moment the water for ablution was poured over their hands."[51] This aspect of ritual purification is one of the main tenets of Sufi mysticism and is included as one of the aspects of the "tenfold Path" of Najmuddin Kubra (twelfth century).[52]

In Judaism, there are extensive acts of purification, including ablutions, as the entire tradition is based on the separation of pure and impure, holy and profane. In the *midrash,* which is part of the oral tradition, there is a story of the sage Yohanan ben Zakkai who told his students, "It is not the dead that defiles nor the water that purifies! The Holy One, Blessed be He, merely says: 'I have laid down a statute, I have issued a decree. You are not allowed to transgress My decree.' "[53]

Yohanan ben Zakkai's point is that the laws regarding purification are not necessarily logical. There is no rational way to comprehend why immersion in water, or sprinkling a little here and there, should in any way purify the soul. Nor is there a reason why we enter the realm of spiritual impurity by touching shoes, hair, or certain parts of the body, by going to the toilet, or being in the presence of a dead person, by having a seminal emission, or by menstruation. The logical conclusion is that many of these conditions are the result of hygienic concerns or the products of pure superstition. When the rules of the game eliminate our rationality, our inclination is to dismiss the game.

Even the most skeptical rationalists encounter experiences beyond their explanation. For example, many people have had long-term relationships with another person, sharing the same dwelling and perhaps even the same bank account. Then one day the two decide to get married. A ceremony takes place, vows are offered and accepted, and all of a sudden everything changes. The house is the same, the finances are the same, but everything has a new flavor. What happened? Who can explain what it means to our inner nature to exchange vows of surrender, fidelity, and lifetime dedication? Yet, this is what the ritual involves, penetrating to the root soul, changing forever each individual. Even if the couple one day separates and follow different paths, the fact of the binding of souls will never change; it is an eternal process.

The power of ritual purification is enormous. Each time the spirit is unfettered from some burden, it can soar ever higher. The broader our spiritual perspective, the greater the effect of future purification. This can be a cumulative process, reaching ever higher domains of liberation, and is the idea behind the practice of ablutions.

ABLUTIONS

Ablutions can consist of sprinkled water, a ritual washing of hands or feet, or a total immersion. In Judaism, the total immersion must be done in a body of "living water," either a specially designed *mikvah,* or a pond, river, or lake where water freely comes and goes. This is not a time for washing with soap. In fact, many traditions require a person to be spotlessly clean prior to a ritual purification.

Unless we are following a specific traditional ritual, the major factor that makes this an ablution is our intention. We can make up our own ritual, as long as our minds are directed toward things like the removal of spiritual impediments, karmic attachments, residuals of wrongful behavior, release from clinging encumbrances. This intention can also be directed toward the immediate future as a preparation for prayer or for practice. It can be a practice done once a day or it can be repeated throughout the day. It can be a ritual every time we eat or go to the bathroom, or prior to every meditation period.

Ablutions are rarely treated as the sole form of spiritual practice, except in unique forms of yoga where one enters a body of water, like the Ganges river, and spends hours in extensive spiritual cleansing of internal organs. Usually, ablutions are an adjunct to the primary practice, a spiritual method of preparing ourselves. The insight we gain in the process is an understanding of the true nature of pure and impure, holy and profane. This lends impetus to our ongoing practice. It deepens our resolve, for we all cherish the goal of casting off the soiled garments of mundane existence in order to clothe ourselves in the fine apparel of spiritual purity and cleanliness.

FORGIVENESS AND
LOVING KINDNESS

One of the greatest burdens we carry along the path of spiritual development is guilt. None of us has lived the life of a saint; we have left considerable debris behind. There are many ways to perform rites of purification, but at times our guilt is so pervasive we need to use direct and powerful methods to cleanse ourselves. Some purification comes from simply dipping the fabric of our being in the waters of ablution. However, we may carry other stains that require a scrubbing board and strong detergent.

It is not easy and may not even be possible to be absolved of all of our misdeeds. The karmic effects of some acts reverberate strongly throughout our lives. Each tradition has its own method for dealing with this. There are practices of prayer, repentance, and redemption; there are acts of charity; and there is the belief in future lives to clean up the karma of the past. Despite the fact that there are many methods based on many different ideologies, all traditions agree that something can be done. Indeed, many spiritual paths focus on this process of gaining forgiveness and developing loving kindness.

In Western tradition, God is viewed as all-merciful and all-compassionate. If it were not for this quality, we could not survive; the repercussions of our acts would surely crush us. The idea of a vengeful God is a misunderstanding of the Scripture. The greatest divine "punishment" is separation. Whenever death is mentioned as a punishment, it is referring to a spiritual death that comes from cutting off the nourishment to the soul. Yet, the fact that the physical body lives on is a sign of the mercy and compassion of the divine, since nothing can exist for even a moment without this vitalizing force.

It is also important to realize that the word *punishment* is somewhat of a misnomer. The implication is that God punishes. A more enlightened perspective is that we punish ourselves, so to speak, in that our acts themselves cause the separation.

Thus Western tradition believes that right up to the moment of our death, there is a chance for redemption. The Eastern traditions follow a different course to reach the same conclusion: there is always the possibility of breaking through the illusions of this reality into our true nature. Enlightenment is always within a hairsbreadth. Merely remove a veil and we will see the truth.

Guilt causes a tight state of mind that can be released only through forgiveness. This state often expresses itself through anger, hatred, or other negative characteristics while at the core is a sense of guilt. Guilt can serve a valuable purpose by keeping us on a clear path, but when it constricts us, it becomes a major impediment to all spiritual development. This is why a large number of practices are specifically directed to developing forgiveness.

Forgiveness is a big issue. In Western tradition we may be focused on the forgiveness of God. In the East, it may be the means of gaining forgiveness from karmic justice. We may be interested in others forgiving us or we may need to forgive others. Finally, a great deal of spiritual psychology is directed toward self-forgiveness.

Symbolically, forgiving is represented by an open hand; it is a letting go. Any holding on implies that somebody is doing the holding, and that means a certain sense of separation and alienation. Letting go is the essence of forgiveness.

"One should forgive, under any injury," it says in the Hindu epic the *Mahābhārata*. "It has been said that the continuation of the species is due to man's being forgiving. Forgiving is holiness; by forgiveness the universe is held together. Forgiveness is the might of the mighty; forgiveness is sacrifice; forgiveness is quiet of mind. Forgiveness and gentleness are the qualities of the Self-possessed. They represent eternal virtue."[54]

In Judaism, the forgiveness practice is called *teshuvah,* which means repentance. Literally it means "returning," to go back to God. The focus here is not on self-forgiving, but on the forgiveness of the All Merciful God. The practice of *teshuvah* takes many forms. It has to do with accepting the yoke of the traditional Jewish laws, but it also involves a wide variety of acts that repair the spiritual damage we cause ourselves. The repair performed through *teshuvah* also assuages the collective guilt of all humankind since the beginning of time.

Some of the outward practices of *teshuvah* are the performing of good deeds, assisting the needy, giving loans without interest, helping people support themselves, being respectful to parents, teachers, and the elderly, doing any act of compassion or loving kindness. The inward practices, the kinds of things we might accomplish on retreat, begin with searching our memory carefully for every action which might have caused harm. It could be a physical act, a product of "evil" speech such as slander or gossip, or it could be in the subtler realm of harmful thoughts.

After identifying our wrongful acts, speech, or thoughts, we search our hearts to find the place where we regret what we did. This is a place where in the deepest sense we are ashamed. The more heightened our awareness and sensitivity, the deeper our shame, for we understand the impact of the most trivial actions. When we have attained a level of regret, we promise never consciously to do such a thing again. We may also add a prayer that we be prevented from unconsciously or accidentally doing so.

This process of identification, regret, and positive assertion provides a method for working to repair the spiritual parts that are broken in us and in the world. Rebbe Nachman says: "Repentance never stops. It is a continuing process."[55] This is an important point. Forgiveness is not in the goal but in the process. The process is the end in itself. It is like being in a dark room and wanting to turn on the light switch. We may strike a match and discover that there is no light switch, but the match provides the light we need. When one match burns out, we need to strike another, and yet another. This is the process of forgiveness. There is no light switch except perhaps an ultimate one that becomes apparent when there is universal messianic consciousness. Until that time, striking the match is the process and the end itself; each step along the way has its own light.

These practices of repentance and forgiveness can be done as visualizations or contemplations; there are many variations on the theme of forgiveness. As long as we follow the basic formula of identification, regret, and commitment not to repeat the act, the only limit to contemplation or visualization is our imagination.

In Christianity there is a strong emphasis of working on ourselves to forgive others. There is the well-known practice of "turning the other cheek" and also the idea of Christian charity. Forgiveness plays a major role in essential Christianity as it is closely related to unconditional love. In a Christian retreat format, a basic practice is not only to forgive ourselves, but to find true forgiveness in our hearts for anything done to us by another person that directly or indirectly harmed us.

A one-pointed meditation in Theravāda Buddhism called *mettā*, the loving kindness meditation, is directed toward forgiveness. It deals both with forgiving ourselves and forgiving others. The idea is to use our feelings of loving kindness as a focal point for concentration when sitting in meditation. This not only helps to release the tightness of the mind, it sends out loving energy and thereby affects the world. It is very powerful and can be the primary practice of a retreat, or it can supplement other practices of concentration or mindfulness.

The *mettā* meditation begins with visualizing ourselves and recognizing those parts that feel constricted. This helps us understand the constricted places in others. Then we visualize the parts of ourselves that are kind, soft, open, and loving. This helps us go to the heart of loving kindness throughout the meditation. We keep returning to this part of ourselves.

Then we say inwardly: "If I have harmed anyone knowingly or unknowingly, I ask their forgiveness." We visualize those people we have knowingly hurt and ask for their forgiveness. This is next followed by the statement: "If anyone has harmed me knowingly or unknowingly, I freely forgive them." Once again, we visualize those who may have harmed us and we offer forgiveness.

Throughout this meditation, the idea is to find feelings of gentleness, warmth, openness, softness, and a general sense of "letting go" within ourselves. We can deepen these feelings through visualizations such as hugging a cuddly tiny kitten, a soft furry puppy, or whatever tugs at our heartstrings. Once we open the feeling, we extend to ourselves all the love and compassion we can give to innocent, vulnerable creatures. We try to reach that place of our own pureness, innocence, and vulnerability. Then we may think about what we really need for ourselves and what we really want at this moment, and we say these things, such as: "May I be happy. May I be peaceful. May I be free."

This is a meditation in which we take all the time we need. It should not be rushed. We allow ourselves the opportunity to explore these feelings, letting forgiveness and loving kindness fill our hearts.

Then we think of someone we love. Visualize that person and say: "Just as I want to be happy, may you be happy. Just as I want to be peaceful, may you be peaceful. Just as I want to be free, may you be free." Feel our loving kindness extend outward. If this person ever harmed us, let us extend forgiveness to our loved one.

Then think of people in the neighborhood. Some we may know well, others we hardly know. Repeat the visualization for these people as a group: "Just as I want to be happy, may all of you be happy. Just as I want to be peaceful, may all of you be peaceful. Just as I want to be free, may all of you be free." Let the feelings of loving kindness spread even wider.

Now repeat the process for parents, whether alive or not. Repeat it for family and extended family, selecting individuals as they come to mind. Then reach for people about whom there may be some hard feelings. We search our memories for people who really hurt us or who we harmed. Often at this point someone will arise in the visualization, and we find ourselves thinking, "Anyone but him!" or "I could never forgive her!" Now is the time to work the hardest, to let go, to try our utmost to find a glimmer of understanding and forgiveness for this person. We can only try. If it does not work this time, maybe it will be a little easier in the next *mettā* meditation.

When we have visualized as many individuals as we can during this meditation, we open up to our nation, all beings in the world, and all beings in the universe: "Just as I want to be happy, may all beings be happy. Just as I want to be peaceful, may all beings be peaceful. Just as I want to be free, may all beings be free."

Feel the experience of being completely open, forgiving, and filled to the brim with loving kindness.

This is a wonderful meditation practice which not only deepens concentration but opens wide the heart. Some retreatants spend months doing just this practice, with variations that carry them deeper and deeper into the realm of accepting themselves and others. The most attained practitioners in *mettā* are like highly polished mirrors with only the filter of love. When we look at them we see ourselves as if filled with love. Everything else is forgiven. There is no consciousness given to any of the imperfections. The full emphasis is on the parts of us that have loving kindness and when these are accentuated, we can feel only gentleness and warmth toward ourselves and everything that is around us.

HATHA YOGA

Only a few generations ago, yoga was viewed as something exotic, a mysterious method used by Hindus to attain levels of extreme asceticism. Caricatures often portrayed men in loincloths lying on beds of nails or walking on carpets of burning coals. In this half of the century, yoga has become popularized and is now offered in daily television programs. Leotards have replaced the loincloth, and lithe females have replaced bearded fakirs.

Both views, the early one of occult magic and the current one of yoga as exercise, are somewhat off the mark. The traditional Hindu perspective of yoga is that any technique that binds the individual to the divine is considered yoga, and anything that unifies what we think we are with who we really are is regarded as yoga. Thus, yoga is a broad concept that includes diverse practices.

Traditionally there were four principal yogas: *jñāna,* the exploration of the intellect to its farthest limits; *bhakti,* a love-oriented, devotional concentration on the divine or someone through whom the divine is perceived; *rāja,* the "royal" yoga of inner concentration; and *karma,* action that is undertaken solely for the divine, without any sense of personal identity. These four original domains have been supplemented with many specialty practices such as mantra yoga, sahaja yoga, agni yoga, japa yoga, laya yoga, tantric yoga, and hatha yoga.[56] This broad concept of yoga extends to the development of new yogic practices, which is exemplified by a contemporary popular work that discusses dream yoga.[57]

When most Westerners encounter the idea of yoga, they usually center on hatha yoga. This is often misunderstood as a method of stretching in various positions, keeping the body limber and relaxing areas of tension. It is indeed an effective technique to accomplish these ends. However, hatha yoga was designed originally as a systematic purification of a psychic structure composed of energy centers located in the body. Obviously, the practices involve physical purification as well, but the objective is to open channels for the flow of energy from its source point up to the highest level of human potential.

In Western terms, this is difficult to comprehend. Hatha yoga is not a process amenable to scientific inquiry. It is true that some effects can be measured. Experiments with meditators have shown how heart rate, blood pressure, body temperature, general metabolism, and other physical features are affected by hatha yoga, meditation, or other yogic practices, but the central process of moving "energy" remains inaccessible to scientific exploration.

The idea of psychic purification is equivalent in many ways to the idea of acupuncture meridians. Acupuncture often works wonders in situations that normal allopathic medicine cannot remedy; its effectiveness has been proven time and again. Yet it works on a mysterious system of fourteen channels (meridians) of energy flow, where hundreds of specific points are charted for purposes of treatment with needles. When the scientific world of anatomy and physiology overlays these points with its own charts, nothing correlates. From a Western medical perspective, acupuncture makes no sense; yet it works.

Another system is outlined in the yogic map of the body, which is composed of six psychic energy centers called *chakras* (Sanskrit for "wheel"; also known as the astral lotuses), plus a seventh that is not accessible except through divine grace. Each *chakra* has a general location and is identified with specific qualities. The energy flow of the body is through *nādīs,* channels similar in concept, but not in location, to acupuncture meridians.

As with all ancient systems, opinions diverge on how the *chakras* are organized. Some hold that there are more, or fewer, than six *chakras;* the location in the body is a matter of dispute, as are the qualities or levels of consciousness associated with each. Nonetheless, there is general agreement that all life has a dimension related to levels of consciousness that supersede the physical plane, and this dimension is accessible for the process of purification, leading to the realization of higher levels of consciousness.

The mysterious internal system, which is the core of hatha yoga, is not unique to Eastern tradition. In the West, the Kabbalah specifically relates energy points to different areas of the body. So too in Sufism, with six centers in the body called *lataif* (the subtle ones) that are closely associated with the concept of *chakras.*[58]

The point here is not so much a comparison of these esoteric systems, which is an excellent subject for a separate investigation; rather it is to acknowledge that there are general parallels in many traditions that relate to the essence of life flowing through channels in the living body. This essence can be used as a focus of concentration and it can be refined through various spiritual practices.

The Hindu system of *chakras* has been developed more extensively than most other systems, and thus we will focus on it, using one of the more commonly accepted descriptions of the fundamental *chakras*.

The root *chakra* is called the *mūlādhāra* and is located near the base of the spine. It is often viewed as the center of survival needs. It is here that the *kundalinī* power lies coiled like a serpent, the primordial energy that must ultimately be aroused for access to the higher realms. The masters warn, however, that this must be done with great care, for the power of *kundalinī* unleashed without the proper vessels to contain it will drive a person mad and lead to certain death.

Although all of us yearn for enlightenment, it is good to remember that magnified light instantly burns through tinder or tissue but a material like metal may not burn at all. Even a laser beam can be contained by the right material. Spiritual practices are designed to build the psychic material to contain the light of *kundalinī*, which far exceeds the power of a laser. It is worthwhile to keep in mind that we are building vessels to hold this light. This is valuable to help temper our desire for instant gratification. At the same time it gives us encouragement to remain steady in our practice, constantly strengthening our internal vessels to utilize the light.

The second *chakra*, called *svādhisthana*, is located just above the first, in the sexual organs. As the *kundalinī* begins to rise, it immediately activates and arouses the sexual power center. For many people, the spiritual path ends right here. The exquisite nature of this new power, frequently confused with love, is seductive and often irresistible. Some tantric practices use this energy to break through to higher realms. Most people in the West do not have the self-discipline to follow esoteric tantric practice; moreover, it is often promoted by individuals who themselves are not coming from a higher level of consciousness and use this merely as a tool of seduction. On all levels, we need to come to grips with sexuality in life, particularly when engaged in spiritual pursuits. Many religious traditions deal with this issue by introducing broad regulations of constraint, edicts of separation, or complete abstinence. In this age of more permissive sexuality, these stipulations seem overly repressive and downright archaic. Yet, almost all spiritual traditions have something significant to say about sexuality. These traditions acknowledge that when our essential energy is diverted too much at this stage of development, the potential for broadened awareness can be stunted. The spiritual aspirant cannot ignore this issue. How we ultimately deal with it is a personal question. Often there is an ongoing process of exploration to find the proper balance between the severity of abstinence and the excessiveness of indulgence.

The third *chakra, manipūra,* is often identified with the solar plexus; it represents power, motivation, and drive. If the flow of energy gets bottled up at this point, the result is aggression and self-centeredness. In this situation, there is considerable personal effort put into controlling or manipulating others and an urge for financial or political power.

In the sixties, when there was a great emphasis on spiritual practice, it was possible to observe this natural cycle. This led to a sexual "revolution." Then came the increase of venereal diseases in the seventies, and the plague of AIDS in the eighties reversed the revolution into an environment of greater self-containment. The result has been an expansion of the focus on personal power along with financial accumulation. The yogic principle is that if this too can be restrained, then the psychic energy will move up to the higher, more enlightened levels of consciousness.

The primeval nature of the first three *chakras* is so substantial that we usually spend most of our time in meditation and retreat working with the thoughts and emotions connected with them. It is not at all uncommon to see people "stuck" in the second *chakra*, obsessed with sexuality, or in the third *chakra*, on a personal power trip. At times the dominant nature of these repetitive thoughts and emotions can deceive the individual into believing he or she will never escape these lower realms.

Although it is true that some people do not escape, this is due to their acceptance and identification with a false frame of reference. Assignment to the lower *chakras* is never a preordained condition. It can always be overcome. On the spiritual quest we need to recognize that these apparent fixations are only stations along the path. They need to be acknowledged for what they are: nothing more than the obsessions of a conditioned mind. Sooner or later, through steady effort and solid practice, the patterns will melt away.

The "heart" *chakra*, called *anāhata*, is the center of loving feelings toward ourselves and humanity. This is the point of integration between the lower *chakras* and those that open us to the highest levels of consciousness. The saints who were known for their exalted acts of loving kindness were operating from this center. This is where we expand from self-consciousness into a recognition and relationship with others. It is where compassion, sympathy, and caring are empowered. When the *kundalinī* power is focused on this level, even without going higher there is extraordinary benefit to humankind.

There are three more *chakra* levels. The fifth level, located in the throat, called *visuddha,* is the point of separation between physical manifestation and the intangible realms. When the life force is centered at this level, the illusory nature of all things becomes apparent. Moreover, the power of thought and speech is recognized for its potency. It is said that the gift of healing finds its source here.

The sixth *chakra,* located in a place behind the lower forehead, between the eyebrows, sometimes called the "third eye," is known as *ājñā.* It is sometimes associated with the pineal gland. The door of the "sixth sense," at times given the misnomer of intuition, it is actually a place of "knowing" the connections between the microcosm of our existence and the macrocosm of all creation. This is a level of profound awareness of how everything fits together in the awesome continuing flow of the universe.

There is a form of yoga meditation where the entire concentration is focused on this *chakra,* the third eye, visualizing the rise of *kundalini* from the base of the spine up to this point. When these first six *chakras* are completely open, then at a certain point, through grace, the *kundalini* power will erupt through to the final stage, the thousand-petal lotus, *sahasrāra,* the crown of the head, the original point of the fontanelle. At that instant the self dissolves in divine unification, the ultimate state of consciousness that is all-inclusive, all one.

The flow of energy through the *chakras* is a focal point for many practices. It is often used in visualization and also appears in movement and mantra practices, as we will see. Hatha yoga is specifically directed to the opening of the *nadī* channels through breathing techniques, called *prānāyāma,* and postures, called *āsanas. Prānāyāma* has been described in the chapter on breath; hatha yoga is best known for its *āsanas*.

Many books on yoga can give guidance to a beginner. Audio and video tapes are available as well as television programming in selected areas. The problem with learning this way is that the emphasis is usually on the physical aspects of hatha yoga. The physical awareness focuses on the posture itself, the muscles involved, how yoga helps blood flow, aids digestion, and is good for constipation. Often very little is mentioned about the channeling of life forces, the purification of emotions, and, if you will, a solvent for mental constipation.

It is useful to find an authentic yoga teacher who is spiritually inclined or to attend a yoga retreat that will instill good lifelong habits. Quite often books describe and picture advanced postures that are well beyond the skills of most practitioners. This is like discussing how to run a high hurdle race with a person who has never worn track shoes.

The hatha yoga reality for most people is to learn a simple routine of basic *āsanas* that can be done in a relatively short time on a daily basis. It is helpful in the early stages to attend weekly lessons, or a few days of a yoga intensive. This will help us develop good habits and may also be worthwhile to avoid injuries.

As with every practice, the key to the usefulness of hatha yoga for spiritual development rests on our attitude while practicing. If we go through a fifteen-minute routine early in the morning, all the while planning the day's activities or reflecting on what happened last night, we may be stretching some muscles and tendons, but we are not accomplishing much on the finer levels. In fact, it is possible that after a session like this we could end up more tense, angry, and closed than when we began.

One of the basic principles of hatha yoga is learning how to relax. When a person learns judo, or any martial art that involves flying bodies, the first instruction is directed toward learning how to fall. If we do not know how to fall, injury is almost certain. Moreover, the confidence of being able to fall well is an essential element that we need to engage whole-heartedly in the practice. In yoga, the key to every posture is knowing how to relax. The essential spiritual benefit comes through the relaxation.

Specific exercises are directed solely to relaxation, such as standing with legs spread and letting the body hang forward as far as it will go without straining, or lying flat on the back with legs slightly spread and palms up. There are also self-guided relaxations, where we use visualization to relax different parts of the body. These techniques slowly reveal the experience of deep relaxation on a number of different levels. Once revealed, it is easier to relax in positions that normally would induce body tension.

When we have learned the correct movements to enter into and hold a yoga posture, there are three basic areas of concentration for every *āsana:* we need to focus on the breathing, on consistent and smooth performance, and finally on relaxation throughout.

There is a tendency to hold the breath when doing physical activities and this is a cue that tension is building. Concentration on breathing is actually a relaxation exercise. The same is true for smooth, flowing performance. The awareness of smooth movement helps to alleviate tension in constricted parts of the body. It also keeps the mind from wandering, for it is very demanding to have constant fluidity in movement.

The focus on relaxation throughout the practice of yoga helps us maintain a continuous body scan, picking up any tension that arises despite steady breathing and fluid motion. This is usually a habitual, unconscious tension that we have patterned into everything we do. It often comes as a surprise to discover how much we bite our lips, clench our jaws and fists, tense our stomachs, or tighten parts of our legs as our natural reaction to physical effort or mental strain. One of the benefits of hatha yoga is learning how to break old patterns on both the physical and mental level so that new, more harmonic relationships can develop.

Some retreatants prefer to use hatha yoga as their primary practice, constantly moving to more difficult *āsanas*. An entire retreat can be filled with this form of yoga. More commonly, hatha yoga is used as a complement or change of pace for a more sedentary type of meditation. Often, on retreat, we spend a great deal of the time sitting. Many retreatants in this situation use a movement meditation in counterpoint. Hatha yoga is an ideal for this purpose. It maintains a high degree of concentration while allowing the body to stretch and readjust.

Some teachers are opposed to mixing disciplines. Nevertheless, if we have a practice that we do daily as part of a regular routine, particularly a physical practice, we must give serious consideration before eliminating that practice as part of a retreat. Changing the rhythms of a steady practice may be harmful. It is important to take up questions like this with the retreat guides.

MOVEMENT

The stereotyped image of a person in meditation is someone sitting quietly, motionless. Yet there are a large number of meditation practices that involve movement. In many retreats, movement-oriented meditation makes up at least half the schedule, in some retreats it is the dominant form.

The goal of most spiritual practice is to integrate it into our ordinary lives. This state is sometimes called "*samādhi* with open eyes." In the West particularly, we do not idealize living in a forest or cave for the rest of our lives. Rather, our aim is to build a light within, to recondition ourselves so that we can adapt better to the daily situations of our lives and perhaps help others in the process.

Sitting quietly is excellent for building this inner light. Quite often, however, people who sit come to distinguish the experience of sitting from the rest of their lives. There is a tendency to separate the inner work accomplished in a sitting meditation from the experience of normal engagement, which is filled with distraction, confusion, and often chaos. One reason is that activity in the world always involves motion of some kind, while sitting is relatively still. It therefore becomes advantageous to develop a skill in moving meditation to enhance bringing the meditative mind to everyday life.

Yoga, as described in the preceding chapter, has aspects of motion. There is the dynamic aspect of entering into and releasing out of a pose. Part of the concentration is directed to smoothness of motion and conscious control of all parts of the body. When we begin to focus our attention to movement in this way, there is no difference between entering an *āsana,* taking our place on a yoga mat, or even sitting down to a meal. The consciousness of smooth, steady motion is a powerful concentration that we can bring to what are normally mundane activities.

Movement meditation can be subtle, as in extremely slow walking, noticing every minuscule body action in the process; it can be ritualistic, as in t'ai chi chuan or a Japanese tea ceremony; it can be free form, as in some sacred dances; and it can be extremely energetic, as in many martial arts. The meditative aspect of an activity is centered in the intention and consciousness of the individual. As Ram Dass points out: "When the way of the martial arts is pursued to its highest point, the practitioner loses all trace of his ego in the perfection of his movements. To reach this point requires as intense a self-discipline as any sitting meditation. . . . For a master of hatha yoga, t'ai chi, or Sufi dancing, movement is stillness."[59]

One of the most straightforward movement meditations is simple walking. There are a wide variety of walking meditations. Already mentioned in the chapter on visualization were special walks innovated by Sufi Sam where the meditator envisions himself or herself to be the embodiment of unique energy at the time of the walk. This was included among visualization work because of its focus, but it is also a movement meditation.

There are many traditional walking meditations. In

MOVEMENT

Zen, the walking form of *zazen* is called *kinhin*. Philip Kapleau describes it from his teacher's introductory lectures:

> Kinhin *is performed by placing the right fist, with thumb inside, on the chest and covering it with the left palm while holding both elbows at right angles. Keep the arms in a straight line and the body erect, with the eyes resting upon a point about two yards in front of the feet. At the same time continue to count inhalations and exhalations as you walk slowly around the room. Begin walking with the left foot and walk in such a way that the foot sinks into the floor, first the heel and then the toes. Walk calmly and steadily, with poise and dignity. The walking must not be done absent-mindedly, and the mind must be taut as you concentrate on the counting. It is advisable to practice walking this way for at least five minutes after each sitting period of twenty to thirty minutes.*[60]

The description goes on to show that there are differences even among various Zen groups:

> *You are to think of walking as* zazen *in motion. Rinzai and Soto [the two main schools of Zen practice] differ considerably in their way of doing* kinhin. *In Rinzai the walking is brisk and energetic, while in traditional Soto it is slow and leisurely; in fact, upon each breath you step forward only six inches or so. . . . Further, the Rinzai sect cups the left hand on top of the right, whereas in the orthodox Soto the right hand is placed on top. . . . Now, even though this walking relieves the stiffness in your legs, such relief is to be regarded as a mere by-product and not the main object of* kinhin.[61]

Compare this description with a *Vipassanā* style described by Joseph Goldstein:

> *The walking meditation is done by noticing the lifting, forward, and placing movement of the foot in each step. It is helpful to finish one step completely before lifting the other foot. "Lifting, moving,*

SPIRITUAL PRACTICE

*placing, lifting, moving, placing." It is very simple. Again it is not
an exercise in movement. It is an exercise in mindfulness. In the
course of the day, you can expect many changes. Sometimes you
may feel like walking more quickly, sometimes very slowly. You
can take the steps as a single unit, "stepping, stepping." Or
you may start out walking quickly and, in that same walking
meditation, slow down until you are dividing it again into the three
parts. Experiment. The essential thing is to be mindful, to be aware
of what's happening.*[62]

We see that Goldstein is less concerned with form and
much more with attentiveness. His description continues:

*In walking, the hands should remain stationary either behind the
back, at the sides, or in front. It's better to look a little ahead, and
not at your feet, in order to avoid being involved in the concept of
"foot" arising from the visual contact. All of the attention should be
on experiencing the movement, feeling the sensations of the lifting,
forward, and placing motions.*

In many *Vipassanā* retreats, the schedule is alternated
evenly between sitting and walking. We may sit for
forty-five minutes and then walk for forty-five minutes.
Approximately six hours are spent each day sitting and
another six hours in walking meditation. The schedule
remains the same every day for between a week and three
months. New meditators often have more trouble quieting their minds while walking than while sitting. This is
natural as we are more inclined to be reflective or
contemplative while sitting, whereas when we are walking we are usually going somewhere. The walking
meditation in *Vipassanā* is specifically designed to give the
meditator a clear message that she or he is going nowhere.
We walk back and forth, between two walls, over the
same rug or floor boards. After considerable practice, the
walking meditation will equal the experience of sitting

quietly, and for many it will become the preferred practice.

Disciplined movement, such as t'ai chi chuan and Japanese tea ceremony, have strong meditative components. T'ai chi chuan is a practice that has quite a few styles, some of which look like graceful dances, others the appearance of a defensive martial art. All styles use a characteristic set of movements, each representing an aspect of nature, requiring excellent balance and a constant awareness of the elements of yin and yang: contraction and expansion, inward and outward, pulling and pushing. Japanese tea ceremony is much more subtle but also works with the elements of yin and yang. Its movements follow a ritual form, which is less obvious than that of t'ai chi chuan to the untrained eye. A bowl of powdered green tea is whisked into a foam and served, and every movement of the server from the entry into the tea room until departure is carefully choreographed to bring harmony and tranquillity into the moment.

In all forms of meditation that require movement, the practitioner rapidly discovers that a confused or busy mind invariably leads to awkwardness. Continued effort in the practice, working to get the movements smooth, learning to coordinate the breathing, leads to a calming effect on the mind. This in turn improves the practice and, as with all spiritual discipline, leads to higher levels of consciousness.

A superb explanation of this process comes from a t'ai chi chuan master, Jou, Tsung Hwa:

> To seek the empty in the solid is to find Hsu, or "the void." To seek nonaction in action is to find Jing, or "stillness." The pursuit of Hsu-Jing is the highest level and final goal of t'ai chi chuan. The movement in t'ai chi chuan emphasizes using one's awareness rather than one's strength. . . . . T'ai chi chuan's principle of using stillness

*in motion in order to master action by nonaction implies that each
outward form should project an inward perception of stillness. . . .
One's aim is to become more peaceful inside in order to affect the
outside. Gradually outer movements will reflect inner direction and
total awareness. As a result, one's spirit will blossom and become
peaceful.*[63]

There is a similar mystical quality in the practice of
Japanese tea ceremony. This is described by Soshitsu Sen,
Grand Master of the Urasenke school of tea:

*The principles of tea Rikyu [the most revered Japanese tea
master, sixteenth century] set forth are harmony, respect, purity,
and tranquillity. Harmony is the oneness of host and guest with the
flowing rhythms of nature. . . . Respect is the sincerity of heart that
allows one to have an open relationship with the other participants,
humbly recognizing their dignity. . . . Purity is removing the dust
of the world from one's heart and mind. . . . Tranquillity comes
with the constant practice of harmony, respect, and purity in
everyday life. In this state of mind, having found peace within
oneself, a bowl of tea can truly be shared with another.*[64]

Another aspect of movement is its relationship to the
universe, the cosmic dance. In Hinduism, Shiva sometimes appears as the king of dancers, representing the
entire spectrum of life's rhythms and cycles, birth and
death, creation and destruction. Throughout history,
"sacred dances" have been used, reflecting universal
ideals, invoking magic, petitioning for power. They
would often lead to rapture, ecstasy, and sublime joy.

The Baal Shem Tov was an advocate of the spiritual
function of dance. He encouraged it to help the dancer
attain *hitlahavut* (enthusiasm) and *devekut* (union with
God). He taught that "the dances of a Jew before his
creator are prayers." His great grandson, Rebbe Nachman of Breslov, believed that to dance in prayer was a

sacred command.[65] Today, at special events, holidays, weddings, and other festivities, we can often find Hasidim, who normally are extremely sedate, dancing in sweet ecstasy, raising sparks of holiness.

In Sufism, a distinct attraction to dance is found among some groups, particularly the whirling dervishes of Mevlevi. It is said that, "All of Rumi's poetry abounds with symbols taken from music and mystical dance; for him, the dance was a life-giving movement, part of the heavenly dance in which the stars and the angels take part."[66]

Concern exists that dancing may induce an ecstatic state that will daze the retreatant and the true fruits of a meditative practice will be lost. There are times when the experience of sublime joy may actually derail a meditator from the true path of liberation. We are often drawn to a pleasant experience as an end in itself. This is one of the traps along the spiritual path and must be treated with considerable caution.

Even though methods may be disputed, the principles remain that movement used as a spiritual practice is a different form of stillness; it requires strong attentiveness and results in increased inner balance. Meditation in motion enhances our general perspective and awareness. When doing any action, our mindfulness is improved through the practice of movement meditation.

It is often recommended that a movement practice be included in a retreat schedule. We must determine for ourselves as time goes along what ratio of moving to sitting works best. We may find that the ratio will change from one retreat to another. At times extended sitting will be the most beneficial and other times movement will work best.

Walking exercise can be learned fairly quickly. Not

much instruction is needed, although it is helpful to consult with a teacher when problems arise. More disciplined movement meditation, such as t'ai chi chuan should be learned from a teacher and not out of a book, for there are always nuances in movement that cannot be transmitted except through a teacher.

Once we gain a degree of mastery in movement meditation, it begins to flow into daily life. This is the time when the work done in meditation and retreat begins to pay off. The more we can integrate everyday activity with the mind state that is attained on retreat, the more balanced and harmonic will be our moment-to-moment existence. The idea that "Now it is time to meditate" or "Now it is time to take a retreat" is an idea that perpetuates a sense of duality between the physical and the spiritual, the mundane and the sacred. True enlightenment is the process of integrating these concepts so that we approach the spiritual aspect of all things and every thought and action has its sacred nature.

MANTRA

The power of the Word has intrigued mystics from the beginning of recorded history. Sound has always been considered awesome, for it is the vehicle through which all creation takes place. Whereas light may be related to the primordial essence, the creation does not manifest except through sound. In kabbalistic terms, sound is the garment, the vessel without which light remains formless.

The early Jewish sages noted that "with ten utterances the world was created."[67] This idea came from the number of times we see in the Creation story of Genesis; "And God said . . . ." This occurs nines times before the end of the sixth day of creation. The tenth is related to the highest mystery, which cannot be uttered, the crown of the Tree of Life. Many sages say it is implied in the opening words of Genesis: "In the beginning, God created. . . ."

Each of the ten utterances is related to the Tree of Life, each an indispensable component in creation. From the Jewish mystical perspective, everything in the universe is related to ten primordial building blocks, which are called *sefirot*. Each of the *sefirot* has its own sound; each is equated with a specific vowel in the Hebrew language. These vowel sounds have similarities to the vowel sounds in most languages. For example, it is fascinating to note that the English language has precisely ten vowel sounds, a long and a short intonation for each of the five vowels. In other words, each time we pronounce a vowel, we are resonating with one of the building blocks of creation. This is the basis for the significance of using mantra as a spiritual practice. There are thousands of classical mantras.

The use of a mantra is often thought to be the practice of repeating a word or series of words, which thereby benefits concentration and builds a kind of trance state. This can in fact result from the use of a mantra, but it misses the most salient feature of a mantra, which is the vibrational quality of its sound.

It is true that all sound has power. The question we must address is how we choose to work with this power. The sounding of vulgar words can raise negative thoughts. The sound of a challenge can raise fear. The sound of an insult can invoke enough anger to lead to physical violence. The sound of a lie can influence someone for life. The sound of slander can destroy a relationship forever. A mantra formed of threats, insults, lies, or slander is not likely to do much for our soul.

Most words have neutral attributes. This is not to say that they are lacking in a divine quality. Perhaps a highly developed person could repeat the words "donkey, donkey, donkey . . ." over and over and gain some extraordinary benefit from this mantra. Most of us, however, would not gain much from the constant repetition of such words.

Even words and phrases that have a spiritual content can be misused in a mantra if our intention is not clear. Simply taking one of the holy names of God and repeating it will not assure us of anything. This does not mean that we need to be in a state of euphoria when saying a mantra. Rather it is a question of intention. We may even be bored while repeating a mantra, but if it has a sacred quality, we may still accomplish a great deal as long as there is true sincerity in our effort.

A beginning meditator or retreatant can use a mantra to great advantage. In the early stages of developing concentration, it is difficult to work on abstract levels. Making sound is a powerful means of gaining focus. It is easy to do and has an almost immediate effect.

There is a tendency for meditators in the West to be attracted to esoteric mantras in unfamiliar languages. This is perfectly fine, for the mantra has its own power. As we learn more about the meanings of the words, new levels of effectiveness are attained. The more we can bring to a mantra, the more we receive from it.

Perhaps the most famous mantra, the one most used for thousands of years, is the word "*OM.*" The mantra appears in the *Mandūkya Upanishad,* one of the oldest teachings of India. The syllable *OM* is related to the supreme One, without a second, known as the Self. (This is not the self with which we identify and wish to dissolve, it is the Self—capital S—that represents the Godhead.)

The *Mandūkya Upanishad* teaches: "This Self, beyond all words, is the syllable *OM.* This syllable, though indivisible, consists of three letters: A-U-M." The language of the teaching becomes difficult to decipher at this point but Joseph Campbell helps us understand the meaning of AUM: "The element A denotes Waking Consciousness and its world (what has become); the element U, Dream Consciousness and its world (what is becoming); the element M, Deep Dreamless Sleep, the unconscious state (what will become); while the fourth

element—the silence before, after, and around AUM—
denotes that absolute, unqualified, unconditioned state-
that-is-no-state of 'consciousness in itself.' "[68]

Another way to understand the three parts of AUM is
that of "the Absolute, the Relative, and the relation
between them. . . . *OM* is the ultimate word that can be
uttered, after which there remains nothing but silence
. . . the sound of all sounds."[69] Clearly, the individual
who is trained in this deeper appreciation of *OM* is going
to work with the mantra in a different way from someone
who sits as a beginner.

The same holds for "*Om mani padme hum*," another
famous Sanskrit mantra that centers on *OM*. "*Mani*
means jewel, therefore a precious thing, the Doctrine.
Padme means 'in the lotus,'. . . the world which enshrines
the doctrine . . . or . . . the spirit in whose depths he who
knows how to take soundings [mantras] will discover
Knowledge, Reality, and Liberation, these three being
one. . . . *Hum* is an ejaculation denoting defiance."[70]
Thus the literal translation is "*OM*, the jewel in the lotus,
hum." This is a more assertive way of saying *OM*, in a
major mantra of Tibetan Buddhists.

In Sufism many mantras use the name of God. The
most common *dhikr* is the mantra, "There is no God but
God," which in Arabic sounds: "*Lā il'lā ha illā Allah-
Hu*." Notice the predominance of the sound of "AH,"
which is also the first sound of the AUM. When we
reflect upon associations with the divine in many languages, the number of times the sound AH appears seems
beyond a chance occurrence. Consider: Rām (r-AH-m),
Krishna (krish-n-AH), Shiva (shiv-AH), Buddha (Bood-
AH), Ātman (AH-t-m-AH-n), and as we saw above,
Allah (AH-l-AH). Many names of the divine do not have

this sound, or anything close to it, but there seem to be an unusual number that do.

It is also notable that the patriarchs and matriarchs of Western tradition in their original Hebrew pronunciation all have this sound: Avraham (AH-vrAH-hAHm), Yitzhak (yitz-hAHk), Yakov (yAH-kov), Sarah (sar-AH), Rivka (riv-kAH), Leah (lay-AH), and Rachel (rAH-chel). Indeed we find in the Torah that Avraham was originally named Avram, and Sarah was originally named Sarai.[71] Each had their name changed by God at the turning point of their lives. The addition of the extra AH sound for each touches upon the mystery of how sound manifests and this is the key in mantras.

Mystics would not find it surprising that this sound is more associated with the divine than others. In Kabbalah it is correlated with the topmost *sefirah*. In Hindu mysticism it is the first vowel of the source of all sound. In the Sufi Order of the West, the sound is associated with the heart chakra.[72] This Sufi group places great emphasis on different mantra sounds as they resonate in various chakras and cause alchemical transformations. The A of AUM, for example, begins in the heart, the U carries it upward through the throat, and the M goes out the crown chakra.

We need to be meticulous in the way we pronounce a mantra, or for that matter any prayer or scripture. The content of a prayer and the intention behind it are only part of the necessary components; the actual sounding of the words with their proper enunciation is also a major ingredient.

This is an approach that confounds rationality, yet its quintessential meaning is at the core of every mantra. The content of the mantra, as was pointed out, is of critical importance. It must have a sacred substance. But the power of the mantra is in the actual saying of it, sounding it out, sending that vibration through the body and into the universe. The meaning of the mantra and its primordial essential sound become one, as described in the famous opening line of St. John's Gospel: "In the beginning was the Word, and the Word was with God, and the Word was God."[73]

In Kabbalah, pronouncing a word correctly makes the difference between gaining access to power and a futile exercise. We can invoke the support of angels not just by knowing their correct names but by saying them precisely. This power is so awesome, there are some names of God that were never spoken except by the High Priest, who in days of old underwent special purification to prepare for this task. If he attempted the name of God while stained by the slightest impurity, he would die immediately upon uttering it. In the Talmud it says that certain names of God could be transmitted only once every seven years, so as to keep them secret and properly respected.[74]

It is important to note the difference between mantra and prayer. In prayer, our intention and sincerity are the cardinal attributes; it does not necessarily matter how clearly the prayers are enunciated or what language is used. Often it is better to use our own language than follow a formula. Although a mantra also requires good intentions and sincerity, the emphasis is placed on the words themselves. A prayer does not have to be repetitious; a mantra, by definition, always repeats. A prayer usually has elements of praise, thankfulness, or supplication; a mantra is often recited purely as a devotional activity.

Although we are making a distinction here between

prayer and mantra to allow for a general understanding, many mystics combine the two. They would assert that a prayer is not only dependent upon intention and sincerity, but that the words do in fact need to be enunciated properly, that sound is an influential part of prayer. Some people believe that a prayer should not be said in the vernacular but rather in the traditional tongue: Hebrew for Jews, Latin for Catholics, Sanskrit for Hindus, and so forth. Although most people prefer the vernacular because it means something to them, there is something to be said for the intrinsic power built into the pattern and melody of established prayers said in the traditional manner, and there is a great deal to consider regarding the power of the spoken word. Thus, despite the differentiation that is suggested here, it is worthwhile to maintain awareness of the power of sound when offering a prayer, to vocalize the words clearly. Nevertheless, this should not keep us from praying in our own language, spontaneously, or silently.

Some mantras are also prayers. The well-known Christian mantra called the Jesus Prayer is an example. There are variations on this mantra/prayer, but essentially it says: "Jesus Christ, have mercy on me, a sinner." Some shorten it to "Christ have mercy" or "Lord have mercy" (*Kyrie eleison*). When used as a mantra, this is repeated continuously throughout the day, until it becomes part of the breath and runs on its own momentum.

Another widespread mantra/prayer is saying the rosary. The "Hail Mary" is repeated fifty times in the standard rosary; this is done thousands of times in a person's life. Because of its popularity, the rosary comes quickly to the lips of many practitioners with only the slightest hint of association.

The potential of a mantra's effectiveness lies in this kind

of internalization. The constant repetition is a method of setting up a wave in the universe, concentrated upon the person who is the epicenter. The immediate effects may be substantial, but the long-range effects, if the mantra can be extended, will result in a complete transformation. The objective in many mantra practices is to repeat a mantra until the vibration sinks into the heart and becomes an integral part of the meditator's energy flow.

Since the nature of mantra is repetition, we often find ourselves bored when doing the practice. As with all spiritual endeavor, we must constantly gently coax ourselves back into concentration. Indeed, experienced meditators do not measure success by the length of time they can maintain a mantra but rather by the willingness they have to return to it, with minimum self-judgment, each time the mind wanders. With this kind of consistency, sooner or later the mantra blends into our lives.

When the mantra becomes internalized, it is no longer necessary to vocalize it. At first this would seem a contradiction to what we have said about physical vibratory levels and the need to enunciate clearly. However, the entire body can make a more profound vibration than the vocal cords once the sound has been properly set in motion. It is much like the phenomenon of sympathetic harmonics in music. If we play a constant note in a room with a stringed instrument tuned to that note, the instrument will begin to vibrate by itself in the note's frequency. So too the harmonics of the body. Once the wave has been clearly and strongly established, to the extent that the mantra becomes internalized, then it will continue even more powerfully without the vocalization.

It was noted earlier that there is a tendency for Western meditators to be attracted to mantras from the East. It is sometimes advantageous to utilize mantras in our own language or in our own root tradition to achieve the higher levels of internalization. We have greater capacity to integrate something that we are familiar with on an intuitive level than something that has to be first learned intellectually. We often have buried treasure in our own homes that we miss because we are constantly booking voyages to exotic lands.

A retreat is a good time to explore the power of mantras. If it is to be a mantra in a strange language, it is necessary to have someone teach it for rhythm and pronunciation. If in our own language, it can be started alone. The Scriptures, particularly the Psalms, are a rich source of mantras for Western meditators.

It is a good idea to set a schedule whereby the mantra is repeated either for a fixed period such as half an hour or a fixed number of times. The number of repetitions should be fairly large, within one's time constraints. Sometimes people use beads on a string to keep count, but counting on the fingers is just as good. Distinctive numbers are often used for mantras, usually centering around one hundred, two hundred, three hundred, five hundred, one thousand, and fifteen hundred. Some mantras are done ten thousand times a day. This requires skill, and we should not take on too much in the beginning.

Once we begin to appreciate the power of the mantra and the potency of sound, we begin to take more care with our verbal expression in the everyday world. This can have a purifying effect that will benefit us in future practice. Thus the mantra can help our daily lives in a number of ways: It builds concentration along with a sense of being connected with the divine forces, and it helps us to be more watchful and skillful in our use of speech.

CONTINUITY

This final chapter discusses how all our practices on retreat can be brought into the world. We will not only improve our quality of life and lighten our load of anxiety with this practice, we can also attain increasingly expanded awareness. It is the practice of practices, called continuity.

Each of us has a switching mechanism in our mind that allows us to move from one state of mind to another in an instant. We may be deeply engaged in a book, but a telephone call will cause us to connect with the world immediately. We may be having a nice conversation with friends, but we will lose our temper promptly when a child spills something. We may be completely absorbed in a chore, but a beep from the clock will swiftly dissolve our concentration.

Not only do we have the ability to change focus at lightning speed, we also forget rapidly what seemed to be our entire world during the time it engaged us. Within minutes we can enter a completely new inner universe and leave the other behind like a spaceship passing through a time warp. The solar system that was previously our entire frame of reference now exists only as a distant reflection.

The Buddhist perspective is that this impermanence is

the nature of all creation. Things are never the same from one instant to the next. In fact, the surprising thing is not that we have the ability to switch our mind state, but that we have the ability to maintain a mind state, to continue a thought for more than an instant. Thoughts are constantly falling away, yet somehow we are able to maintain coherent ideas. Moreover, we have the facility to remember, which is a miraculous phenomenon if each and every moment the world is completely new. What is it that is remembering and what is there to remember?

The image that the Buddhists use to work with this paradox is the idea of a flame being passed from candle to candle. We cannot say the flame is the same from one candle to the next, yet each is dependent upon the one just before it. Not only does this account for the potential transmission of thought but also for memory, because each flame has a quality of the original flame as far back as one wishes to travel. Extinguish one candle in the line and the rest must now depend upon a new source.

The metaphor of the passing flame applies to our daily lives. Normally the flame of one thought is being snuffed out and another takes over. It too is extinguished, and the process continues, with constant switching in thought patterns. Any stimulus can act to snuff out a flame and begin a new one. As stimuli are constantly impinging upon us, from our environment and our own bodies, this process happens tens of thousands of times each day on the conscious level and billions of times in the unconscious realms.

We find that two opposing principles are at work. There is the universal principle of impermanence, that things are constantly changing. This in many ways is related to the theory of entropy, that the universe is continuously losing energy and running down. The opposing principle is of coherence, that energy continues to pass along, like dominoes falling, until something interrupts the flow. There is always a flow of some kind, even though its course may be completely erratic. This is related to the theory of the conservation of energy. No matter how many changes take place, the amount of energy in the universe remains the same.

The universe functions with opposing forces. The force of gravity, pulling objects together, is balanced by the law that objects in motion tend to go in a straight line. One balances the other, and this causes orbits. Theoretical physics says that gravity will ultimately overpower the orbit, but then other factors engage and everything will begin again. This view, of course, is dependent upon which theory is current at the time. Yet all agree that the dynamic tension of opposing forces is a fundamental principle of the universe.

This is an important basis for spiritual work. Many of the ideas of mysticism, when taken out of context, seem to imply a sense of futility. If there is no "I," no "me," no "self," then "Why do I need to try so hard to understand; why should I try to grow, learn, improve myself, or help others? If it is all one huge illusion, a make-believe world that does not really exist, then why do I need to work toward peace, care about suffering, worry about the environment? If things are constantly changing and nothing is ever certain, what is the use of trying to end disease, starvation, or acts of brutality?"

These ideas of non-self, illusion, and impermanence are universal, yet each must be viewed in holistic terms as one element in dynamic tension with an opposing force. The idea of non-self meets its opponent in the concept of soul, which is known by different names in various traditions. Even in Buddhism, which does not acknowledge the existence of a soul per se, there is the concept of the Unborn, the Unconditioned, or the universal Buddha nature, all of which when carefully analyzed have strikingly similar attributes to descriptions of the soul.

The idea of illusion or *māyā* meets its opposition in the principle of karma, the vibratory energy that radiates from every act. It is the tension of this paradox that provides the basis for all our acts of loving kindness, our compassion, and our efforts to repair the world. The mystic does not stop with the statement that the world is an illusion but suggests that behind it are infinite levels of illusion that repeat to a vanishing point. The suggestion is that every reality has its illusory aspects, and every illusion has a deeper reality. This does not give us much to grasp. It is a *koan* for deeper meditation, and it provides a continuous tension for the reality/illusion paradigm.

This also applies to the tension developed between impermanence and coherence. Constant change takes place in every aspect of creation, yet paths of continuity provide the adhesive for things to stick together. Without continuity, we would not be able to think, there would be no causal relationships, nothing would work. This idea of continuity leads to one of the most profound spiritual practices we can undertake.

It is a practice simple to describe and exceedingly difficult to follow. Continuity is the practice of maintaining meditative consciousness throughout every period of a retreat. That's all there is to it. From the moment we awaken to the moment of falling asleep, we engage in some form of meditative practice. When this is working properly, there is even a level of awareness in our dreams; the practice continues awake or asleep.

Before dreams were mentioned, the practice sounded

manageable as long as we applied continuous effort. The idea of practicing while dreaming, however, adds a new dimension. It means that effort is only part of the equation. Somehow, the consciousness of practice must permeate our being so thoroughly that it becomes an instinctive aspect of moment-to-moment awareness.

When we are successful in this process, we join forces with the principle of coherence. This not only brings a steadiness to the overall practice but dramatically affects the quality of our life. Most of the time, we are tossed on the stormy seas of change—now here, now there, moody, up and down, all over the place. Problems occur when we try to hold on to some states of mind or resist others, not recognizing the nature of change. This attempt to hold on or resist can generate a new level of pain.

The steadiness of continuity does not affect the universal nature of change. There is still a stormy sea out there. Rather, it gives us a new perspective of this change. We neither hold on nor resist; we weather everything because we know for certain it will change very soon, no matter what. This is like pouring oil on the water; there are still waves but they do not seem as violent. This is the power of continuity. In the maintenance of a constant practice we gain enormous insight into the nature of change and its counterpart, coherence.

Some practices lend themselves more to continuity than others. Focus on the breath, mindfulness, devotion, prayer, awareness of movement, and mantras are practices conducive to the structure of continuity. Any meditative practice that can fill the space of the "between times" is useful in this work. What are we doing from the moment we stop a sitting meditation and begin a walking meditation? What are we doing between the bed and the bathroom, between the bathroom and the kitchen, between the kitchen and the sitting cushion? What are we thinking about when we brush our teeth, put on our clothes, look out the window, switch on a light, or prepare some food?

What we do most of the time in these and other innocuous activities is what is known in the vernacular as "spacing out." This is a good description of our mind state. We are absent from the act at hand, we have learned how to deal with things in a rote manner. We are very accomplished at pretending to be here doing something or listening to somebody when actually we are somewhere beyond the stars, creating and discovering new worlds. We have convinced ourselves that this is not only normal but a useful escape from the mundane activities of life.

This is sometimes true. It can be useful to hide out in a private world in order to ease some of the burden of daily life. The problem arises when we are patterned this way and know no other. Then when our private world turns ugly, we are caught in it with no apparent escape. In addition, when we are in that other world, we are not "here," and we miss the exquisite experience of how things are actually happening in the moment. We miss the beauty, the simultaneity, and the presence of the divine force.

The hallmark of the enlightenment process is in being "here" and not "there." Indeed, the focal point of continuity is in being here at all times. The famous message of Ram Dass to "Be here now" is what results when one is adept in this practice. It is laborious in that it requires great perseverance—we are up against lifelong patterns—but it is a major enlightenment practice because it can break through our basic conditioning.

The secret of success in continuity practice is to eliminate any sense of failure. From the moment we begin, we are successful. The only measure of success is this moment, right now. Are we here? If we are here, our practice is perfect.

The fact that we have just returned from out yonder, or that we might take off again in a few seconds, is not relevant. Without this practice, we would always be spaced out. We would rarely experience being here. Thus, each moment we are able to break the pattern, we have succeeded.

There is another level to this understanding. Each time we break a pattern, it becomes easier to break it next time. Each moment we are successful in continuity practice is like a small deposit in the "enlightenment account." With continuous effort, the account slowly grows. Somewhere along the way it begins to collect interest. The payoff, in the end, can be tremendous.

Attempting continuity practice in everyday life also has rich rewards. Most of the time, however, we do not have a strong enough spiritual center to maintain the practice without being smothered by the old patterns of coping, interacting, and relating. After a while, we simply forget and fall asleep.

On retreat it is a different story, which is one of the great advantages of retreat. It is inherently supportive to the kind of effort required to build a strong practice. It is an ideal environment to work on continuity. Not only do we have the advantage of silence and solitude, but knowing that the retreat is for a fixed time gives us strength to overcome a great deal of resistance. We do not like to change old patterns and will do anything to avoid this restructuring. By telling ourselves that the practice is only for a short time, we can usually build tolerance to deal with the discomfort.

After we gather a large enough account, we begin to

gain the new insights the continuity practice elicits. If it is a long retreat and we have many successful moments, the benefits will overflow into everyday life. After many retreats the continuity practice becomes accessible to us on a regular basis. With it we are able to acquire powers of observation and a quality of life that gives us an entirely new perspective.

On retreat the continuity practice works as a center of gravity throughout the day, keeping us focused while switching from one form of meditation to another. When it is time to get up from our sitting position, the tendency is to stand without knowing how it happened. Continuity requires that we observe ourselves in motion, keeping it smooth, maintaining consciousness as the muscles contract and expand, the bones change position, and we find our balance. Sometimes it is helpful to look around as we walk, to touch and feel things along the way. This helps keep us in the moment.

When we go to the bathroom, we are always observing how the body moves and what is happening in our minds. As we begin to brush our teeth, we narrow our attention to catch each subtle thought, each rising inclination. We monitor our movements in reaching for the toothbrush and the toothpaste. Sometimes it is helpful to imagine a broken finger or only having one hand to appreciate the complexity of this seemingly simple act. When we brush, how conscious can we remain of the tactile sensation, the engagement of arm and hand, the taste, the feeling of the gums? Soon it becomes an amazing act. Thousands of impressions converge upon us. How is it that we usually miss all of this? It is because we have accepted our conditioning as what life is about, and thus pass most of our time in a world oblivious to the wonder of each moment.

A solid concentration meditation, such as mantra or breathing exercises, can be brought out of a retreat and integrated into daily life as a continuity practice. We fill in the gaps with a soft internal mantra or a conscious breath. Soon we find that there are many more gaps than we imagined, and our practice sharpens our awareness. It can also be useful for calming and harmonizing our lives.

Other continuity practices are actually more adaptable to everyday life than retreat. One of them, for example, is what is called "right speech" in Buddhism, or *shmirat lashon ha-ra* (guarding against gossip) in the Jewish tradition. With this practice, we are constantly aware of what is being said in normal communication. We carefully separate gossip from useful conversation.

It is astonishing how much of our communication is idle gossip. Even when we think what we are saying is harmless, dangerous seeds are often planted. The continuity practice is to avoid all gossip, either conveying it or listening to it. This sounds much easier than it really is. Many people discover that over fifty percent of their daily conversation is somehow related to gossip. Moreover, it is extremely difficult to stop others from gossiping without insulting them. Some sages believe that the ability to master this practice is sufficient in itself to raise a person to an exceptional level of awareness.

Many ethical and moral practices can be used for continuity in the same way as right speech. We can make commitments to act or relate in ways that will not only benefit others but also help us to repattern our thoughts, speech, or actions. It might be charity work that overflows into our daily lives, or watching our thoughts to nullify unfair judgments or criticisms as they arise, or even the simple act of picking up every loose piece of paper we see littering the streets. The effort involved to maintain this kind of commitment is a continuity practice that greatly benefits our spiritual progress.

Continuity practice may also involve restraint. It is not uncommon for retreatants to come to realize the degree to which their minds are affected by all external stimuli. This is particularly true of the evocative impressions that appear daily on television, radio, and in the print media. When we are sitting quietly, we often experience advertising themes playing through our minds. Sometimes we remember scenes from horror movies. Thus, sometimes a daily continuity practice is nothing more than choosing more carefully the external stimulation to which we wish to be exposed.

People who become immersed in the spiritual quest may decide to undertake more compelling continuity practices. At times, a meditator gets very serious about his or her practice and commits to the precepts of a traditional path. Some of these paths involve leaving the mundane world altogether and joining a monastery or nunnery. Some paths mean moving to an ashram or spiritual community, and some can be accomplished in a delicate balance of being in the world but not caught by it. Traditional paths have a tremendous amount to offer, but they are also extremely demanding.

We *can* become completely absorbed in continuity practice without taking on robes. When moment-to-moment awareness is brought to the Buddhist practice of mindfulness, an enormous power is accumulated that transforms us completely. In the West, continuity practice often involves maintaining God-consciousness every moment. It is such a prevalent idea, a large number of major teachers have spoken of it in one way or another. One Christian monk made this principle the singular practice of his entire life. Brother Lawrence of the Resurrection, who lived in Paris in the seventeenth century, wrote the following:

> Having found different methods of going to God and different practices to attain the spiritual life in several books, I decided that they would serve more to hinder than to facilitate me in what I was seeking—which was nothing other than a means to be wholly God's. This made me decide to give all to gain all; so after having given all to God in satisfaction for my sins, I began to live as if there were no one in the world but Him and me. . . . I adored Him as often as I could, keeping my mind in His holy presence and recalling it as often as it wandered. I had no little difficulty in this exercise, but I kept on despite all difficulties and was not worried or distressed when I was involuntarily distracted. I did this during the day as often as I did it during the formal time specifically set aside for prayer; for at all times, at every hour, at every moment, even in the busiest times of my work, I banished and put away from my mind everything capable of diverting me from the thought of God.[75]

Overall, continuity practice on retreat is the most difficult and the most rewarding. It builds will and concentration, it opens deep levels of insight, and it is the transition practice that helps us bring our meditation and retreat consciousness into every moment of our lives.

Mastery on the spiritual path is often defined by the extent to which someone is able to maintain continuity, the cornerstone of spiritual development. Once we are unable to distinguish between meditation, retreat, and the simple chores of daily existence, we know that we have attained a new level of excellence on this wondrous spiritual voyage called life.

EPILOGUE

THE VISION OF EZEKIEL

And it was in the thirtieth year, in the fourth month, on the fifth of the month. . . . I saw visions of God.

I saw, and behold a stormy wind . . . a great cloud and flashing fire, and a Glow round about, and from its midst a vision of the Speaking Silence, in the midst of the fire.

And from its midst was the form of four Chayot [Living Creatures]. . . . Each one had four faces and every one had four wings. Their feet were straight, and the soles of their feet were like those of a calf's foot, and they shined like a vision of polished copper. . . .

The form above the heads of the Chayot was that of a firmament, looking like a fearsome ice, spread out about their heads. . . .

Above the firmament that was over their heads, like a vision of a sapphire, was the form of a Throne, and over the form of the Throne, there was a form like a vision of a Man, on it from above.

And I saw a vision of the Speaking Silence like a vision of fire. . . . This was the vision of God's Glory. I saw it, and I fell on my face. Then I heard a voice speak.

It said to me, "Son of man, stand up on your feet, and I will speak to you." Then a spirit came in me, and it spoke to me. It stood me on my feet, and I heard that which spoke to me.[76]

Ezekiel 1:1–2:2

NOTES

NOTES FOR "THE TRADITION OF SPIRITUAL RETREAT"

1. *The Jerusalem Bible* (Jerusalem: Koren Publishers, 1984) Exodus 34:28–30.

2. Louis Ginzberg, *The Legends of the Jews,* vol. 3, (Philadelphia: Jewish Publication Society of America, 1982) pp. 114–117.

3. William James, *The Varieties of Religious Experience* (New York: Viking Penguin, 1982) p. 380. Originally published in 1902.

4. Quoted in Ben Zion Bokser, *The Jewish Mystical Tradition* (New York: Pilgrim Press, 1981) p. 2.

5. Quoted in Gershom Scholem, *Major Trends in Jewish Mysticism* (New York: Schocken Books, 1946) p. 4.

6. Philip Kapleau, *The Three Pillars of Zen* (New York: Anchor Books, 1980) p. 13.

7. Shunryu Suzuki, *Zen Mind, Beginner's Mind* (New York: Weatherhill, 1970) p. 75.

8. Yūhō Yokoi with Daizen Victoria, *Zen Master Dōgen* (New York: Weatherhill, 1976) p. 32.

9. Ibid.

10. Robert Kornman, *Vajrayana: The Path of Devotion* in *Buddhist America,* ed. Don Morreale (Sante Fe, New Mexico: John Muir Publications, 1988) pp. 198–202.

11. Luke 6:20.

12. Thomas Merton, trans., *The Wisdom of the Desert* (New York: New Directions, 1960) p. 52.

13. Matthew 18:2–4.

14. Matthew 3:16–17.

15. Mark 1:12–13.

16. See James, *Varieties of Religious Experience*, abridged from footnotes on pp. 410–11.

17. R. M. Bucke, *Cosmic Consciousness* (New York: E. P. Dutton, 1969) p. 187. First published 1901. Quote is from Jacob Boehme, *Works*, vol. 4, *The Way to Christ*, pp. 75–76.

18. Quoted in James, *Varieties of Religious Experience*, p. 418 (his italics).

19. J. K. Kadowaki, SJ, *Zen and the Bible*, trans. Joan Rieck (London and New York: Arkana, 1989) p. 128.

20. Bartoli-Mitchel, *Vie de Saint Ignace de Loyola*, quoted in James, *Varieties of Religious Experience*, p. 410.

21. Kadowaki, *Zen and the Bible*, p. 128.

22. E. Allison Peers, trans., *Spiritual Canticle*, (New York: Doubleday/Image, 1961) p. 15.

23. E. Allison Peers, trans., *The Autobiography of St. Teresa of Avila* (Garden City, New York: Doubleday, 1960) p. 91.

24. Ibid., p. 80.

25. Ibid., p. 91.

26. Teresa of Avila, *The Interior Castle*, trans. K. Kavanaugh and O. Rodriguez (New York: Paulist Press, 1979) pp. 185–86.

27. Martin Buber, comp., *Ecstatic Confessions*, ed. Paul Mendes-Flohr, trans. Esther Cameron (San Francisco: Harper & Row, 1985) p. 127.

28. Ibid., p. 88.

29. Clifton Wolters, trans., *The Cloud of Unknowing* (Harmondsworth, England: Penguin Books, 1961) p. 51.

30. Bucke, *Cosmic Consciousness*, p. 324.

31. Ibid.

32. Ibid.

33. Ibid., p. 325.

34. Ibid., pp. 325–26.

35. Ibid., p. 328.

36. Ibid., pp. 328–29.

37. Ibid., p. 329.

38. Ibid., p. 324.

NOTES

39. Merton, *Wisdom of the Desert,* p. 55.

40. John G. Bennett, *Long Pilgrimage* (Clearlake, California: Dawn Horse Press, 1983) p. 20.

41. Ibid., pp. 15–20.

42. Ibid., pp. 80–81.

43. Ibid.

44. David Godman, ed., *Be As You Are: The Teachings of Sri Ramana Maharshi* (London & New York: Arkana, 1985) pp. 1–3.

45. Ibid., p. 84.

46. Ibid.

47. Ibid., pp. 175–78.

48. Buber, *Ecstatic Confessions,* p. 16.

49. *Mahatma Gandhi,* (New Delhi: Government of India Press, 1969) Introduction.

50. *See* William L. Shirer, *Gandhi* (New York: Washington Square Press, 1979) p. 221.

51. Ram Dass, *Journey of Awakening* (New York: Bantam Books, 1985) pp. 131–32.

52. Paramahansa Yogananda, *Autobiography of a Yogi* (Los Angeles: Self-Realization Fellowship, 1975) p. 503.

53. Shirer, *Gandhi,* p. 169.

54. Ibid., p. 164.

55. *The Koran,* trans. N. J. Dawood, ed. Betty Radice, (Harmondsworth, England: Penguin, 1979) Sura 7:138/143.

56. Ibid., p. 9.

57. Bucke, *Cosmic Consciousness,* pp. 126–27.

58. James, *Varieties of Religious Experience,* p. 403.

59. Ibid., p. 404.

60. Annemarie Schimmel, *Mystical Dimensions of Islam* (Chapel Hill: University of North Carolina Press, 1978) p. 91.

61. Ibid., p. 95.

62. James, *Varieties of Religious Experience,* p. 404.

63. Buber, *Ecstatic Confessions,* p. 30.

64. Ibid., p. 17.

65. Scholem, *Major Trends in Jewish Mysticism,* pp. 15–16.

66. R. J. Zvi Werblowsky, *Joseph Karo: Lawyer and Mystic*

(Philadelphia: Jewish Publication Society of America, 1977) p. 66. Author's italics.

67. Scholem, *Major Trends in Jewish Mysticism*, p. 136.

68. Ibid., p. 137.

69. Ibid., p. 150.

70. Ibid., p. 151.

71. Ibid.

72. Ibid.

73. Ibid., p. 152.

74. Ibid.

75. Bokser, *Jewish Mystical Tradition*, pp. 153–54.

76. Werblowsky, *Joseph Karo*, p. 69.

77. Ibid., pp. 69–70.

78. The first letter of *Elohi* is an aleph, of *Rav* a resh, and of *Yitzhak* a yod. The letters aleph-resh-yod spell Ari.

79. Bokser, *Jewish Mystical Tradition*, p. 142.

80. See *Jewish Encyclopedia* (Jerusalem: Keter Publishing House Jerusalem Ltd., 1972) Luria, Vol. 11 p. 573.

81. Ibid., Israel Ben Eliezer, Vol. 9 p. 1050.

82. Aryeh Kaplan, *Meditation and Kabbalah* (York Beach, Maine: Samuel Weiser, 1986) p. 274.

83. Abraham Joshua Heschel, *A Passion for Truth*, (New York: Farrar, Straus & Giroux, 1986) p. 56.

84. Ibid., p. 92.

85. Ibid., p. 143.

86. *Pirke Avot*, 2:5.

87. Ibid., 3:13.

88. Heschel, *A Passion for Truth*, p. 215.

89. *Abraham Isaac Kook*, trans. Ben Zion Bokser (New York: Paulist Press, 1978) p. 232.

90. Ibid., pp. 233–34.

91. Ibid., p. 234.

92. Ibid., pp. 210–202.

NOTES FOR "SETTING UP A RETREAT"

1. Quoted in Rabbi Nathan of Breslov, *Advice*, trans. Avraham Greenbaum (Jerusalem: Breslov Research Institute, 1983) p. 163.

2. Ibid., pp. 164–65.

3. *The Jerusalem Bible,* 1 Kings 19:4–13.

4. Godman, ed., *Be As You Are: The Teachings of Sri Ramana Maharshi,* p. 89.

5. Ibid., chapter on silence, p. 105ff.

6. John White, ed., *The Highest State of Consciousness* (New York: Anchor Books, 1972) p. 40.

7. Burton Watson, trans., *The Complete Works of Chuang Tzu* (New York: Columbia University Press, 1968) p. 69.

8. Exodus 20:8.

9. The Song of Songs 5:2.

10. Maimonides, *Guide of the Perplexed,* trans. M. Friedlander (New York: Hebrew Publishing, Part III, Chap. 51, p. 287.

11. Schimmel, *Mystical Dimensions of Islam,* p. 243.

12. Ibid.

13. Quoted in Peter Matthiessen, *Nine-Headed Dragon River,* (Boston: Shambhala, 1986) p. 60.

14. Genesis 6:9.

15. Quoted in R. J. Zvi Werblowsky, *Joseph Karo: Lawyer and Mystic,* p. 60.

16. Jack Kornfield, in *Buddhist America,* ed. Don Morreale (Sante Fe, New Mexico: John Muir Publications, 1988) p. xxiii.

17. P. D. Ouspensky, *In Search of the Miraculous,* (New York: Harcourt, Brace & World, 1949) p. 42.

18. Ibid., p. 161.

19. *Pirke Avot* 2:4.

20. Godman, *Be As You Are,* pp. 2–3.

21. Viktor E. Frankl, *Man's Search for Meaning* (New York: Simon & Schuster, 1963) pp. 56–57.

22. Ibid., pp. 62–63.

NOTES FOR "SPIRITUAL PRACTICE" AND "EPILOGUE"

1. Paul Reps, *Zen Flesh, Zen Bones,* (New York: Anchor Books, 1957) p. 34.

2. *The Jerusalem Bible,* Genesis 2:7.

3. Schimmel, *Mystical Dimensions of Islam*, p. 401.
4. Ven. Ajahn Chah, *A Taste of Freedom* (Thailand: Bung Wai Forest Monastery, 1982) pp. 5–6.
5. *Bhagavad Gita* 4:29, quoted in Paramahansa Yogananda, *Autobiography of a Yogi* (Los Angeles: Self-Realization Fellowship, 1975) p. 276.
6. Ibid., p. 362.
7. Taisen Deshimaru, *Questions to a Zen Master,* trans. Nancy Amphoux (New York: E. P. Dutton, 1985) p. 104.
8. Ibid., p. 105.
9. Kapleau, *The Three Pillars of Zen,* p. 14.
10. Aryeh Kaplan, *Meditation and the Bible* (York Beach, Maine: Samuel Weiser, 1981) p.37.
11. A. C. Bhaktivedanta, Swami Prabhupada, *Bhagavad Gita As It Is* (Worcester, England: Bhaktivedanta Book Trust, International Society for Krishna Consciousness, 1968) p. 264.
12. Ibid., pp. 265–66.
13. Ibid., p. xxvii.
14. Christmas Humphreys, *Buddhism* (New York and Harmondsworth: Penguin Books, 1978) p. 120. First published in 1951.
15. Ibid., p. 156.
16. Ibid.
17. Thomas Merton, trans., *The Wisdom of the Desert* (New York: New Directions, 1970) p. 20.
18. Schimmel, *Mystical Dimensions of Islam*, p. 172.
19. Ibid., p. 173.
20. Ibid., p. 174.
21. Rebbe Nachman, *Advice,* comp. Rabbi Nathan of Breslov, trans. Avraham Greenbaum, (Jerusalem: Breslov Research Institute, 1983), pp. 275–99. Selections from the chapter on prayer.
22. Teresa of Avila, *The Interior Castle,* trans. Kavanaugh and Rodriguez, p. 38.
23. Ibid., pp. 116–17.
24. Buber, comp., *Ecstatic Confessions,* ed. Mendes-Flohr, trans. Cameron, p. 79.

NOTES

25. Ibid., pp. 72–73.
26. Yogananda, *Autobiography of a Yogi*, p. 145.
27. William James, *Varieties of Religious Experience*, p. 464.
28. Ibid., pp. 467–70.
29. Roberto Assagioli, M.D., *Psychosynthesis* (New York: Penguin, 1987) p. 145.
30. Titus Burckhardt, *Alchemy* (England: Element Books, 1986) p. 142.
31. Scholem, *Major Trends in Jewish Mysticism*, pp. 153–55.
32. Ibid.
33. Ibid.
34. John Blofeld, *The Tantric Mysticism of Tibet*, (Boston: Shambhala, 1987) p. 89.
35. Ibid., pp. 89–90.
36. Ibid., p. 92.
37. Arnold Mindell, *Working On Yourself Alone* (London and New York: 1990) p. 65.
38. Wolters, trans., *The Cloud of Unknowing*, p. 20.
39. *Pirke Avot*, 3:22.
40. Merton, *The Wisdom of the Desert*, p. 42.
41. Fritz Meier, *Transformation of Man in Mystical Islam*, in *Man and Transformation*, ed. Joseph Campbell, Bollingen Series, (Princeton, New Jersey: Princeton University Press, 1980) p. 47.
42. Schimmel, *Mystical Dimensions of Islam*, p. 172.
43. Ibid., p. 6.
44. Wolters, trans., *Cloud of Unknowing*, p. 53.
45. Chah, *Taste of Freedom*, p. 10.
46. Edward Conze, *Buddhism: Its Essence and Development* (New York: Harper & Row, 1975) p. 107. *See also* Chah, *A Still Forest Pool*, Kornfield and Breiter, ed. and comp., p. 23.
47. Suruttama, *Theravada: Thus Have I Heard*, in *Buddhist America*, ed. Don Morreale, pp. 13–14.
48. Joseph Goldstein, *The Experience of Insight*, (Boston: Shambhala, 1983) p. 20.
49. Mircea Eliade, *Mystery and Spiritual Regeneration*, in *Man and Transformation*, Campbell, p. 12.

50. Schimmel, *Mystical Dimensions of Islam,* p. 341.

51. Ibid., p. 149.

52. Ibid., p. 255.

53. *Numbers Rabbah,* 19:8.

54. Yogananda, *Autobiography of a Yogi,* p. 513.

55. Nachman, *Advice,* p. 312.

56. Jean Herbert, in André Van Lysebeth, *Yoga Self-Taught,* trans. Carola Congreve (New York: Harper & Row, 1973) pp. 7–10, introduction.

57. *See* Frances Vaughan, *The Inward Arc* (Boston: Shambhala, 1986) pp. 168ff.

58. *See* S. R. Sharda, *Sufi Thought* (New Delhi: Munshiram Manoharlal Publishers, 1974), p. 72.

59. Ram Dass, *Journey of Awakening* (New York: Bantam Books, 1985) p. 80.

60. Kapleau, *Three Pillars of Zen,* pp. 36–37.

61. Ibid.

62. Golstein, *Experience of Insight,* pp. 4–5.

63. Jou, Tsung Hwa, *The Tao of Tai-Chi Chuan,* ed. Shoshana Shapiro (Warwick, New York: Tai Chi Foundation, 1980) p. 214.

64. Soshitsu Sen, *Chado* (New York/Tokyo: Weatherhill/Tankosha, 1979) pp. 3–4.

65. *See* Dance, *Encyclopedia Judaica* Vol. 5, p. 1267.

66. Schimmel, *Mystical Dimensions of Islam,* p. 318.

67. *Pirke Avot,* 5:1.

68. Joseph Campbell, *Creative Mythology: The Masks of God* (New York: Viking Press, 1968) p. 647.

69. Thomas Merton, *The Asian Journals of Thomas Merton,* ed. Naomi Burton, Brother Patrick Hart, and James Laughlin (New York: New Directions, 1975) p. 390.

70. Ibid.

71. *See* Genesis 17:5, 17:15.

72. Sufi Order, *Toward the One* (New York: Harper & Row, 1974) p. 232.

73. John 1:1.

74. *See Kiddushin* 71a.

75. Brother Lawrence of the Resurrection, *The Practice of*

the Presence of God, trans. John J. Delaney (New York: Image/Doubleday, 1977) p. 87.

76. Kaplan, *Meditation and The Bible,* pp. 44–45. The Hebrew word *Chashmal* is translated by Kaplan as "Speaking Silence," which he equates with the "still small voice." He notes that *chashmal* is made up of two words, *chash,* meaning "silence," and *mal,* indicating "speech." He says, "At this level, the prophet experiences the 'speaking silence.' This is the level of silence through which he can hear the word of God or see a true divine vision" (p. 41).

SAMPLE SCHEDULES

There are as many potential schedules as there are meditators. Following are the outlines of four schedules, each with its own personality. They give us a taste of the range, but by no means should they suggest limits. These outlines are primarily to guide the person who has never experienced a retreat schedule.

EXAMPLE OF A TIGHT SCHEDULE

Good for making progress on a short retreat but also works well for long retreats.

5:00 AM	Wake-up
5:30–6:15	Sitting meditation
6:15–7:00	Walking meditation
7:00	Breakfast in silence
7:45–8:30	Tidy up
8:30–9:15	Sitting meditation
9:15–10:00	Walking meditation
10:00–10:45	Sitting meditation
10:45–11:30	Walking meditation
11:30–12:15	Sitting meditation
12:15 PM	Lunch in silence

1:00–2:00	Rest—take notes
2:00–2:45	Sitting meditation
2:45–3:30	Walking meditation
3:30–4:15	Sitting meditation
4:15–5:00	Walking meditation
5:00	Light meal/snack
5:30–6:15	Sitting meditation
6:15–7:00	Walking meditation
7:00–8:00	Inspirational Reading
8:00–8:45	Sitting meditation
8:45–9:30	Walking meditation
9:30–10:15	Sitting meditation
10:15	Bedtime

Approximately 6½ hours for sleeping; Nine sits, at 45 minutes each, equals 6¾ hours daily; Seven walking meditations, equals 5¼ hours daily; Total 12 hours of meditation daily.

This is typical of *Vipassanā* schedule. There is little time to encourage mental wandering. At first this may seem severe, but it soon becomes a comfortable rhythm and many practitioners will follow this practice for weeks or months, adding meditation periods in the early morning or after the normal bedtime as the need for sleep diminishes.

EXAMPLE OF A LOOSE SCHEDULE

The type of schedule many beginners prefer, offering some discipline but not compelling too much constraint.

SAMPLE SCHEDULES

5:00–7:00 AM	Wake-up, cleanup, morning exercise, quiet time, some sitting meditation
7:00–9:00	Breakfast, cleanup, notes
9:00–12:00	Morning meditations
12:00–1:00 PM	Lunchtime
1:00–3:00	Rest, stroll, gaze, contemplate
3:00–6:00	Afternoon meditations
6:00–7:00	Suppertime
7:00–9:00	Read and make notes
9:00–10:00	Last meditation of the day

This schedule provides for seven to eight hours of meditation daily and represents a more relaxed approach. Compared to our active daily lives, this kind of retreat will provide much-needed silence and spiritual revitalization. After a while, however, a retreatant will usually want to design a more challenging and rigorous schedule. Yet there will also be instances when an experienced retreatant will back away from a compelling schedule for a day or two and use this kind of format to relax a little while still maintaining a modicum of discipline.

EXAMPLE OF A SCHEDULE EMPHASIZING PRAYER

4:15 AM	Wake-up
4:30–5:00	Ablutions
5:00–5:30	Quiet preparation for prayer

SAMPLE SCHEDULES

5:30–7:00	Morning prayers
7:00	Breakfast
7:30–8:30	Cleanup
8:30–11:00	Meditation or chores
11:00–11:30	Preparation for midday prayers
11:30–12:30	Midday prayers
12:30 PM	Lunch
1:00–2:00	Rest
2:00–5:00	Meditation or chores
5:00	Preparation for evening prayers
5:30–6:00	Evening prayers
6:00	Supper
7:00–9:00	Inspirational reading and notes
9:00	Last meditation, followed by bedtime prayers

ONE OF MY FAVORITE PERSONAL SCHEDULES

3:00 AM	Wake-up
3:30–4:30	Sitting meditation
4:30–5:00	Walking meditation
5:00–6:00	Sitting meditation
6:00–7:00	Morning prayers
7:00–7:30	Yoga
7:30	Very light breakfast
8:00–8:30	Cleanup
8:30–8:50	Twenty-minute nap
9:00–10:00	Sitting meditation
10:00–11:00	Walking meditation
11:00–12:00	Sitting meditation
12:00–12:30 PM	Yoga or moving meditation
12:30–1:00	Midday prayers
1:00	Lunch: main meal

SAMPLE SCHEDULES

2:00–3:00	Rest, stroll, take notes
3:00–4:00	Sitting meditation
4:00–5:00	Walking meditation
5:00–6:00	Sitting meditation
6:00–6:30	Yoga or moving meditation
6:30	Light evening snack
7:00–8:00	Sitting meditation
8:00–9:00	Inspirational reading
9:00–10:00	Sitting meditation
10:00	Bedtime

RECOMMENDED READING
FOR RETREATANTS

There are many guidebooks of instruction in various traditions and practices. A complete bibliography would fill a number of volumes. This is a brief list of books that are particularly inspiring or that contain helpful descriptions of retreat practices. Each tradition has produced many classics that may not be mentioned here. If a book appears on this list, the meditator may rest assured that it has been used successfully on retreats.

Aitken, Robert. *Taking the Path of Zen*. Berkeley: North Point Press, 1982.

Arberry, A. J. *Sufism*. New York: Harper & Row, 1950.

Arberry, A. J., trans. *Muslim Saints and Mystics*. Oxon, England: Routledge and Kegan Paul, 1966.*

Attar, Fariduddin. *The Conference of the Birds*. Berkeley: Shambhala, 1971.

Augustine, Saint. *Confessions*. New York: Viking Penguin, 1961.

Behari, Bankey. *Sufis, Mystics and Yogis of India*. Bombay: Bhavan's Book University, 1962.*

Bennett, John G. *Long Pilgrimage*. Clearlake, California: Dawn Horse Press, 1983.

Ben-Amos, D., and Mintz, J. R. *In Praise of the Baal Shem Tov*. New York: Schocken Books, 1970.

Boehme, Jacob. *Mysterium Magnum*. London: Watkins, 1924.*

Bokser, Ben Zion. *Abraham Isaac Kook*. New York: Paulist Press, 1978.

*Esoteric books from small publishing houses may be available through special mail order.

RECOMMENDED READING

————. *The Jewish Mystical Tradition.* New York: Pilgrim Press, 1981.

Brown, Raphael, trans. *The Little Flowers of St. Francis.* Garden City, New York: Doubleday, 1958.

Buber, Martin. *Tales of the Hasidim.* New York: Schocken Books, 1947. Two volumes.

————. *The Legend of the Baal Shem.* New York: Schocken Books, 1955.

————, comp. *Ecstatic Confessions.* Edited by Paul Mendes-Flohr. Translated by Esther Cameron. San Francisco: Harper & Row, 1985.

Chah, Ven. Ajahn. *A Taste of Freedom.* Thailand: Bung Wai Forest Monastery, 1980.*

————. *A Still Forest Pool.* Edited by Jack Kornfield and Paul Breiter. Wheaton, Illinois: Theosophical Publishing House, 1985.*

Chögyam Trungpa. *The Myth of Freedom.* Berkeley: Shambhala, 1976.

Deshimaru, Taisen. *Questions to a Zen Master.* Translated by Nancy Amphoux. New York: E.P. Dutton, 1985.

Dionysius the Areopagite. *The Divine Names.* Surrey, England: Shrine of Wisdom, 1957.*

Faris, Amin Nabih, trans. *The Mysteries of Purity.* Lahore: Muhammad Ashraf, 1966.*

Foster, R. J. *Celebration of Discipline: The Path to Spiritual Growth.* New York: Harper & Row, 1978.

Frankl, Viktor E. *Man's Search for Meaning.* New York: Simon & Schuster, 1963.

al-Ghazzālī, Abu Hamid. *The Alchemy of Happiness.* Claud Field, trans. Lahore: Muhammad Ashraf, 1964.*

Gibran, Kahlil. *The Prophet.* New York: Alfred A. Knopf, 1923.

Ginzberg, Louis. *The Legends of the Jews.* Philadelphia: Jewish Publication Society of America, 1982. Six volumes.

Godman, David, ed. *Be As You Are: The Teachings of Sri Ramana Maharshi.* London and New York: Arkana, 1985.

Goldstein, Joseph. *The Experience of Insight.* Boston: Shambhala, 1983.

Goleman, Daniel. *Varieties of the Meditative Experience.* New York: E. P. Dutton, 1977.

RECOMMENDED READING

Govinda, Anagarika. *Foundations of Tibetan Mysticism, According to the Esoteric Teachings of the Great Mantra, Om Mani Padme Hum.* New York: Samuel Weiser, 1969.

Herrigel, Eugen. *Zen in the Art of Archery.* New York: Pantheon Books, 1953.

Heschel, Abraham Joshua. *The Sabbath.* New York: Farrar, Straus & Giroux, 1951.

Hesse, Hermann. *Siddhartha.* New York: New Directions, 1951.

Ignatius, Saint. *The Spiritual Exercises of St. Ignatius.* Translated by Anthony Mottola. Garden City, New York: Doubleday, 1964.

Jacobs, Louis. *Hasidic Prayer.* New York: Schocken Books, 1972.

———. *Hasidic Thought.* New York: Behrman House, 1976.

James, William. *The Varieties of Religious Experience.* New York: Viking Penguin, 1982.

John of the Cross, Saint. *Spiritual Canticle.* Translated by E. Allison Peers. New York: Image/Doubleday, 1961.

Jou, Tsung Hwa. *The Tao of Tai-Chi Chuan.* Edited by Shoshana Shapiro. Warwick, New York: Tai Chi Foundation, 1980.*

Kadowaki, J. K. *Zen and the Bible.* Translated by Joan Rieck. London and New York: Arkana, 1989.

Kaplan, Aryeh, trans. *Rabbi Nachman's Wisdom.* New York: Sepher-Hermon, 1973.

———. *Meditation and the Bible.* York Beach, Maine: Samuel Weiser, 1981.

———. *Meditation and Kabbalah.* York Beach, Maine: Samuel Weiser, 1986.

Kapleau, Philip. *The Three Pillars of Zen.* Garden City, New York: Anchor/Doubleday, 1966.

Khan, Hazrat Inayat. *The Sufi Message of Hazrat Inayat Khan.* London: Barrie & Jenkins, 1970. Twelve volumes.*

Khan, Pir Vilayat. *Sufi Masters.* Paris and New York: Sufi Order, 1971.*

———. *Toward the One.* New York: Harper & Row, 1974.

Krishnabai, Mother. *Guru's Grace: Autobiography of Mother Krishnabai.* Translated by Swami Ram Dass. Kanhangad, India: Anandashram, 1964.*

Krishnamurti, J. *Think on These Things.* New York: Harper & Row, 1970.

RECOMMENDED READING

Langer, Jiri. *Nine Gates.* Cambridge, England: James Clarke & Co., 1961.

Lawrence, Brother. *The Practice of the Presence of God.* Garden City, New York: Doubleday, 1977.

Levin, Meyer. *Classic Hassidic Tales.* New York: Viking Penguin, 1975.

Levine, Stephen. *A Gradual Awakening.* Garden City, New York: Anchor/Doubleday, 1978.

Lysebeth, Andre Van. *Yoga Self-Taught.* New York: Harper & Row, 1973.

Mahasi Sayadaw. *Practical Insight Meditation.* Santa Cruz, California: Unity Press, 1972.*

Mascaro, Juan, trans. *The Bhagavad Gita.* New York: Viking Penguin, 1962.

Meher Baba. *Discourses.* Walnut Creek, California: Sufism Reoriented, 1967; also published by Sheriar Press, Myrtle Beach, South Carolina. Three volumes.*

Merton, Thomas, trans. *The Wisdom of the Desert.* New York: New Directions, 1960.

———. *The Asian Journal of Thomas Merton.* New York: New Directions, 1968.

Mindell, Arnold. *Working on Yourself Alone.* London and New York: Arkana, 1990.

Mukerji, A. P. *The Spiritual Instructions of Swami Muktananda.* Clearlake, California: Dawn Horse Press, 1974.*

Nachman of Breslov, Rebbe. *Advice.* Translated by Avraham Greenbaum. Jerusalem: Breslov Research Institute, 1983.

Osborne, Arthur, ed. *The Teachings of Ramana Maharshi.* New York: Samuel Weiser, 1962.

Paramananda, Swami. *Secret of Right Activity.* Cohasset, Massachusetts: Vedanta Center, 1964.*

Peers, E. Allison. *The Autobiography of St. Teresa of Avila.* Garden City, New York: Doubleday, 1960.

Pennington, Basil. *Centering Prayer: Renewing an Ancient Christian Prayer Form.* New York: Doubleday, 1982.

Prabhavananda, Swami. *How to Know God: The Yoga Aphorisms of Patanjali.* Translated by Christopher Isherwood. New York: Signet, 1969.

RECOMMENDED READING

Ram Dass. *Be Here Now*. New York: Harmony Books, 1971.

———. *The Only Dance There Is*. Garden City, New York: Doubleday, 1974.

———. *Grist for the Mill*. Berkeley: Celestial Arts, 1987.

Reps, Paul. *Zen Flesh, Zen Bones*. Garden City, New York: Doubleday, 1957.

Schachter, Zalman. *Fragments of a Future Scroll*. Germantown, Pennsylvania: Leaves of Grass Press, 1975.*

Schimmel, Annemarie. *Mystical Dimensions of Islam*. Chapel Hill: University of North Carolina Press, 1978.

Scholem, Gershom. *Major Trends in Jewish Mysticism*. New York: Schocken Books, 1946.

Sivananda, Swami. *Japa Yoga*. Himalyas, India: Divine Life Society, 1972.*

Steinsaltz, Adin. *Beggars and Prayers*. New York: Basic Books, 1979.

Suzuki, Shunryu. *Zen Mind, Beginner's Mind*. New York: Weatherhill, 1970.

Teresa of Avila. *The Interior Castle*. Translated by K. Kavanaugh and O. Rodriguez. New York: Paulist Press, 1979.

Underhill, Evelyn. *Mystics of the Church*. Cambridge, England: James Clarke & Co., 1925.

Vivekenanda, Swami. *Raja Yoga*. New York: Ramakrishna-Vivekananda Center, 1955.*

———. *Karma Yoga and Bhakti Yoga*. New York: Ramakrishna-Vivekananda Center, 1973.*

Waddell, Helen. *The Desert Fathers*. Ann Arbor: University of Michigan Press, 1972.

Watts, Alan. *The Way of Zen*. New York: Pantheon Books, 1957.

Wolters, Clifton, trans. *The Cloud of Unknowing*. Harmondsworth, England: Penguin, 1961.

Yogananda, Paramahansa. *Autobiography of a Yogi*. Los Angeles: Self-Realization Fellowship, 1975.

Yogeshananda, Swami. *The Visions of Sri Ramakrishna*. Madras, India: Sri Ramakrishna Math, 1973.*

Yokoi, Yūhō, and Daizen, Victoria. *Zen Master Dōgen*. New York: Weatherhill, 1976.

INDEX

ABOUT THE AUTHOR

Rabbi David A. Cooper has studied mysticism for close to forty years. He has participated in extended meditation retreats in many traditions, including Buddhism, Sufism, Hinduism, and Judaism. He is best known for his teachings in meditation and Kabbalah. In addition to being a rabbi and meditation teacher, he has had a variety of occupations, including being a licensed charter sailboat skipper in the Caribbean, a certified acupuncturist, a pilot, and a successful political consultant in Washington, D.C.

Rabbi Cooper and his wife, Shoshana, are well-known spiritual guides. During the 1980s, they lived in the Old City of Jerusalem, Israel, for eight years, immersed in the study of Kabbalah. They teach meditation and have led weeklong silent retreats at various centers across the nation, including Omega, Mount Madonna, Lama Foundation, and Elat Chayyim. Cooper is the author of a popular book on Kabbalah, *God Is a Verb* (Riverhead), and also authored the best-selling audiotape series *The Mystical Kabbalah* (Sounds True). Currently David and Shoshana live in the Rocky Mountains, not far from Boulder, Colorado.

About SKYLIGHT PATHS Publishing

Through spirituality, our religious beliefs are increasingly becoming *a part of* our lives, rather than *apart from* our lives. Nevertheless, while many people are more interested than ever in spiritual growth, they are less firmly planted in *traditional* religion. To deepen their relationship to the sacred, people want to learn from their own and other faith traditions, in new ways.

SkyLight Paths sees both believers and seekers as a community that increasingly transcends traditional boundaries of religion and denomination. Many people want to learn from each other, *walking together, finding the way.*

The SkyLight Paths staff is made up of people of many faiths. We are a small, highly committed group of people, a reflection of the religious diversity that now exists in most neighborhoods, most families. We will succeed only if our books make a difference in your life.

We at SkyLight Paths take great care to produce beautiful books that present meaningful spiritual content in a form that reflects the art of making high quality books. Therefore, we want to acknowledge those who contributed to the production of this book.

PRODUCTION
Bronwen Battaglia, Bridgett Taylor, David Wall

COVER DESIGN
Drena Fagen

PRINTING AND BINDING
Versa Press, East Peoria, Illinois

From Our Friends at Jewish Lights

MEDITATION FROM THE HEART OF JUDAISM
Today's Teachers Share Their Practices, Techniques, and Faith
Edited by *Avram Davis*

A "how to" guide for both beginning and experienced meditators, *Meditation from the Heart of Judaism* will help you start meditating or help you enhance your practice. 22 masters of meditation explain why and how they meditate. *A detailed compendium of the experts' "Best Practices"* offers practical advice and starting points.

6" x 9", 256 pp. HC, ISBN 1-879045-77-X **$21.95**; PB, ISBN 1-58023-049-0 **$16.95**

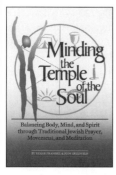

MINDING THE TEMPLE OF THE SOUL
Balancing Body, Mind & Spirit through Traditional Jewish Prayer, Movement & Meditation
by *Tamar Frankiel* and *Judy Greenfeld*

This new spiritual approach to physical health introduces readers to a spiritual tradition that affirms the body and enables them to reconceive their bodies in a more positive light. Relying on Kabbalistic teachings and other Jewish traditions, it shows us how to be more responsible for our own psychological and physical health. Focuses on the discipline of prayer, simple Tai Chi–like exercises and body positions, and guides the reader throughout, step-by-step, with diagrams, sketches and meditations.

7"x 10", 184 pp. Quality Paperback Original, illus., ISBN 1-879045-64-8 **$16.95**

Audiotape of the Blessings, Movements & Meditations (60-min. cassette) **$9.95**
Videotape of the Movements & Meditations (46-min. VHS) **$20.00**

THE ENNEAGRAM AND KABBALAH
Reading Your Soul
by *Rabbi Howard A. Addison*

What do the Enneagram and *Kabbalah* have in common? Together, can they provide a powerful tool for self-knowledge, critique, and transformation?

How can we distinguish between acquired personality traits and the essential self hidden underneath?

6" x 9", 167 pp., Quality Paperback Original,
ISBN 1-58023-001-6 **$15.95**

Spiritual Inspiration
From Jewish Lights . . . The Kushner Series

EYES REMADE FOR WONDER
A Lawrence Kushner Reader
Introduction by Thomas Moore

A treasury of insight from one of the most creative spiritual thinkers in America. Whether you are new to Kushner or a devoted fan, this is the place to begin. With samplings from each of Kushner's works, and a generous amount of new material, this is a book to be savored, to be read and reread, each time discovering deeper layers of meaning in our lives. Offers something unique to both the spiritual seeker and the committed person of faith.

6" x 9", 240 pp. Quality PB, ISBN 1-58023-042-3 **$16.95**; HC, ISBN -014-8 **$23.95**

GOD WAS IN THIS PLACE & I, i DID NOT KNOW
Finding Self, Spirituality & Ultimate Meaning
by *Lawrence Kushner*

Who am I? Who is God? Kushner creates inspiring interpretations of Jacob's dream in Genesis, opening a window into Jewish spirituality for people of all faiths and backgrounds.

In a fascinating blend of scholarship, imagination, psychology and history, seven Jewish spiritual masters ask and answer fundamental questions of human experience.

"Rich and intriguing." —*M. Scott Peck, M.D., author of* The Road Less Traveled

6" x 9", 192 pp. Quality Paperback, ISBN 1-879045-33-8 **$16.95**

HONEY FROM THE ROCK
An Easy Introduction to Jewish Mysticism
by *Lawrence Kushner*

"Quite simply the easiest introduction to Jewish mysticism you can read."

An introduction to the ten gates of Jewish mysticism and how they apply to daily life.

6" x 9", 176 pp. Quality Paperback, ISBN 1-879045-02-8 **$14.95**

THE RIVER OF LIGHT
Spirituality, Judaism, Consciousness
by *Lawrence Kushner*

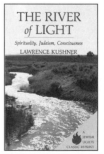

A "manual" for all spiritual travelers who would attempt a spiritual journey in our times. Taking us step by step, Kushner allows us to discover the meaning of our own quest: "to allow the river of light—the deepest currents of consciousness—to rise to the surface and animate our lives."

6" x 9", 192 pp. Quality Paperback, ISBN 1-879045-03-6 **$14.95**

Spiritual Inspiration
From Jewish Lights ...The Kushner Series

•AWARD WINNER•

INVISIBLE LINES OF CONNECTION
Sacred Stories of the Ordinary
by *Lawrence Kushner*

Through his everyday encounters with family, friends, colleagues and strangers, Kushner takes us deeply into our lives, finding flashes of spiritual insight in the process. This is a book where literature meets spirituality, where the sacred meets the ordinary, and, above all, where people of all faiths, all backgrounds can meet one another and themselves. Kushner ties together the stories of our lives into a roadmap showing how everything "ordinary" is supercharged with meaning—*if* we can just see it.

6" x 9", 160 pp. Quality Paperback, ISBN 1-879045-98-2 **$15.95**; HC, ISBN -52-4 **$21.95**

THE BOOK OF WORDS
Talking Spiritual Life, Living Spiritual Talk
by *Lawrence Kushner*

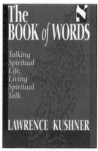

Kushner lifts up and shakes the dust off primary religious words we use to describe the spiritual dimension of life. The *Words* take on renewed spiritual significance, adding power and focus to the lives we live every day. For each word Kushner offers us a startling, moving and insightful explication, and pointed readings from classical Jewish sources that further illuminate the concept. He concludes with a short exercise that helps unite the spirit of the word with our actions in the world.

•AWARD WINNER•

6" x 9", 152 pp. Beautiful two-color text. Quality Paperback, ISBN 1-58023-020-2 **$16.95**;
HC ISBN 1-879045-35-4 **$21.95**

•AWARD WINNER•

THE BOOK OF LETTERS
A Mystical Hebrew Alphabet
by *Lawrence Kushner*

In calligraphy by the author. Folktales about and exploration of the mystical meanings of the Hebrew Alphabet. Open the old prayerbook-like pages of *The Book of Letters* and you will enter a special world of sacred tradition and religious feeling. More than just symbols, all twenty-two letters of the Hebrew alphabet overflow with meanings and personalities of their own.

Rabbi Kushner draws from ancient Judaic sources, weaving talmudic commentary, Hasidic folktales, and kabbalistic mysteries around the letters.

"A book which is in love with Jewish letters."
—*Isaac Bashevis Singer* (לז)

• Popular Hardcover Edition •
6" x 9", 80 pp. Hardcover, two colors, inspiring new Foreword
ISBN 1-879045-00-1 **$24.95**

• Also available in a Deluxe Gift Edition *($79.95)* and Collector's Limited Edition *($349.00)* •
Call 1-800-962-4544 for more information.

Spirituality from Jewish Lights

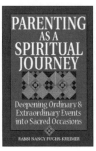

PARENTING AS A SPIRITUAL JOURNEY
Deepening Ordinary & Extraordinary Events into Sacred Occasions
by *Rabbi Nancy Fuchs-Kreimer*

A perfect gift for the new parent, and a helpful guidebook for those seeking to re-envision family life.

Draws on experiences of the author and over 100 parents of many faiths, revealing the transformative spiritual adventure that parents can experience while bringing up their children. Rituals, prayers, and passages from sacred Jewish texts—as well as from other religious traditions—are woven throughout the book.

"This is really relevant spirituality. I love her book."
—*Sylvia Boorstein, author of* It's Easier Than You Think *and mother of four*

6" x 9", 224 pp. Quality Paperback, ISBN 1-58023-016-4 **$16.95**

STEPPING STONES TO JEWISH SPIRITUAL LIVING
Walking the Path Morning, Noon, and Night
by *Rabbi James L. Mirel & Karen Bonnell Werth*

How can we bring the sacred into our busy lives? Transforms our daily routine into sacred acts of mindfulness. Chapters are arranged according to the cycle of each day—and the cycle of our lives—providing spiritual activities, creative new rituals, meditations, acts of *kavannah* (spiritual intention) and prayers for any lifestyle, to help us embrace God's creation every moment.

6" x 9", 240 pp. HC, ISBN 1-58023-003-2 **$21.95**

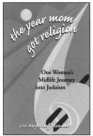

THE YEAR MOM GOT RELIGION
One Woman's Midlife Journey into Judaism
by *Lee Meyerhoff Hendler*

A frank, thoughtful, and humorous "spiritual autobiography" that will speak to anyone in search of deeper meaning in their religious life. The author shares with the reader the hard lessons and realizations she confronted as a result of her awakening to Judaism, including how her transformation deeply affected her lifestyle and relationships. Hendler's journey is a powerful reminder that anyone, at any moment, can deeply embrace faith—and face the challenges that occur along the way.

6" x 9", 208 pp. HC, ISBN 1-58023-000-8 **$19.95**

MOSES—THE PRINCE, THE PROPHET
His Life, Legend & Message for Our Lives
by *Rabbi Levi Meier, Ph.D.*

How can the struggles of a great biblical figure teach us to cope with our own lives today? A fascinating portrait of the struggles, failures, and triumphs of Moses, a central figure in Jewish, Christian, and Islamic tradition. Drawing upon stories from *Exodus*, *midrash* (finding contemporary meaning from ancient Jewish texts), the teachings of Jewish mystics, modern texts, and psychotherapy, Meier offers new ways to create our own path to self-knowledge and self-fulfillment—and face life's difficulties head-on.

6" x 9", 224 pp. HC, ISBN 1-58023-013-X **$23.95**

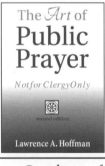